The·Master·Musicians

SCHUMANN

Series edited by Stanley Sadie

The Master Musicians Series

Titles available in paperback

Bach *Malcolm Boyd*
Bartók *Paul Griffiths*
Beethoven *Denis Matthews*
Bizet *Winton Dean*
Britten *Michael Kennedy*
Dufay *David Fallows*
Grieg *John Horton*
Haydn *Rosemary Hughes*
Mahler *Michael Kennedy*
Mozart *Eric Blom*
Rossini *Richard Osborne*

Schoenberg *Malcolm MacDonald*
Schubert *John Reed*
Schumann *Joan Chissell*
Sibelius *Robert Layton*
Richard Strauss *Michael Kennedy*
Tchaikovsky *Edward Garden*
Vaughan Williams *James Day*
Verdi *Julian Budden*
Vivaldi *Michael Talbot*
Wagner *Barry Millington*

Titles available in hardback

Bach *Malcolm Boyd*
Bartók *Paul Griffiths*
Berlioz *Hugh Macdonald*
Bruckner *Derek Watson*
Dufay *David Fallows*
Dvořák *Alec Robertson*
Franck *Laurence Davies*
Handel *Percy M. Young*
Haydn *Rosemary Hughes*
Liszt *Derek Watson*
Mendelssohn *Philip Radcliffe*
Monteverdi *Denis Arnold*

Mozart *Eric Blom*
Ravel *Roger Nichols*
Schoenberg *Malcolm MacDonald*
Schubert *John Reed*
Schumann *Joan Chissell*
Stravinsky *Francis Routh*
Tchaikovsky *Edward Garden*
Vaughan Williams *James Day*
Verdi *Julian Budden*
Vivaldi *Michael Talbot*
Wagner *Barry Millington*

In preparation

Brahms *Malcolm MacDonald*

A list of all Dent books on music is obtainable from the publishers:

J.M. Dent & Sons Ltd
91 Clapham High Street, London SW4 7TA

The·Master·Musicians

SCHUMANN

Joan Chissell

With eight pages of photographs
and 90 music examples

J.M. DENT & SONS LTD
LONDON

First published 1948
Revised 1956
© Revisions, J.M. Dent & Sons Ltd, 1967, 1977, 1989
First bound as a paperback 1979

Printed and bound in Great Britain
by The Guernsey Press Co. Ltd., Guernsey, Channel Islands.

Typeset by Deltatype, Ellesmere Port

This book is set in 10/11½pt Sabon

British Library Cataloguing in Publication Data

Chissell, Joan
   Schumann.——[5th ed.]
   1. German music, Schumann, Robert, 1810–1856
   I. Title   II. Series
780'.92'4

ISBN 0–460–12588–5

To
MY MOTHER

Preface to fifth edition

Since this book first appeared in 1948, much invaluable new information has become generally available through the publication in East Germany of Schumann's own youthful *Tagebücher*, his *Ehetagebücher und Reisenotizen*, and the still more remarkable *Haushaltbücher* recording every factual detail of his daily life (even each *thaler* earned or spent) from the age of twenty-seven until his mental breakdown in February 1854. To the editors of these copiously annotated volumes, the late Dr Georg Eismann and Dr Gerd Nauhaus, both of the Robert–Schumann–Haus in Zwickau, all Schumann biographers will remain eternally indebted. Though the essential portrait of the composer emerges unchanged, every decade of his life in itself could now fill a whole book twice as long as mine.

I am grateful to my editor and publishers for allowing me, in the inevitably limited space of a revision, to make some relevant biographical amendments besides reappraising several of Schumann's later works on the strength of splendid live performances and recordings in recent years. In conclusion I can only renew thanks to the late Dr Gerald Abraham, Dr Eric Sams, Dr Eliot Slater and Dr Alfred Meyer for their own thought-provoking writings, as also to the late Mr Frank Howes and Miss Barbara Banner at the Royal College of Music for more general advice and help in the book's earliest days.

JOAN CHISSELL

London
May 1988

Contents

Illustrations

Thus it is throughout human life: the goal once reached is no longer a goal, and we aim, and strive, and wish to get higher, until our eyes close, and our exhausted soul lies slumbering in the tomb. . . .

SCHUMANN TO HIS MOTHER
28th April 1828.

1

1810–1830

'On 8th June to Herr August Schumann, notable citizen and bookseller here, a little son' – such was the first public announcement, in the *Zwickauer Wochenblatt*, of the birth at Zwickau, Saxony, of Robert Schumann. The hour of the event was 9.30 p.m., the year 1810 – a notable year in the history of German music.

Inherited characteristics, like early environment, leave their indelible stamp on personality. And from his own parents, Robert's legacy was considerable. Herr August Schumann had not become a 'notable citizen and bookseller' without a great deal of effort; his earlier life was a continuous conflict between the security offered by a business career and the literary and philosophical dictates of his own heart. His own father, an impecunious Lutheran minister, first at Endschütz, then nearby Weida, had destined him for the former. But August succumbed more and more to the lure of poetry, in particular that of Milton and Young, and soon made bold to send some of his own literary efforts to a bookseller called Heinse. Heinse's reply was not encouraging. Yet in 1792, while employed as a grocer's assistant at Leipzig, August enrolled himself as an arts student at the University, where he remained for two or three hard-working months until his all too limited savings were exhausted. Forced back to his parents' home, he began a novel, *Knightly Scenes and Monkish Tales*, again inviting Heinse's criticism. Though still unimpressed, this time Heinse offered practical help in the form of work – the job of clerk in his bookstore at Zeitz. August accepted gladly, and all went well until he lost his heart to Johanna, daughter of his landlord, Schnabel, the municipal surgeon. The engagement was permitted only on condition that August should concentrate on establishing a business of his own, and it speaks well for him that in a year and a half, back with his parents at Weida, his writings (including a commercial handbook, *The*

Merchants' Compendium) earned him enough to buy a small grocery and general store in Ronneburg in 1795. By 1799 he was able to return to books, eventually moving to Zwickau to establish the publishing firm of the Brothers Schumann in partnership with his half-brother, Friedrich. His creative urge nevertheless remained strong, finding outlet in several more works of fiction as well as still more esteemed treatises on mercantile and statistical subjects. He also found time to edit two journals, *The Erzgebirge Messenger* (1808–12) and *Leaves of Memory* (1813–26) as well as to translate Byron's *Beppo* and *Childe Harold*. As a publisher his pocket edition of the classics of all nations confirmed his good taste and vision, just as his best-selling *Picture-Gallery of the Most Celebrated People of all Nations and Times*, military and political, with descriptive text, did his business acumen. His life, therefore, was a record of achievement through struggle, with anxiety once or twice bringing him to the verge of breakdown. From his father Schumann can be said to have inherited his own creative urge, his feeling for literature, a measure of perception and discernment, and a determination to achieve his life's purpose in spite of a none too robust constitution.

Of Schumann's mother it is only possible to obtain a blurred picture. There is little authentic evidence about her life, though according to the memoirs of her grand-daughter, Eugenie, she loved to sing and to coax the young Robert into responding 'with beautiful intonation and in the right rhythm'. Conjectures as to her personality vary with each biographer. Wasielewski describes her as attractive and intelligent, but suffering from provincial education and outlook. His comment on her later days is more revealing: 'She fell into an exaggerated state of romance and sentimentalism, united with sudden and violent passion, and an inclination to singularity, to which conjugal differences may have contributed.' Fuller-Maitland is more outspoken. He accuses her of a too practical disposition and says that though entirely lacking in imagination 'she was much addicted to that kind of romantic sentimentality which is only found to perfection in minds of a thoroughly commonplace type'. Some of her letters and some of Robert's replies would suggest that she was the victim of her own intensely morbid imagination, and that she too frequently played the woman. Other letters, notably that celebrated appeal to

Wieck concerning her son's career, reveal her as a woman of considerable perception and good sense. In all fairness her faults must be attributed to an excessive devotion to her young son, which, as in so many mothers, verged on possessiveness. From her Schumann undoubtedly inherited his acute emotional susceptibility and a strain of melancholy in youth sometimes bordering on the self-indulgent.

From his parentage and early environment it can be seen that Robert was not reared in an atmosphere of ignorance and poverty. On the other hand, he was not born with a silver spoon in his mouth, like his almost exact contemporary and future friend Mendelssohn. His family was eminently middle class and respectable, in their income increasingly reaping the rewards of hard labour, and Robert as a result was a normal, healthy child of average but not outstanding general ability. There is little information about his early escapades with his three elder brothers, Eduard, Carl and Julius, or his sister Emilie, but the affection for them revealed in his latter letters must undoubtedly have been the result of congenial family life throughout his boyhood. As the youngest and most attractive child he was accustomed to a good deal of attention and fondling, and it is highly probable that his merest whim was gratified by his adoring mother.

Niecks suggests that Robert received his earliest education from a young tutor who gave him lessons in exchange for board and lodging at the Schumann household. It is definitely known that at the age of six he went to school, a private preparatory school kept by a Doctor Döhner, where he remained for four years. He then passed on to the Zwickau Lyceum, or Academy, the local high school of about two hundred boys, where he remained till the age of eighteen. In both institutions his appetite and aptitude for work were pre-eminently normal; consequently he was on excellent terms with his companions, and in his younger days his unbounded vitality and boisterous good feeling made him the moving spirit of many games and escapades. Though August Schumann had no musical leanings himself, he seems from the start to have been anxious to repair this deficiency through his son, for at the age of seven it was arranged for Robert to have private piano lessons from Johann Gottfried Kuntzsch, a schoolmaster at the Lyceum, whose musical knowledge and keyboard ability had been acquired entirely through his own effort in his own spare time. In spite of his appointment as organist at St Mary's church and his persistent efforts to stir up musical interest at Zwickau with performances involving choir and orchestra and the consequent union of the town musician and his men with the military band,[1] it is obvious that his love for music far outreached his technical equipment. The actual method by which he initiated Robert into the mysteries of the keyboard would probably have horrified such a teacher as Wieck; but he must be given credit for stimulating the child's interest in a far wider range of music than mere educational piano pieces. In later life Robert must have realized his master's technical short-comings, yet could still express wholly sincere gratitude to Kuntzsch in a letter of 1852 accompanying a laurel wreath sent in honour of the fiftieth anniversary of Kuntzsch's installation as a teacher. At the age of seven or eight Robert composed a set of little dances, and his gift for extemporizing also began to reveal itself. One biographer[2] goes as far as to say:

> Schumann as a child possessed rare taste and talent for portraying feelings and characteristic traits in melody – ay, he could sketch the different dispositions of his intimate friends by certain figures and passages on the piano so that everyone burst into loud laughter at the similitude of the portrait.

If true, this would suggest that even Schumann's earliest creative efforts had tangible connection with the events of his life.

By this time August Schumann seemed determined to foster whatever musical gifts his child possessed, buying him a Streicher grand piano besides organizing an expedition to Leipzig for a performance of *Die Zauberflöte* and another to Carlsbad in the summer of 1819 to hear Ignaz Moscheles, who at that time was enjoying an unchallenged reputation as a pianist. Though Robert was only nine years old, the occasion made a deep and lasting impression on him, and it is interesting to read in one of his subsequent letters to Moscheles, that of November 1851, thanking him for the dedication of a sonata, that he had preserved a concert programme which Moscheles had touched, more than

[1] Haydn's *Creation* in 1802 was his most ambitious effort.
[2] In a supplement, in 1850, to No. 52 of 1848 of the *Allgemeine musikalische Zeitung*.

thirty years ago on that very occasion, as a 'sacred relic'. From this experience Robert returned to his own piano with redoubled energy, and we next hear of him playing many duets with another boy of his own age, Friedrich Piltzing, son of the leader of a regimental band stationed at Zwickau. This boy was also a pupil of Kuntzsch, and again the latter must be praised for giving the boys not only original four-hand compositions by Hummel, Weber and Czerny, but also arrangements of symphonies and overtures of Haydn and Mozart – and most notably of Beethoven, whose music was then known only to the discerning few. Kuntzsch was well aware of Robert's instinctive musicianship. When conducting a public performance of Schneider's *Weltgericht* in 1821, he allowed the boy of eleven to play the piano accompaniment. This experience of concerted music-making inspired Robert to make similar experiments in his own home. Among the collection of music which August Schumann was acquiring for his son there appeared one day by mistake the overture to Righini's *Tigrane*, complete with orchestral parts. Undaunted, Robert gathered together as many of his friends as could play an instrument (they amounted to two violins, two flutes, two horns and a clarinet) and directed a performance of this work with himself filling in as many missing parts on the piano as he could manage. This led to similar unprofessional performances of works not too difficult for these eager young people, and, still only in his eleventh or twelfth year, Robert himself composed a setting of the 150th Psalm for voices and orchestra, also an Overture and Chorus (with words beginning 'Wie reizend ist der schöne Morgen'), augmenting his orchestral forces with as many of his friends as could sing. The only audience were members of the Schumann family, and August, with his customary unobtrusive understanding and kindness, presented the music-makers with music stands to faciliate their efforts.

At the Lyceum concerts Robert frequently appeared as both reciter and pianist, and seems to have had greater success in the latter capacity. On one occasion when nearly fifteen, he performed various variations by Moscheles and Herz with such easy assurance that Kuntzsch, realizing that the boy had far outstripped his own limited powers, declined to give him any more lessons. August Schumann, by this time determined that his son should have the best instruction possible, wrote to ask Weber if he would accept Robert as a pupil. The reply was unfavourable, however, for Weber was then busy on the composition of *Oberon*. This was the last thing August was able to do for his son, for in August 1826 he died, just two months after Weber's own death. He left Robert a comfortable 10,000 or so thalers, with a further provision for whatever university expenses might arise.

It may seem from this account of Robert's early days that his whole mental horizon was occupied with music. But literature made equal claims, and here August Schumann was able to act more directly as his son's mentor, supplementing his school reading with books from the bookshop. Little robber plays, acted by himself and his friends, were among Robert's first creative efforts. As he grew older he embarked on several more ambitious dramatic projects, in turn historical, comic and horrific, and compiled a poetic anthology including many poems of his own as well as keeping an intimate record of his own awakening susceptibilities in diaries and notebooks – one colourfully entitled *Hottentottiana*. Most important of all for him was his auto-biographical story, *Juniusabende und Julitage*. 'My first work, my truest and my finest', he subsequently claimed, 'how I wept as I wrote it and yet how happy I was!' At a more practical level he assisted (when only fourteen) with the text for his father's *Picture-Gallery of the Most Celebrated People of all Nations and Times*, and shortly before leaving school he took an active part in the preparation of a new edition of Forcellini's *Lexicon Totius Latinitatis*, a publication undertaken by his brother Carl.

All this led him to play a very active part, from the age of fifteen onwards, in his school's German Literary Society, which had for its excellent maxim: 'It is the duty of every man of culture to know the literature of his country.' The society held regular meetings to achieve this purpose, and also to encourage and criticize its own members' essays in authorship. Robert's letters to Emil Flechsig, an old school friend now at Leipzig University, reveal his literary standing and taste during this last year of his schooldays. His acquaintance with Greek and Latin classics was extensive, even if not profound, and his opinions of Sophocles, Horace, Homer, Plato, Tacitus, Sallust, Cicero and Caesar betoken a lively mentality in a schoolboy of eighteen. Of his own countrymen, Schiller occupied a high place in his esteem, but Goethe he confessed as yet beyond his understanding. It was romantic literature which had the most direct and personal appeal for him. Spitta mentions Schulze, Franz von Sonnenburg and Byron as among his favourite authors, but all of them were eclipsed by his overwhelming passion for Jean Paul Richter, whose ideology and sentiment were the embodiment of his own as yet hazy and undefined fancies. His early letters not only contain numerous references to his idol, but are themselves extravagant imitations of the novelist's peculiar style and imagery, such as that to Flechsig in July 1827:

> All those joyful hours which I spent with you, my old friend, came thronging before my soul, and with a saddened spirit I went forth to be with Nature, and I read your letter, read it ten times over; while a last kiss from glowing lips was touching the sweetly fading green of the wooded heights; golden cloudlets floated in the pure aether, and——

At this point he was interrupted by a visitor, otherwise there is no telling where his vision might have led him.

If the outward expression of his feelings appeared but a play of fine-sounding words, the inner emotions which prompted them were entirely sincere at the time of writing. Robert was, in fact, in the painful throes of adolescent susceptibility, and the slightest tremor reacted on his exposed and defenceless heart with the intensity of an earthquake. It was the beginning, but only the beginning, of that acute sensibility which was sometimes, in his twenties, to push him to manic-depressive extremes. There was a concrete reason for his already apparent streak of melancholy, for the year of 1826 had been doubly tragic: not only had his father died in August, but shortly beforehand his nineteen-year-old sister, Emilie, had drowned herself. Even though her suicide was directly attributable to typhus fever after a distressing skin disease, it did not pass lightly over her young brother. Calf-love also brought its own pleasure and pains. He had worshipped the beauty of a certain Liddy Hempel to find only mental and spiritual barrenness beneath; he had experienced 'absorbing passion' for a Nanni Patsch, causing his feelings to overflow to Flechsig in customary imitation of Jean Paul:

> O Friend! were I but a smile, how would I flit about her eyes! were I but joy, how gently would I throb at her pulses! yea, might I be but a tear, I would weep with her, and then if she smiled again, how gladly would I die on her eyelash, and gladly, gladly, be no more!

But soon his emotional temperature subsided into 'pure divine friendship and reverence, like devotion to the Madonna'.

Nevertheless, in spite of his growing tendency to introspection, with its attendant loneliness of spirit, it must not be assumed that Robert completely shut himself off from the everyday world and its earthier pleasures. His letters to Flechsig also describes lively excursions into the countryside, made in the company of casual friends rather than what he could have called soul-mates. One letter tells of a particularly hilarious climax to a winter's journey, when after consuming large quantities of food and grog at an inn, his friends entertained the peasants with recitations and he with improvisations on the piano. Finally, the merriment ended with a dance:

> . . . we whirled the peasant girls about in rare style. I danced a waltz with that gentle, modest Minchen of the Müllers', while Walther made believe to play. Old Müller and his wife joined in the dance, the rustics stamped their feet; we rejoiced and rushed about, staggering among the legs of the clodhoppers, and then took a tender farewell of the whole company by imprinting smacking kisses on the lips of all the peasant girls, Minchen and the rest.

Letters and diary entries at this time reveal that he was fully sexually awakened, and sometimes censorious of his indiscretions. He had also acquired an expensive taste for champagne and cigars. His happiest moments during these last schooldays were nevertheless those spent in the house of C. E. Carus, a Zwickau merchant, but a keen friend of music and all who loved it. In later life Schumann described its atmosphere as being all joy, serenity and music. It was there that he grew to know and love the less frequently heard music of Haydn, Mozart and Beethoven, especially their quartets. And it was there that he met other artists and friends of music, including Agnes Carus, wife of Dr Ernst Carus (a nephew of C. E. Carus). She was a gifted amateur singer, and in her home at Colditz, quite near Zwickau, he would accompany her and even compose songs for her,[1] enjoying her attractive personality as much as their music-making.

But in spite of the sympathy accorded him in these surroundings, he lacked a father's strong hand and good sense – he even lacked a mother's understanding, for at this critical time she was

[1] Including *Lied für XXX* (Schumann's words), *Verwandlung* (Schulze), *Sehnsucht* (Ekert) and a translation of Byron's 'I saw thee weep'.

persuading him against his own inner conviction that far more rewarding than the precarious life of an artist of any kind was the security offered by the profession of law. Working on her son's warm, youthful affection for her, and supported by his guardian Rudel, an astute merchant, she eventually bent his will to her own; and after his final examination at the Lyceum on 15th March 1828 he was dispatched to Leipzig to make necessary arrangements at the University for entering as a student of law. To Robert, there was drama in the situation:

> Here I am, without guide, teacher or father, flung helplessly into the darkness of life's unknown [he wrote to Flechsig], and yet the world has never seemed fairer than at this moment, as I cheerfully face its storms. Flechsig, you must stand my friend in the whirl of life, and help me if I fail.

In spite of family ties at Zwickau, in spite of but tepid interest in his career, Schumann's arrival at Leipzig opened up new vistas for him. He first made arrangements for his future lodgings, deciding to live with Flechsig, now a divinity student, and Moritz Semmel, a law student, who was his sister-in-law Therese's brother. He then had to matriculate as a student of law, which took place on 29th March. And in the company of his two friends he saw many new sights and many new faces. One evening, in a tavern, Semmel introduced him to a certain Gisbert Rosen, a law student who was about to complete his studies at Heidelberg, and from this chance meeting grew one of Schumann's most valued youthful friendships. A common enthusiasm for Jean Paul was their immediate point of contact, but they soon discovered their temperaments to be so finely attuned in most matters that Schumann's spontaneous reaction was to invite his friend to come back with him to Zwickau, where they stayed for a fortnight, enjoying the wedding festivities of Schumann's brother, Julius, in the meantime. And then, still loath to end this delightful new-found companionship and eager to explore the beauties and historic wealth of Bavaria, Schumann arranged to accompany Rosen as far as Munich on a somewhat indirect route to Heidelberg. Setting off by stage-coach, their first call was Bayreuth, the one-time home of Jean Paul and to Schumann and Rosen a holy city of consequence. They visited many places immortalized by the novelist and received a portrait of him from his widow. They stopped again at

Augsburg, where they stayed for a few days with Dr Kurrer, a chemist, who at Zwickau had been August Schumann's closest friend. Here Schumann's susceptible heart was made to beat more quickly by their host's charming daughter, Clara, and his departure was hastened only by letters of introduction to Heine given him by a friend of the Kurrers. At Munich the two travellers lost no time in calling on Heine, whose ironic wit had already won him considerable fame, though a comparatively young man of thirty-one. Although unaware that one of his visitors was destined to breathe new life into his own verses, he was remarkably courteous to them both in spite of their youth, and received them a second time that day at the Leuchtenberg Gallery. By this time it was essential that Rosen should at once go on to Heidelberg and Schumann back to Leipzig. It is not known if the parting cost Rosen as much heartache as it did Schumann, but writing to Rosen of his lonely return Schumann said:

> My journey by Ratisbon was confoundedly dull, and I missed you terribly in those ultra-Catholic regions. I never care about describing my travels, let alone when they arouse unpleasant feelings, which are better effaced from our recollections. I will merely say that I thought of you most affectionately, that both sleeping and waking sweet Clara's image was always before my eyes and that I was heartily glad to see my dear native town of Zwickau once more.

But his joy to be home was at once dispelled by his anxiety to be away again. He stayed only three hours to collect up his luggage and, disappointing all his family who were longing for a detailed account of his holiday in what were unknown regions to them, he was soon back again in a corner of the stage-coach travelling to Leipzig, though, he confessed, weeping bitterly.

If as a Zwickau schoolboy Schumann found that Leipzig epitomized all his longings for freedom and a wider life, now he was firmly established there, it was only Zwickau that he wanted. All his first student letters speak of an intense homesickness, a longing for his family and for the Zwickau countryside and open air. Leipzig he describes at various times as 'disgusting', 'this infamous nest', and he writes:

> It is hard to find nature here. Everything is ornamented by art. There is no valley, no mountain, no wood, where I can thoroughly lose myself in my own thoughts, no spot where I can be alone,

unless it is locked up in my own room, with an everlasting noise and uproar going on below.

Consequently the accounts of his activities are frequently interspersed with melancholy reflections, in Jean-Paulian idiom, on the irretrievable past, such as 'Alas, why do we appreciate happiness only after it has left us, and why does each tear one sheds contain either a dead pleasure or a vanished blessing?' There were no material reasons for his unhappiness. His lodgings he described as excellent, and it was even remarked among his associates that they were far more comfortable and elegant than the usual student's abode. Then there were student clubs open to him, in which he could indulge in fencing, drinking, and exchange of ideas; and in these first student days his allowance appeared to be adequate, in not over-plentiful, for all his needs. His mother sent him frequent parcels and letters, and even promised that he should have riding lessons.

The immediate cause of all the trouble was his own sensitive temperament, which tended to place a barrier between himself and this strange new world and inhibit all his natural desire for companionship. He frequently confessed that he felt miserable among people who did not understand him, and whom he could not care for. As to his fellow students in general, he was rather disillusioned by their lack of vision and of serious purpose in life, and he deplored their wild and hazy notions about nationality and Germanity. Schumann himself did not grow young till he was a little older: at this time he was still his mother's spoilt son. He mentions Flechsig and Semmel as his customary friends, but complains that 'Flechsig never cheers me up, if I am sometimes depressed, he ought not to be so too, and might be humane enough to brighten me up'. He admired the strong personality of a philology student called Götte (and wrote sensible letters to him in the holidays) and might have made friends with Schütz and Günther 'were they less narrow-minded'. He also frequently writes that he was not intimate with many families. It was Rosen whom he pined for; Rosen, who, had he been at Leipzig, might have cured Schumann's spiritual loneliness and altered the whole picture of Leipzig for him. As it was, Schumann was always wishing himself at Heidelberg with his friend.

Then deeper, gnawing him like some malignant canker, was his dislike for the profession of law. If on Schumann's departure to

Leipzig his mother breathed a sigh of relief that her wayward child had at last a settled purpose in life, her mental peace must have been short-lived. His first letter to her, written on 1st May 1828, had this significant ending:

> I am perplexed beyond measure by the choice of a study. Chilly jurisprudence, with its ice-cold definitions, would crush the life out of me from the start. Medicine I will not, theology I cannot study. Thus I struggle endlessly with myself and look in vain for someone to tell me what to do. And yet – there is no help for it; I must choose law.

It seems that for a while Schumann did attempt to take an intelligent interest in the subject, for his next letters to his mother all mention that he attended lectures regularly, with the qualification that he took notes mechanically; and in his letter of 4th July to his guardian he was the dutiful ward *par excellence*: 'I have certainly decided on law as my profession, and shall work hard at it, however dry and uninteresting the beginning may be.' A letter to his mother dated 4th August, full of plans for going to Heidelberg, must have again disturbed her, for he speaks of being already rusty at Leipzig and in need of better professors. On 22nd August he writes that he often goes to lectures (no longer is it 'regularly'), although a letter to Rosen only eight days earlier said that he had not been to a single lecture yet. Was he exaggerating to his friend or hiding the truth from his mother? His subsequent published letters to her from Leipzig carefully avoid all references to his work, and, as if he were conscious of his shortcomings, they are full of ardent affection expressed with luxuriant emotional imagery, such as he knew would both please and appease her.

The reason for this guilty silence was undoubtedly the result of an incident which occurred in July of that year. As soon as he reached Leipzig, Schumann had hired a piano so that he could practise and improvise at will, and with its help he had also composed several keyboard works, and still more important, some settings of poems by Kerner, Ekert, Goethe, Byron and Jacobi. In July he sent these songs for criticism to Gottlob Wiedebein, musical director at Brunswick, who won great fame, if only in his lifetime, for his one book of published songs. For Schumann, Wiedebein's songs had special significance, since the words were those of Jean Paul, whose 'mystic utterances only became clear and intelligible to me when seen through the magical garb of your tone-pictures', as he wrote as introduction to his letter. The essence of Wiedebein's kindly, candid reply is now of historic interest:

> Your songs have many, sometimes very many shortcomings; but I should call them sins, not so much of the spirit as of nature and youth, and these are excusable and pardonable where pure poetic feeling and genuine spirit shines through. And it is precisely that which has pleased me so much.

Schumann's effusive letter of thanks ended with this significant remark: 'Live as happily as you deserve to do, for you have given happy moments to a great many people, *and to me my happiest.*'

Throughout all his schooldays he had shown a constant pleasure in music and literature, and in the background of his adolescent mind there had always been a great longing for some elusive thing just beyond his eyes' horizon. At the time of leaving school this longing was still not clearly enough defined for him to oppose his mother's wishes more stubbornly; but here at Leipzig it gradually began to take more definite shape – and then Wiedebein made it clear once and for all. Music alone could give him lasting satisfaction. 'But yet in my own heart I am not quite so joyless,' he writes to his mother on 31st August, 'and what my fellow creatures cannot give me is given me by music. My piano tells me all the deep sentiments which I cannot express.'

He had by this time renewed acquaintance with his old Colditz friend, Dr E. A. Carus, now appointed Professor of Medicine at Leipzig University, and more especially with his wife, Agnes. In the sympathetic atmosphere of their home Schumann was drawn out of his shell and introduced to several people after his own heart. Among these were Marschner, the operatic composer, and, of outstanding importance, Friedrich Wieck, who was Leipzig's leading piano teacher. Schumann wasted no time in starting lessons with him, but after over three years with no instruction at all he found it hard to adapt himself to the 'quiet, cold, well-considered, restrained conquest of technique', as Wieck afterwards described it, and also to a systematic study of harmony and counterpoint which was part of this excellent teacher's comprehensive system. But Wieck persevered with him, not only because he liked him, but because he also perceived that his pupil had unusual latent ability. As for Schumann, he enjoyed this new musical environment so much that many hours due to the lecture room were spent in Wieck's house, and quite a lot of them in the company of Wieck's gravely attractive little daughter of nine, who was herself a pianist and a brilliant advertisement for her father's method. Among his fellow students, Schumann had discovered a cellist, Glock, and a violinist, Täglichsbeck, and with himself at the piano (often in shirt-sleeves with cigar in his mouth) the three would make music together in the evenings at his own lodgings. Sometimes they were joined by Sörgel, another student, who played the viola; and when they considered themselves rehearsed and ready for performance, Wieck would be invited as guest of honour. A special study was made of Schubert's B flat major piano trio, for at this time Schubert was Schumann's god, inspiring both the C minor piano quartet and the Eight Polonaises for Piano Duet[1] which he wrote for these musical evenings with his friends. When Schubert died towards the end of 1828, Schumann's sobbing was heard by Flechsig throughout the night. Then there were the celebrated Gewandhaus concerts to go to, and in one letter Schumann even spoke of performing a four-hand concerto with Emilie Reichold, in his estimation Leipzig's best young pianist, at one of the next season's concerts. Certainly his first Leipzig winter had its full share of illicit musical enjoyment for him. Yet his restless nature still yearned for new experiences, and the move to Heidelberg eventually took place in May 1829, after a lively holiday at Zwickau.

The change of air brought about a complete change of heart. From the very first day of the long south-westward journey it seems as if the lonely visionary came down from his watch-tower and threw himself into the vortex of life with hedonistic abandonment. On the coach drive to Frankfort Schumann found the perfect companion in Willibald Alexis, the author, and instead of going direct from Frankfort to Heidelberg, he seized the opportunity to accompany Alexis as far as Coblenz on his way to Paris, and in consequence they crossed the Rhine together and sailed up from Bingen through the picturesque Rheingau to Coblenz. He absorbed all the loveliness of the natural scenery and all the grandeur of old cities, and yet showed equal delight in the

[1] Unpublished until Karl Geiringer edited the work for Universal Edition in 1933.

vagaries of his oddly assorted travelling companions, his food and his wine, and the hundred little humorous incidents which a few months before would have been beneath his notice. At Frankfort the urge to play the piano was so strong that he walked into a music shop, telling them he was tutor to a young English lord who wished to buy a piano. After playing for three hours, much 'stared at and applauded', he told them he would inform them in a day or two whether his lordship would buy the instrument. By that time, of course, he was already at Rüdesheim, drinking Rüdesheimer! His letter to his mother describing the journey is full of good spirits, humour, intelligent observations and direct word-pictures of what he saw, without any sentimental, would-be philosophical wrappings to them. He refers to his 'divinely merry mood' and summarizes the whole excursion as 'this short but most enjoyable little episode in my journey through life'. And Heidelberg was no less fair in his eyes. There was his old friend Rosen, unexpectedly able to stay a year longer at the University, to welcome him, and they were soon to be joined by Semmel. Then there was Heidelberg itself. His own description of it best reveals its assuaging beauty:

> And yet, my bright little Heidelberg, you are so lovely, so innocent and idyllic, and if one may compare the Rhine and its rocky hills to a fine, strong man, so the Neckar valley might be likened to a lovely girl. There everything is massive and rugged, vibrating in old Teutonic harmonies; here everything breathes a soft melodious song of Provence.

The reason he gave his mother for coming to Heidelberg University, almost a year before, was that the best German jurists of the day, Thibaut and Mittermayer, were among its lecturers. As a Saxon citizen he had to take his degree at Leipzig University, which insisted on Saxon Law, and he realized he would have to return there eventually, as at Heidelberg it was possible to study only Roman law and the Pandects. But from his first few letters home his mother must have felt that the period away from Leipzig was to prove a blessing in disguise. 'I am very jolly and at times quite happy,' he wrote to her on 17th July:

> I am industrious and regular, and enjoy my jurisprudence under Thibaut and Mittermayer immensely, and am only now beginning to appreciate its true worth, and the way in which it assists all the

highest interests of humanity. And good heavens! what a difference there is between the Leipzig professor, who stood at his desk at lectures and rattled off his paragraphs without any sort of eloquence or inspiration, and this man Thibaut, who, although about twice as old as the other, is overflowing with life and spirits, and can hardly find words or time to express his feelings.

In the same letter he mentioned that the standard of music was much lower at Heidelberg than at Leipzig, so that although his practice had been much neglected, his own piano playing was considered quite exceptional. This reference to music is but casual, with no more significance than his comparison of the cost and standard of living in the two towns, or his description of the many eligible young ladies about, or of his friends and the 'scores of other acquaintances to whom I bow in the street and talk conventional commonplaces'. In short, he was beginning to enjoy rubbing shoulders with common humanity, and was in consequence becoming a man of the world. His indulgence was soon to alarm his family, for on top of his already increased expenses he now asked them, with masterly plausibility, for a considerable sum of extra money to enable him to spend his whole summer vacation exploring Switzerland and Italy. As usual, they eventually acceded, and he travelled south through wonderful Swiss alpine scenery to Milan, then east to the Adriatic and Venice, and back through Innsbruck and Augsburg, not arriving at Heidelberg till the middle of October. In spite of love-sickness at Milan, this time for a beautiful Englishwoman, sea-sickness at Venice and characteristic shortage and borrowing of money the whole time, he considered the journey a success, and came back with an impression of Pasta singing Rossini at La Scala printed indelibly on his mind.

Throughout the winter of 1829–30 life continued to offer him good things which he accepted with wide-open arms, irrespective of expense or good sense. His letters describe numerous acquaintances and friends, sleighing parties, balls, his increasing popularity and his title of the 'Heidelberg favourite'. And demands for money became increasingly frequent and inconsiderate. In a letter to his mother of 24th February 1830 he first tells her of his large bills at the bootmaker's and the tailor's, and continues:

Then I must eat and drink; and I play the piano, and smoke, and sometimes, but not often, drive to Mannheim. I also require money for lectures, and want books and music, all of which costs a terrible lot of money. Those confounded fancy balls, tipping various people, subscriptions to the museum and cigars – oh, those cigars! – the piano tuner, the laundress, the shoeblack, candles, soap, all my dear friends who expect a wretched glass of beer, the man at the museum who brings me the newspapers! I should absolutely despair if I were not on the verge of desperation already!

His begging letters to his guardian, though no less urgent, are worded with diplomatic reticence and skill.

In this whirlpool of pleasure music and law appeared to be reconciled, but underneath the rift was soon to widen again. A letter to Wieck written in November 1829 reveals that in his secret self the longing for music was as strong as ever. It speaks of his systematic practice and his overmastering desire to release on manuscript paper the multitude of ideas imprisoned in his mind; it mentions his continued delight in Schubert, who used music paper as other people might use a diary, and it requests that a mass of new music and copies of the *Musikalische Zeitung* should be sent to him at Heidelberg. Piano practice occupied all his spare time, and sometimes he would begin very early and play for as long as seven hours if he had promised to entertain his friends in the evening. His improvisations astonished everyone, but Schumann's main concern was to improve his technique. Even when on excursions into the surrounding countryside he would take a dumb keyboard with him. The climax of his efforts at Heidelberg was a big concert, with the Dowager Grand Duchess of Baden in the audience, at which he played Moscheles's 'Alexander' variations with such success that 'there was absolutely no end to the "bravos" and "encores" and I really felt quite hot and uncomfortable'. Added to all this, he made renewed attempts at composition. Intrigued by the discovery that friends in both Heidelberg and Mannheim shared the surname Abegg, capable of translation into musical notation, he planned a set of variations for piano and orchestra on a theme generated by those five notes. In the event, however, the work emerged as a piano solo subsequently chosen for publication as his Opus 1. Most other projects remained incomplete, though sketches from this period were incorporated in later keyboard works, notably *Papillons*.

All this tended to divert much time and attention from Thibaut.

But he was usually on excellent terms with his professor, as the latter was himself an enthusiastic amateur musician, who had even written a book on *The Purity of Musical Art*. Some of his speculations on musical subjects were beyond Schumann and, more important, his conservative taste at times offended Schumann's progressive outlook; but for the most part there was keen sympathy between them, and Schumann was a regular participator in the weekly orgies of music-making at his house, where about seventy people would sing choruses from Handel and other old music, with Thibaut himself accompanying at the piano. But above all Thibaut deserves credit for making it perfectly clear to Schumann that he not only had no interest in law, but no ability for it either. The spring of 1830 found him asking his family for another six months at Heidelberg, as if anxious to prolong this delightful, irresponsible life, and fearful to pronounce the decision at which he had long since arrived in his heart. On Easter Sunday he went to Frankfort with two friends to hear Paganini, and the effect of that violinist's playing was comparable only with the impression made on him by Moscheles eleven years earlier; and it undoubtedly moved him a step nearer his ultimate goal. Matters came to a head on 30th July. There is no better approach to the drama of the situation than through the letters of the three people concerned. First, Schumann to his mother:

HEIDELBERG,
30th July 1830, 5 a.m.

GOOD MORNING, MAMMA!

How shall I describe my bliss at this moment? The spirit lamp is hissing under the coffee pot, the sky is indescribably clear and rosy, and the keen spirit of the morning fills me with its presence. Besides, your letter lies before me and reveals a perfect treasury of good feeling, common sense and virtue. My cigar tastes uncommonly good; in short, the world is very lovely at times, if one could only always get up early.

There is plenty of blue sky and sunshine in my life at present, but my guide, Rosen, is wanting. Two more of my best friends, the v. H.'s, from Pomerania (two brothers), went off to Italy a week ago, and so I often feel very lonely, which sometimes makes me happy, sometimes miserable – it just depends. One can get on better without a sweetheart than without a friend; and sometimes I get into a regular fever when I think of myself. My *whole life* has been a twenty years' struggle between poetry and prose, or, if you like to call it so, Music and Law. There is just as high a standard to be reached in practical life as in art. In the former the ideal consists in the hope of plenty of work and a large extensive practice; but what sort of prospect would there be in Saxony for such a fellow as myself, who is not of noble birth, has neither money nor interest, and has no affection for legal squabbles and pettiness? At Leipzig I did not trouble my head about my career, but went dreaming and dawdling on and never did any real good. Here I have worked harder, but both there and here have been getting more and more attached to art. Now I am standing at the crossroads and am scared at the question which way to choose. My genius points towards art, which is, I am inclined to think, the right path. But the fact is – now, do not be angry at what I am going to say, for I will but gently whisper it – it always seems to me as if you were putting obstacles in my way. You had very good reasons for doing so, and I understood them all perfectly, and we both agreed on calling art an 'uncertain future and a doubtful way of earning one's bread'. There certainly can be no greater misery than to look forward to a hopeless, shallow, miserable existence which one has prepared for oneself. But neither is it easy to enter upon a career diametrically opposed to one's whole education, and to do it requires patience, confidence and quick decision. I am still at the height of youth and imagination, with plenty of capabilities for cultivating and ennobling art, and have come to the conclusion that with patience and perseverance, and a good master, I should in six years be as good as any pianist, for pianoforte playing is mere mechanism and execution. Occasionally I have much imagination and possibly some creative power. . . . Now comes the question: 'To be, or not to be,' for you can only do *one* thing well in this life, and I am always saying to myself: 'Make up your mind to do one thing thoroughly well, and with patience and perseverance you are bound to accomplish something.' This battle against myself is now raging more fiercely than ever, my good mother. Sometimes I am daring and confident in my own strength and power, but sometimes I tremble to think of the long way I have traversed and of the endless road which lies before me. As to Thibaut, he has long ago recommended me to take up art. I should be very glad if you would write to him, and he would be very pleased too, but unfortunately he went off to Rome some time ago, so probably I shall never speak to him again.

If I stick to law I must undoubtedly stay here another winter to hear Thibaut lecture on the Pandects, as every law student is bound to do. If I am to go in for music, I must leave this at once and go to Leipzig, where Wieck, whom I could thoroughly trust, and who can tell me what I am worth, would then carry on my education. Afterwards I ought to go to Vienna for a year, and if possible study under Moscheles. Now I have a favour to ask you, my dear mother, which I hope you will grant me. *Write yourself to Wieck and ask him point blank what he thinks of me and my career*. Please let me have a SPEEDY answer, deciding the question, so that I can hurry on my departure from Heidelberg, although I shall be very sorry to leave it and my many kind friends and favourite haunts. *If you like you can enclose this letter to Wieck. In any case the question must be decided before Michaelmas*, and then I shall pursue my object in life, whatever it may be, with fresh vigour and without tears. You must admit that this is the most important letter I have ever written, so I trust you will not hesitate to comply with my request, for there is *no time* to be lost.

Goodbye, dear mother, and do not fret. In this case heaven will help us only if we help ourselves.

Ever your most loving son,
ROBERT SCHUMANN.

Then his mother to Wieck:

ZWICKAU,
7th August 1830.

HONOURED SIR,

According to the request of my son, Robert Schumann, I take the liberty of applying to you in regard to the future of this dear son. With trembling and deep anxiety I seat myself to ask you how you like Robert's plan, which the enclosed letter will explain. It is not in accordance with my views; and I freely confess that I have great fears for Robert's future. Much labour is needed to become a *distinguished* musician, or even to earn a living by music; because there are too many great artists before him; and, were his talent ever so marked, it is, and ever will be, uncertain whether he would gain applause, or earn a secure future. . . .

He has now studied for almost *three* years, and had many, very many wants. Now, when I thought him almost at the goal, I see him take another step, which puts him back to the beginning – see, when the time has come for him to prove himself, that his little fortune is gone, and that he is still dependent. Whether he will succeed . . . alas! I cannot tell you how sad, how cast down, I feel when I think of Robert's future. He is a good soul. Nature gave him intellectual endowments such as others must struggle to attain, and he is not disagreeable in appearance. He has enough money to pursue his studies without distress, enough of which still remains to support him respectably until he is able to provide for himself; and now he would choose a profession which should have been begun ten years earlier. If you, honoured Sir, are yourself a father, you will feel that I am right, and that my distress is not groundless. My other three sons are greatly displeased, and absolutely insist that I shall not consent; but I would not force him, if his own feelings do not lead him; for it is no honour to begin again as a scholar, after three wasted years, and spend his few thaler upon an *uncertainty*.

All rests on your decision – *the peace of a* LOVING MOTHER, THE WHOLE HAPPINESS FOR LIFE of a young and inexperienced man, who lives but in a higher sphere, and will have nothing to do with practical life. I know that you love music. Do not let your feelings plead for Robert, but consider his years, his fortune, his powers and his future. I beg, I conjure you, as a husband, a father and a friend of my son, act like an upright man and tell me your opinion frankly – what he has to fear or to hope.

Excuse the distraction of my letter: I am so overcome by all that has passed that I am soul-sick; and never was a letter so hard for me to write as this. May you be happy! and send an answer soon to your

Humble servant,
C. SCHUMANN, NÉE SCHNABEL.

And finally, Wieck's reply to her:

LEIPZIG,
August 1830.

HONOURED MADAM,

I hasten to answer your esteemed favour of the 7th inst., without further assuring you in advance of my warmest sympathy. But my answer can only be quite short, since I am pressed by business of various kinds, and since I must talk over the greater part of it with your son, if a satisfactory result is to be attained. My suggestion would be that in the first place (for many and far-reaching reasons for which I hope to persuade your son) he should leave Heidelberg – the hotbed of his imagination – and should return to our cold, flat Leipzig.

At present I merely say that I pledge myself to turn your son Robert, by means of his talent and imagination, within three years into one of the greatest pianists now living. He shall play with more warmth and genius than Moscheles and on a grander scale than Hummel. The proof of this I offer you in my eleven-year-old daughter, whom I am now beginning to present to the world. As to composition, our Cantor Weinlig will no doubt be sufficient for present needs. But:

1. Robert very mistakenly thinks 'that the whole of piano playing consists in pure technique'; what a one-sided conception! I almost infer from this, either that he has never heard a pianist of genius at Heidelberg or else that he himself has advanced no farther in playing. When he left Leipzig he knew better what belongs to a good pianist, and my eleven-year-old Clara will show

21

him something different. But it is true that for Robert the greatest difficulty lies in the quiet, cold, well-considered, restrained conquest of technique, as the foundation of piano playing. I confess frankly that when – in the lessons which I gave him – I succeeded, after hard struggles and great contradictoriness on his part, after unheard-of pranks played by his unbridled fancy upon two creatures of pure reason like ourselves, in convincing him of the importance of a pure, exact, smooth, clear, well-marked and elegant touch, very often my advice bore little fruit for the next lesson, and I had to begin again, with my usual affection for him, to expound the old theme, to show him once more the distinctive qualities of the music which he had studied with me, and earnestly to insist on my doctrines (remember that I cared only for Robert and for the highest in art). And then he would excuse himself for the next week or fortnight or even longer; he could not come for this or that reason, and the excuses lasted – with a few exceptions – until he went to a town and to surroundings which in truth are not designed to restrain his unbridled fancy or quiet his unsettled ideas. Has our dear Robert changed – become more thoughtful, firmer, stronger, and may I say calmer and more manly? This does not appear from his letters.

2. I will not undertake Robert (that is if he means to live wholly for art in the future) unless for a year he has an hour with me almost every day.

Why? For once I ask you to have unquestioning confidence in me. But how can I do this now that I have a business at Dresden as well, and at Christmas am going to found a similar one in Berlin, Vienna and probably also in Paris? What will Robert's so-called Imagination-Man say to it if the lessons (lessons in touch, with an unemotional theme) have to be stolen from me and he is left to himself for from three to six weeks, to go on in the right direction? Honoured lady, neither of us can tell that; Robert himself knows best; he alone can say if he really has any determination.

3. Without committing myself further at present, I declare that the piano virtuoso (if he does not happen to be the most famous composer whose name has been honoured for years) can earn his living only if he gives lessons – but then, very easily and well. Good, intelligent teachers who have received an all-round education are wanted everywhere, and it is known that people pay 2–4 thaler an hour in Paris, Vienna, St Petersburg, Berlin, etc.; and 6–8 thaler in London. I am educating my daughter to be a teacher first of all, though – child as she is – she is already far superior to all other women pianists in the world, for she can improvise freely – yet I do not allow this to mislead me in any way. Robert would be able to live very comfortably in such places, as a piano teacher, since he has a small income of his own. For I should be sorry to think that he will eat up his capital.

But I wish to know if Robert will decide at once to give lessons here, since teaching needs years of training? Robert surely remembers what I demand from a good piano teacher? That is one question which I cannot answer; nor can I say whether Robert also himself can answer it.

4. Can Robert determine to study dry, cold theory, and all that belongs to it, with Weinlig for two years? With instruction in the piano I always combine lessons in the practical study of simple chords by means of which I impart a beautiful and correct touch, etc. etc. – in a word, everything that is not and never will be found in any piano school.

Has Robert condescended to learn even this small amount of theory, although in any case my lessons are sufficiently interesting? I must say, No. Will Robert now decide like my Clara to give some hours every day to writing exercises in three- and four-part composition? It is work which almost wholly silences the imagination – at least such a one as our Robert enjoys.

5. If Robert will not do all that I have said, then I ask: What part will he play, and what outlet will his imagination find?

From the frankness with which I have spoken of this, even if it has not been possible to treat it fully, you can easily see that I know how to deserve it later, if your son comes back to Leipzig, when he and Dr Carus can discuss everything with me more fully and we can advise together.

Your son will excuse me for not having answered his letter to me. My business and the education of my daughter must excuse all such neglect on my part, as well as the haste in which I have written this letter.

Most honoured friend, do not be anxious – compulsion is of little use in such matters: we must do our part as parents; God does the rest. If Robert has the courage and the strength to clear away my doubts when he is with me – and they might practically be removed in six months (so that in the contrary case everything would still not be lost) – then let him go in peace and give him your blessing. In the meantime you will be awaiting his answer to these few lines, the writer of which respectfully signs himself

Your most devoted servant,
Fr. Wieck.

For Schumann there was now no looking back. On 24th September he said goodbye to Heidelberg and to himself as a law student for ever. But it was characteristic that his journey to Leipzig was made, not direct, but by an elongated, circular route up the Rhine to Wesel, thence eastward to Detmold to visit his old friend Rosen, who had returned home, fully graduated, in June.

2
1830–1840

Ever since Johann Sebastian Bach held the post of cantor of St Thomas's church from 1723 to 1750, Leipzig had occupied a leading place in the history of German music. As a centre of industry and not the seat of a prince it had always enjoyed considerable independence in promulgating its culture, and in that way had anticipated the general trend towards nineteenth-century middle-class art. From small, occasional concerts held in various coffee-houses and inns had grown *Das grosse Konzert*, a concert society made memorable when Johann Adam Hiller took over musical directorship in 1763. Eighteen years later the society purchased the Gewandhaus (clothhall) building, and the ensuing Gewandhaus orchestral concerts, with their catholic programmes and eminent visiting soloists, were sufficient in themselves to account for a good deal of Leipzig's musical fame. In 1830 Pohlenz was musical director and Matthäi leader of the orchestra. The choir of St Thomas's under Cantor Weinlig would always assist at all choral concerts, and Pohlenz had organized choral societies for the same purpose. Then there was a newer, smaller orchestral society, *Euterpe*, directed by C. G. Müller. Many of its members also played in the Gewandhaus orchestra, but *Euterpe* aimed at being more selective in its choice of programmes and more ready to try out new, manuscript works. Chamber music could also be heard in public, at the regular quartet concerts directed by Matthäi. An enterprising young man of twenty-six, Heinrich Dorn, was musical director of the Leipzig Opera. Furthermore, the celebrated publishers, Breitkopf & Härtel, had their headquarters in the town, which consolidated and strengthened its musical position; and the *Allgemeine musikalische Zeitung*, a musical journal founded by Gottfried Härtel, was responsible for influencing musical taste throughout a large part of Germany.

As a retiring law student of eighteen, Schumann had touched

24

only the fringe of Leipzig's activities. He had been hardly aware of its long-established musical traditions. But now, in the atuumn of 1830, he arrived buoyed up by a big decision, full of determination and confidence in his own ability. It is not surprising that his immediate reactions on being thrown up against this wealth of musical proficiency were extreme. He was lost and bewildered, and his self-confidence changed abruptly into mortification as he looked back on his wasted past and realized the distance which separated his present achievement from the pinnacle of his ambitions. These gloomy thoughts threw him back into himself, and his letters to his mother resume all their old melancholy introspection. Up till December of that year he refers repeatedly to his dejection, restlessness, laziness and indifference, and he writes in November: 'Of my old fire and enthusiasm barely the ashes remain.' His inward conflict was aggravated by increasing financial complications: he had no money for clothes, no money to have his hair cut, no money for postage, no money to have his piano tuned, not even enough money to buy a pistol to shoot himself; yet with characteristic indulgence he had his portrait painted as a present for his mother! He was not blind to his thoughtless method of ordering his affairs, or of the inconsiderate demands he was continuously making on his family. 'This contempt and waste of money is a wretched characteristic of mine,' he writes on 15th December.

> You would not believe how careless I am – I often actually throw money away. I am always reproaching myself, and making good resolutions, but the next minute I have forgotten them, and am tipping someone eight groschen! My being away from home, and travelling about, have much to do with it, but most of the blame attaches to myself and my accursed carelessness. And I fear it will never get any better.

This irresponsibility and thoughtful sincerity were two further irreconcilable characteristics which contributed to his complex personality.

He was at this time living in Wieck's house, Grimmaische Gasse No. 36, as a resident pupil, so that he could enjoy the full benefit of that teacher's daily instruction and constant supervision, which, as may be remembered, was one of Wieck's stipulations before agreeing to take him on at all. From Wieck's letter to

Schumann's mother[1] it is obvious that Wieck was a shrewd judge of character; and that, while appreciating Schumann's unusual musicianship and imagination, he realized there was a certain instability in Schumann's temperament, an over-easy surrender to the impulse of the moment, which might destroy his chance of ultimate success. Wieck was a self-made man – his present influential position had been secured entirely through his own effort by making the most of his opportunities. His peculiar method of piano teaching had been devised by selection and rejection from the methods of Milchmayer and Bargiel, two eminent piano teachers with whom he had come into contact during his varied early life as a general tutor; and his sympathies were always with the more modern 'Clementi' school of pianos and playing, permitting greater powers of expression, rather than the 'Vienna' school, with its light-actioned instruments designed for brilliant display. Furthermore, in his teaching he was a psychologist, always prepared to make allowances for individual temperament. But beneath it all he remained a practical man of the world who could run a piano hire-business and a music lending library with commercial success. Schumann the extravert admired his common sense and firm resolve. But Schumann the visionary often deplored his fundamental commercialism, his opportunism and arrogance, even once going as far as to write in the diary: 'He is a charlatan and models his mannerisms on Paganini's.' So their relationship was in a constant state of flux, with Schumann at one moment full of ambition, resolution and readiness to entrust his whole artistic future to Wieck's guidance, and the next dejected, dissatisfied, and full of plans for leaving him on the slightest pretext, such as temporary absence on tour with Clara. As early as December 1830 he spoke of going to Hummel in Vienna for lessons and appeared innocently surprised at Wieck's indignation over the idea. He describes the incident in a letter to his mother on 15th December:

> The other day I suggested to him [Wieck], in a light and airy kind of way, my plan about Hummel; but he took it ill, and asked me whether I mistrusted him, or what; and whether, as a matter of fact, he was not quite the best master? He saw that I was startled by such unnecessary anger, but we are now quite friendly again, and he treats me most affectionately, like his own child. You can hardly

[1] See pages 21–3.

have a notion of his fire, his judgment, his view of art; and yet, when he speaks in his own or Clara's interests, he is as rude as a bear. . . .

In spite of their continued friendship, Schumann persisted in his idea of going to Hummel, and in August of the following year wrote a letter to the latter criticizing Wieck's teaching without the smallest pretence of loyalty. All his friends were against his going to Hummel, who, they said, was ten years behind the times, but Schumann was adamant, and in the end it was only fate that prevented him.

It may be remembered that Wieck expected his pupils to be not only keyboard virtuosi, but also all-round musicians with a knowledge of harmony and counterpoint. In his earlier relations with Schumann he had found it impossible to make him realize the necessity for this 'dry, cold theory', and now Schumann stubbornly refused to study the same subject with Weinlig, cantor of St Thomas's church, who had taught Richard Wagner for a short time and to whom Wieck had entrusted his own daughter's education. Instead Schumann elected to study with Dorn, the youthful conductor of the Opera, who appeared to represent the progressive as opposed to the academic school of thought. As people, the two were excellent friends, but musically Schumann again proved a difficult pupil. Inwardly he realized that discipline was essential to his musical thinking, yet the slightest check to his fancies was sufficient to arouse a storm of indignation. 'I shall never get on with Dorn,' he writes in January 1832 to Wieck, who was away on a concert tour with Clara,

> he wants to persuade me that music is nothing but fugues. Good heavens, how different people are! But I certainly feel that theoretical studies have a good influence upon me. Formerly I wrote down everything on the impulse of the moment, but now I follow the course of my ideas more, and sometimes stop short and look round to see where I am.

Nevertheless, Dorn realized that he could make no progress with such a wayward mind, and in April 1832 Schumann found himself without any guide save Marpurg's book of theory and Bach's *Well-tempered Clavier*. The latter he not only analysed thoroughly, but also devoured its content with immense appetite. 'The advantage of this [analysis] is great, and seems to have a strengthening moral effect upon one's whole system; for Bach was a thorough man, all over, there is nothing sickly or stunted about him, and his works seem written for eternity,' was his own comment on the process.[1]

A postcript to a letter dated 8th June 1832 from Schumann to Wieck said: 'Six hours ago I began my twenty-third year. In reality it is only my second,' and in that remark lies the clue to a good deal of Schumann's impatience and irritation with every kind of systematic study now forced on him at an age when training would normally have given way to positive achievement. Yet in spite of this feeling of academic frustration, his inner imagination was finding an outlet in its own free way. As he remarks in a letter during the spring of 1832: 'Though I listen to the opinions of experienced men with modesty and diffidence, still I do not blindly accept them.' During 1831 he had published his *Abegg Variations* for piano, also a fanciful collection of little pieces – partly inspired by Jean Paul's *Flegeljahre* – called *Papillons*. The poet Grillparzer, reviewing both publications in the *Wiener musikalische Zeitung*, started:

> It is always pleasant to stand on one's own feet, and to require neither crutches nor the shoulders of others. This is the first time we have met this probably young composer, who is one of the rarities of the age. He follows no school, but draws his inspirations entirely from himself, and does not adorn himself with strange feathers gathered in the sweat of his brow; on the contrary, he has created a new and ideal world for himself, in which he revels almost recklessly, and sometimes with quite original eccentricity.

In writing those prescient words, little did Grillparzer know he was heralding no less a person than the champion of musical romanticism in Germany. And throughout 1831 and 1832 Schumann had composed other piano pieces,[2] including a *Toccata* (Op. 7), an *Allegro* (Op. 8), a set of *Intermezzi* (Op. 4) and some *Studies on Caprices by Paganini* (Op. 3), all of them early manifestations of the new, poetic spirit which was to animate music throughout the nineteenth century. He was aware, too, that he was not standing alone, and in September 1831 he sent a fanciful review of Chopin's *Là ci darem* Variations for piano (Op. 2) to Fink, editor of the *Allgemeine musikalische Zeitung*, in which he paid enthusiastic tribute to a kindred spirit.

[1] In a letter to Kuntzsch, 27th July 1832.
[2] Several were extensively revised before emerging under these titles.

In October 1831, when Wieck left on a long concert tour with Clara, Schumann moved into lodgings of his own. On Wieck's return in May 1832 his house still remained Schumann's second home, for with such an inexhaustible supply of riddles, charades and tales of doubles, robbers and ghosts, Schumann was as much of a favourite with Wieck's younger sons as with Clara herself, now twelve. 'I have been in Arabia during your absence', he had written to her, 'in order to be able to relate all the fairytales which might please you.'

But all further piano lessons were out of the question: Wieck came back to find his pupil scarcely able to play at all. As early as January 1830, when practising six to seven hours daily in a desperate attempt to make up for lost time, Schumann was already complaining of a 'numbed' finger and an aching right hand. By May, 1832, diary entries specify a lamed third finger, while a medical affidavit prepared shortly before to gain him exemption from military service also mentions similar, though less acute, problems with his index finger too. During Wieck's absence he is known to have experimented with a mechanical finger-strengthener (referred to in his diary as the *Cigarren-mechanik*), though whether or not he was the 'famous pupil' to whom Wieck referred in his book, *Clavier und Gesang* (1853) as having had his third and fourth fingers wrecked by recourse to such a gadget remains a moot point. Writing to a Belgian admirer, Simonin de Sire, seven years later, Schumann summarized the whole matter with sound common sense: 'the hand trouble is nothing more than that some fingers (probably from too much writing and playing in earlier times) have become quite weak, so that I can hardly use them. This has often perturbed me. However, heaven now and then sends me a good idea instead, and so I think no more about the matter.'

At the time it nevertheless troubled him enough to try every possible kind of treatment from brandy-and-water bathing, herb poultices and *Tierbäder* (immersing the affected part in the blood of a freshly killed animal) to electricity and homoeopathy. The fact that Dr Hartmann, the homoeopath, prescribed 'a tiny, tiny powder' besides a strict diet with no wine or coffee and very little beer, recently prompted the researcher Eric Sams to claim mercury poisoning as the root of the trouble, – mercury at that time, together with a similar diet, being the common treatment for the syphilis which, in Sams's opinion, was already undermining Schumann's health in other ways too. Challengeable as this supposition has proved, Schumann's diaries nevertheless testify to enough erotically tinged exploits, notably in the context of a regular visitor to his bed called Christel (nick-named Charitas), to suggest that cigars and heavy drinking were not his only youthful indulgences. An entry in May, 1831, even refers to treatment from his medical-student friend, Glock, for what he calls 'the wound', subsequently specified as a sore (possibly torn) tip of the penis. But despite moments of black despair, driving him to wild schemes for taking up the cello (needing left-hand fingers only) or even theology, Schumann gradually came to terms with the disaster, realizing, if at first only gradually, that there was no further doubt as to his real life-work, composition. Even by July 1832 he was able to write to his brother, Julius: 'I cannot tell you how bravely I am making my way, and how happily and industriously I work at my one objective in life.'

The winter of 1832–3 Schumann spent at Zwickau. The main excitement was in November 1832, when Clara came over with her father to play at a concert at which parts of Schumann's G minor Symphony were performed by the local orchestra. Clara took the town by storm, but for Schumann the occasion was not so successful. In all probability the Symphony started off as an exercise in form set by Dorn; but as soon as he heard of the opportunity of having it played, he wrote to Müller, conductor of *Euterpe*, for some lessons in instrumentation. The help was not forthcoming, and much of the work's failure was due to miscalculations of scoring. In a letter to Hofmeister of 17th December he confessed: 'I often put in yellow instead of blue; but I consider this art so difficult that it will take long years' study to give one certainty and self-control'. The revision and continuation of the Symphony took up most of Schumann's remaining time at Zwickau, but after further performances of the first movement at Schneeberg in January 1833 and at Leipzig three months later it was heard no more.

This launching of a large-scale orchestral work, however unsuccessful, was a further step towards attracting public attention. His *Abegg Variations* and *Papillons* had received Grillparzer's favourable notice in the *Wiener musikalische Zeitung* and a more truthful if less enthusiastic review from

Rellstab in the Berlin *Iris*; also, the *Wiener Anzeiger* had made mention of his Paganini Caprices. Though the *Allgemeine musikalische Zeitung* had so far ignored his music, Fink, the editor, had accepted and published his article on Chopin, and the *Comet* had printed his 'Reminiscences of Clara Wieck's Concerts'. Nearly every criticism of his work drew attention to its striking originality – though to many this quality appeared more of a vice than a virtue. So when Schumann returned to Leipzig in the early part of 1833, he came not as an obscure student but as a personality capable of arousing curiosity and interest. His circle of friends grew larger, and many an evening they would meet together, either in the *Kaffeebaum* restaurant or in one of their own rooms, and prolong the pleasures of food and wine with never-ending discussion of topical problems. They deplored the prevalent decadence of music: the public's preference for the superficial virtuoso compositions of the day to the genuine music of the immediate past –the dross of Herz and Hünten to the pure gold of Beethoven and Schubert. They deplored the conservatism and impotence of the musical press. Then one day, to quote Schumann's subsequent account, 'the thought awakened in a wild young heart "Let us not look on idly, let us also lend our aid to progress, let us again bring the poetry of art to honour among men" '. And to do this they resolved to start a new music paper of progressive policy,[1] as a challenge to artistic complacency of every kind, as a help to young artists and, most important, as a champion of that awakening spirit in music, best described in a single word – romanticism. Wieck, when first approached, was sceptical. He had experienced his old pupil's short-lived enthusiasms before and doubted his powers of sustained interest and perseverance in anything. But a maturer sense of responsibility was noticeable in Schumann's approach to this particular undertaking, and Wieck eventually decided to co-operate as one of the paper's directors. Difficulties with the publishing and business aspects of the enterprise delayed the first number till April 1834, when it eventually appeared, with a distinguished list of contributors and Julius Knorr as editor, as the *Neue Leipziger Zeitschrift für Musik*. Very soon the editorship passed into Schumann's hands, and there is evidence of his teeming imagin-

[1] No doubt Schumann recalled Weber's similar aims when founding the *Harmonische Verein* in 1810.

ation on every page. Fanciful pseudonyms were allotted to many of his contributors, but even more mystifying to the reader was his incorporation of all his friends, dead as well as living, into the *Davidsbund*, a fictitious society he had originally created for an unrealized novel, whose purpose was to tease and antagonize the Philistines of art in every possible way. And it was in this *Davidsbund* world that Schumann himself would regularly masquerade as both Florestan and Eusebius, two imaginary characters (borrowed from the unrealized novel) long used in his diaries to argue out his own conflicting viewpoints – and already once introduced to the world in his 1831 article on Chopin's Op. 2. A diary entry for 1827 suggests that the idea came direct from Jean Paul, who 'mirrors himself in all his works, but each time in *two* persons: he is Albano and Schoppe, Siebenkäs and Leibgeber, Vult and Walt, Gustav and Fenk, Flamin and Victor. Only the unique Jean Paul could combine in himself two such different characters: but he is so – always complete opposites, if not extremes, united in his works and in himself.' Schumann's subdivision of his own personality was no mere romantic extravagance. A letter to his mother in May 1832 reveals acute awareness of the opposing claims of his inner spirit and the practical, everyday world. And now in the *Neue Leipziger Zeitschrift für Musik* the sensitive, introspective, poetic dreamer was finally resolved into Eusebius, and the bold, impulsive man of action into Florestan. The rare occasions when the two merged into one integrated personality were marked by the signature of Master Raro, a pseudonym which at other times hid the stable identity of Wieck.

Of all Schumann's friends there was perhaps no one who welcomed his return to Leipzig quite so much as Clara. She was now fourteen, and her performances on the many concert tours she had undertaken with her father all over Germany had won her an enviable reputation as a young pianist of the modern Clementi school. Yet none of the many celebrities she had encountered mattered to her in quite the same way as her old friend Robert, her old 'moon-struck maker of charades'. In June 1833 Schumann writes to his mother:

> Clara is as fond of me as ever, and is just as she used to be of old, wild and enthusiastic, skipping and running about like a child, and saying the most intensely thoughtful things. It is a pleasure to see

how her gifts of mind and heart keep developing faster and faster, and, as it were, leaf for leaf. The other day, as we were walking back from Connewitz (we go for a two or three hours' tramp almost every day), I heard her saying to herself: 'Oh, how happy I am! How happy!' Who would not love to hear that? On that same road there are a great many useless stones lying about in the middle of the footpath. Now, when I am talking, I often look more up than down, so she always walks behind me, and gently pulls my coat at every stone to prevent my falling; meantime she stumbles over them herself!

There was a mature sympathy in her youthfulness, and its warmth opened Schumann's heart and permitted him to reveal his inner nature to her in a way that he found possible with only a few people. Their world was one of music and romance, and no flights of fancy were too extravagant for them. It is pleasant to think of Schumann in his summer lodgings in Riedel's Garden, when an attack of malaria prevented him from visiting Clara, devising what he termed

> a plan of sympathy – this: tomorrow on the stroke of 11 I shall play the *adagio* from Chopin's variations and at the same time I shall think of you very hard, exclusively of you. Now the request is that you should do the same, so that we may see each other and meet in spirit. The place will probably be over the little Thomaspförtchen, where our doubles will meet.

There is a musical memorial of this happy summer of 1833 in Schumann's *Impromptus on a Theme by Clara Wieck*, which was his birthday present to her father in August.

During the autumn Schumann moved from Riedel's Garden to No. 21 Burgstrasse, where he had rooms on the fourth floor. And it was there that he heard of the successive deaths of his much-loved sister-in-law Rosalie and his brother Julius. The double tragedy was more than his constitution could stand; it not only swamped his mind and sterilized his thinking, but also induced serious physical consequences which he described to his mother as 'violent rushes of blood to the head, inexpressible nervousness, shortness of breath, sudden faintness'. In this same letter of 27th November he also writes: 'I will say nothing of the past weeks. I was more like a statue than anything else, without either heat or cold; but by dint of forced work life returned gradually.' For a long time the loneliness and terror of the long winter nights were unbearable to him. Fearing that he might fling himself out of the window he moved down to a first floor flat, and even then persuaded one of his more even-tempered friends, a certain Lühe, to sleep with him to prevent him, in a moment of extreme stress, from taking any other desperate action. It was not till January 1834 that his mind grew calmer, when a growing intimacy with Ludwig Schunke, a young pianist recently come to Leipzig, helped to turn his thoughts away from himself and his melancholy. Schunke realized that distraction was essential to Schumann, and lost no time in introducing him to Carl Voigt, one of Leipzig's rich patrons of the arts, and his wife Henriette, who was herself a talented pianist and one-time pupil of Clementi's pupil Ludwig Berger. Schumann once said that he would rather lose all his friends together than Schunke, and as for Henriette, his regard for her grew into a romantic friendship which partly compensated for the warmth recently lost to him.

Yet his bruised spirit still cried for affection, for some more lasting assuagement; and it was in this emotionally unsatisfied state that during the summer of 1834 his longings came to rest on Ernestine von Fricken. She had come to Leipzig that April to study the piano with Wieck; and as she lived in his house, it was not long before Clara introduced her to the beloved Robert. Ernestine was then nearly eighteen, beautiful in appearance, charming in manner, and the growing attentions of an agreeable young musician of twenty-three undoubtedly caused her to radiate as never before. Schumann was entranced: 'She has a delightfully pure, childlike mind, is delicate and thoughtful, deeply attached to me and everything artistic, and uncommonly musical,' he writes to his mother in July 1834, ' – in short just such a one as I might wish to have for a wife.' Henriette was his other confidante, and made it possible for the two of them to meet alone in her house; while their standing together as god-parents to Wieck's baby daughter[1] seemed to bring them into a closer alliance. Clara, meanwhile, was nonplussed by her Robert's behaviour – even though still a child of fifteen, she could intercept glances and realize painfully that at times her company was not wanted. But Schumann was now thinking primarily of himself. In his mind there still lingered some advice given him by a doctor during his

[1] Wieck remarried in 1828, four years after his first wife left him.

recent breakdown: 'Medicine is no good here. You need a wife'; and in September he became secretly engaged to Ernestine just before she returned to Asch, her home. For a while their separation, broken only by occasional hasty meetings, intensified their love; but during 1835 Schumann's growing realization that Ernestine's personality was not as interesting as he first thought, together with his discovery that she was only an impecunious, adopted illegitimate daughter of Baron von Fricken, brought the affair to a gradual end. While it lasted it was full of intoxicating delight, which Schumann recorded in the musical diary of his life in terms of *Carnaval*, a set of piano variations on the letters A S C H,[1] translated into notes. Even the theme of his *Études symphoniques* was composed by Baron von Fricken. But once it was over, Schumann had no pangs, other than desultory pangs of conscience, for there were distractions of another kind in the air.

In the early autumn of 1835 Mendelssohn arrived at Leipzig, to take over the work of the retiring musical director, Pohlenz. His reputation had preceded him, and the town in consequence was astir with curiosity and expectation. When only twenty-four, Mendelssohn had been invited to conduct the Lower Rhenish Musical Festival, and his success there had led to his appointment as musical director at Düsseldorf. And now, though only twenty-six, he had come to take charge of Germany's leading musical city. Schumann first met him at Wieck's house and immediately succumbed to that charming manner, which had power to enslave all who encountered it. For Mendelssohn had every quality that befitted his upbringing in an environment of culture and ease. His family belonged to the class of moneyed intelligentsia, and their Berlin home was frequented by all the most distinguished writers, poets, artists and musicians of the day. Furthermore, his mind had been broadened and enriched through extensive travel. Schumann, in comparison, felt dwarfed and provincial, and quite overlooking the infinitely richer and deeper range of his own imagination, he soon put Mendelssohn on a high pedestal which the latter, accustomed to such treatment, found wholly acceptable. Personal admiration was matched by artistic admiration, and after Mendelssohn's début at the Gewandhaus on 4th October Schumann wrote an enthusiastic account of the occasion

[1] S being Es = German for E flat, H German for B flat.

in 'Letters of an Enthusiast' in the *Neue Zeitschrift*, condemning only the modern practice of conducting with a baton: 'For my part, I disliked the conductor's stick in the overture as in the symphony. When Matthäi stood at the head of the orchestra, before Mendelssohn, orchestral works were performed without a time-beating conductor.' But Mendelssohn was determined to abolish the old custom of the concert-master directing performances from his seat in the orchestra, and soon made it quite clear that he himself intended to direct orchestral concerts, and not only choral concerts as his predecessors up to the time of Pohlenz had done. Matthäi's death on 4th November made this reform easier, for Mendelssohn was able to appoint his gifted young friend Ferdinand David as leader of the orchestra, permitting intimate co-operation. Mendelssohn's achievements attracted many distinguished visitors to Leipzig during the next few years, and its musical life certainly flourished as never before. In the autumn of 1835 Schumann was able to meet two artists he had long since admired from a distance: first Chopin, who stayed for just one day, and then Moscheles, who had come over from England for a longer period. In Moscheles Schumann had long seen either a possible London correspondent for the *Neue Zeitschrift* or else a means of obtaining one, and had written to him in February for that very purpose, describing the paper's circulation as 'extraordinary and universal'. It was, in fact, absorbing all his time and energies; not only in his own contributions describing the militant activities of the Davidites, but also in private letters to correspondents and general editorial duties. Nevertheless he found time to complete two piano Sonatas in F sharp minor (Op. 11), and G minor (Op. 22), also to work at a third in F minor. The first of the three had the significant dedication: 'To Clara, from Florestan and Eusebius.'

Throughout the autumn of 1835 Wieck's house had remained a happy meeting-ground for all musicians. And Schumann, in consequence, found himself again much in the company of Clara. She was now sixteen, but the many experiences crowded into her life had ripened her personality beyond all relation to her years. Her performance of her own new A minor piano concerto at the Gewandhaus on 9th November, with Mendelssohn on the rostrum, set the seal on all her earlier successes, and there was now no doubting that a great future lay before her as a pianist to whom the poetry of music mattered above all else. Ever since she was a child Schumann had followed up her achievements with whole-hearted admiration; he had watched the gradual unfolding of her mind and her heart, and now, in her eyes, he saw a look which told him the truth about their relationship. She loved him, he loved her, they had always loved each other, and he knew then, in a flash of intuition, that the paths of their lives would one day converge. No word was spoken, but the evening before Clara set out on a concert tour in November, Schumann came to say goodbye, and kissed her as she guided him, light in hand, down the stairs. They met next in December at Zwickau, where Clara was giving a concert, and they kissed again. And in January 1836 Schumann travelled to Dresden, where Clara was on holiday, and in her father's absence they told each other of their love. On 4th February Schumann's mother died, but of this he writes:

> Your radiant image shines through the darkness and helps me to bear everything better. . . . At Leipzig my first care shall be to put my worldly affairs in order. I am quite clear about my heart. Perhaps your father will not refuse if I ask him for his blessing. Of course there is much to be thought of and arranged. But I put great trust in our guardian angel. Fate always intended us for one another. I have known that a long time, but my hopes were never strong enough to tell you and get your answer before. . . . The room is getting dark. Passengers near me are going to sleep. It is sleeting and snowing outside. But I will squeeze myself right into a corner, bury my face in the cushions and think only of you.
>
> Your ROBERT

Schumann was secretly confident that Wieck had always hoped for such a son-in-law, and would now rejoice with them in their happiness. In this he was mistaken. On hearing the news Wieck adopted an attitude which, though incomprehensible to an impulsive young lover such as Schumann, was wholly reasonable to him. His whole life had been devoted to Clara and her music, she was on the threshold of a great career and, most important, she was only sixteen and to him still a child – his child. Drastic measures seemed imperative, so he forbade all further meetings and communications between them while artfully contriving to divert Clara's attention to her new singing teacher, Carl Banck. To drown his sorrows Schumann again turned heavily to drink and, as he admits in the diary, to his old friend Christel. His excesses led to further financial embarrassments and urgent requests for money from Eduard and Carl; and his irregular habits and rowdiness even caused his kindly landlady, the widowed Frau Devrient, to threaten to throw him out. He soon confided in her, and writes:

> Why should I make a moan to you about ruined plans, of deserved and undeserved sorrows, of youthful griefs such as come upon every one of us? – for I, too, have some glorious hours at the piano, talking to delightful people, in the consciousness of an honourable sphere of action and in the hope of accomplishing still greater things. But it is just this exalted state of mind which often ends in presumption, and then I feel inclined to take the world by storm. Then the reaction sets in, followed by artificial means of recuperating one's energies. I know full well what would be the one thing to reconcile such dangerous extremes, and that is – a loving woman.

Musically the winter season of 1836–7 was even more brilliant than the previous one, and in the centre of it all Mendelssohn reigned supreme. His conscientious work with the orchestra, demanding individual perfection from every instrumentalist and especially the wind players, had led to astonishing results. 'The life of the orchestra was quickened by an entirely new pulsation animated by a spirit of which the listeners had formed no previous conception,' was the criticism of a contemporary.[1] To Schumann Mendelssohn's tireless energy and efficiency were almost super-human: 'I look up to him as to a high mountain. He is a real god,' he writes to his family, and a little later: 'Not a day passes without his producing at least a few thoughts that might straightway be engraved in gold.' In September Chopin paid Leipzig another visit, and spent a whole day making music with Schumann. And in a letter to his sister-in-law, Therese, in November Schumann mentions Ludwig Berger, the pianist; Mlle Carl, the singer; Lipinski, the violinist; Stamaty, the pianist; David, the new leader of the orchestra; Walter von Goethe, the poet's grandson; and William Sterndale Bennett, 'a thorough Englishman, a glorious artist and a beautiful and poetical soul', as among the many friends who beguiled him. Particular mention must be made of his friendship with Sterndale Bennett, who had come over from England to enrich his mind in the land of music; also his

[1] Dörffel, the pianist.

enthusiasm for Bennett's music, which modelled itself so faithfully on Mendelssohn. Schumann's *Études symphoniques*,
published in 1837, were dedicated to Bennett, and the quotation
from Marschner's *Ivanhoe* opera *Der Templer und die Jüdin* in
the finale is a compliment to Bennett's England.

But at heart Schumann yearned for Clara only, and it was
during this time that he began the sketches of the great C major
Phantasie, of which the first movement, as he told her on its
completion in 1838, was 'the most passionate thing I have ever
composed – a deep lament, for you'. On 13th August 1837 Clara
gave a recital at Leipzig and included some of Schumann's *Études
symphoniques* in her programme – her only way of speaking to
him; but they could bear the separation no longer, and the next
day, by surreptitious letters, they became secretly engaged. 'So
one little "yes" is all you want? What an important little word it
is! Surely a heart so full of inexpressible love as mine can utter it
freely. I can indeed say it. My inmost soul whispers it unceasingly
to you,' was Clara's answer. And on 13th September, Clara's
eighteenth birthday, Schumann asked Wieck for his consent,
pleading his own improved position in the musical world, his
constancy during the last eighteen months, and promising to
undergo any further test of devotion that Wieck might choose to
impose. But again he met with no success. Wieck's prime
objection remained that Clara was a pianist, and that she could
marry only a husband rich enough to save her from financial
worries and household cares. And at this stage he still undoubtedly acted, so he thought, in Clara's interests; for he had
had nearly ten years in which to discover Schumann's irresponsibility over money, his abrupt changes of mind and mood and his
occasional weakness of will. Once again Schumann was plunged
into suicidal despair. 'Do all you can to find a way out; I will
follow like a child . . .' he writes to Clara on the morning of 18th
September. 'How my poor head swims! I could laugh for very
anguish. This cannot go on much longer – my health will not
stand it. . . . God preserve me from despair. My life is torn up by
the roots.' But that same afternoon he pulls himself together
somewhat:

> If he drives us to extremes by persisting in refusing his consent
> for a year and a half or two years more, we must take the law into
> our own hands. . . . In that case a magistrate would marry us.

Heaven send it may not come to that.... Let me have a few soothing, kind words soon. My picture of you is much clearer and lovelier now than when I wrote this morning, and your thrice repeated 'steadfast' is a message from Heaven's blue.

During the winter of 1837–8 Clara was away with her father on a long concert tour, and in Vienna she experienced the biggest successes of her life and receptions at times overwhelming in their spontaneity. The greatest honour was her election as court pianist to the Emperor of Austria, and Schumann, in consequence, began to make discreet inquiries about the possibility of taking his doctor's degree in philosophy at Leipzig University, thinking that some official standing was now more than ever necessary to him from Wieck's standpoint. Clara's letters to him from Vienna had salutary effects in every way.

> If you only knew how I value your opinions, not only in art, but in everything, and how much your letters cheer me up! So tell me about all that goes on round you, about people, towns and customs. You are very sharp-sighted, and I love to follow you in your reflections. It does not do to get too much absorbed in self and one's own interests, as one is then very apt to lose all insight and penetration into the outer world. There is so much beauty, richness and novelty in this world of ours. If I had said that oftener to myself in former days, I should have done more, and should have got on further,

he writes to her in March. His own life at Leipzig had been much occupied with the paper and also with friends, including two young English girls, Clara Novello, the singer, and Robena Laidlaw, the pianist, both of whom had taken part in public concerts. The Belgian violinist Vieuxtemps had been another distinguished visitor, but perhaps Henselt's company gave Schumann more delight than any other. 'Our first meeting was, I may say, like that of two brothers,' he tells Clara. 'Sometimes there is really something demoniacal about him like Paganini, Napoleon or Madame Schröder.[1] At other times he seemed like a troubadour, you know, with a lovely large cap and feathers.' This was of special interest to Clara, whose recital programmes frequently included Henselt's *Si oiseau j'étais* alongside other 'modern' music by Chopin, Mendelssohn and her own works. When making music in intimate surroundings she was an

[1] Wilhelmine Schröder-Devrient, the famous dramatic soprano.

enthusiastic propagandist for Schumann's compositions, but she realized they were unsuitable for performance before the general public, nurtured as it was on bravura variations. It is interesting to see in one of her letters to Schumann at this time that she begged him to be lucid when writing the string Quartet he had in mind, as it hurt her so much when people did not understand him. But Schumann was now quite impervious to criticism. His mind was overflowing with music which he could fasten down on paper as spontaneously as the ideas occurred to him, and he confessed that, even were he marooned on a desert island, he could not refrain from composing. He explains his present attitude to composition in a letter to Clara on 13th April 1838:

> I am affected by everything that goes on in the world and think it all over in my own way, politics, literature and people, and then I long to express my feelings and find an outlet for them in music. That is why my compositions are sometimes difficult to understand, because they are connected with distant interests; and sometimes striking, because everything extraordinary that happens impresses me and impels me to express it in music. And that is why so few [modern] compositions satisfy me, because, apart from all their faults of construction, they deal in musical sentiment of the lowest order, and in commonplace lyrical effusions. The best of what is done here does not equal my earliest musical efforts. Theirs may be a flower, but mine is a poem, and infinitely more spiritual; theirs is a mere natural impulse, mine the result of poetical consciousness.

In this and other similar statements he revealed that some extra-musical stimulus was nearly always essential to start his musical imagination working at all. Sound-patterns created for their own sake had no justification whatsoever in his eyes; at the same time he was aware that music should never usurp the place of words or paint as a descriptive medium. To him it was first and foremost a subjective language for the expression of thoughts and feelings and all things unattainable and undefinable, made of the stuff of dreams. In consequence his music became the diary of his soul-life, and at this particular time its sole inspiration was Clara. The *Phantasie* (Op. 17) and *Kreisleriana* (Op. 16), completed in 1838, are nothing else in substance than his yearning for her; the *Davidsbündlertänze* (Op. 6) and *Novelletten* (Op. 21), composed in 1837 and 1838 respectively, speak of more varied emotions concerning her; while the *Phantasiestücke* (Op. 12) of 1837 and

Kinderscenen (Op. 15) of 1838 can also be traced back to her – even if less directly. He summarized everything in a letter dated Easter Tuesday 1838: '. . . It is very curious, but if I write much to you, as I am doing now, I cannot compose. The music all goes to you. . . .'

It was at this time that the minds of both Clara and Schumann were much occupied with the thought of settling in Vienna. Money remained Wieck's main bone of contention in opposing their marriage, and Vienna seemed to offer them every chance of doubling their income – both in Clara's concert fees and Schumann's royalties. Consequently the whole of the summer was occupied with plans for transferring the *Neue Zeitschrift* to Vienna, and temporarily leaving the editorship in the hands of Oswald Lorenz at Leipzig, Schumann went there in September to make personal inquiries about obtaining a licence. He knew the Vienna authorities had a reputation for slowness in matters of this kind, but as the paper dealt only with artistic topics and had been circulated in the Austrian states ever since its foundation, he hoped to publish his first Vienna number not later than January 1839. But disappointments awaited him. He revelled in the surrounding countryside and derived a deal of amusement from his experiences; but Vienna, the one-time home of Haydn, Mozart, Beethoven and Schubert, he found to be full of gossips and pettiness, and the celebrated Viennese good nature but a pleasant face. And he sought in vain for artists: 'I mean artists who not only play one or two instruments pretty well, but are large-minded men who understand Shakespeare and Jean Paul,' he writes to his sister-in-law Therese. He had trouble in finding a suitable publisher, became entangled in a mesh of red tape on approaching the censorship and, worst of all, discovered that the brave, progressive policy which differentiated the paper from all others might have to be modified to meet the demands of a troublesome government department. This was beyond all endurance, for in asserting himself as editor during the last few years his main concern had been to keep all his contributors to a strict 'party' line. Zuccalmaglio, who wrote as Wedel, the village sexton, and was perhaps Schumann's most valued contributor, was severely reprimanded for making fun of Berlioz in an article, 'The Prize Symphony', and had to be reminded that the paper stood for youth and progress. Similarly Keferstein, whose association with the paper went back to its foundation, was questioned whether he still had the same interest in the younger generation as he once had. And any writer[1] who genuinely admired the past, or was prepared to attack the Philistines of the present, or who had hopes for the future, was quite sure of having his articles accepted. Schumann had no intention of modifying his views now that the paper's influence was becoming so widely felt, so he abandoned all his Vienna plans and was back at Leipzig by April 1839. Before leaving he accomplished one piece of good work, valued by posterity, if not by his contemporaries. On visiting Schubert's brother, a poor schoolmaster with eight children, he discovered a pile of unpublished manuscripts including several operas, four masses and five symphonies, which he immediately brought to the notice of the publishers Breitkopf & Härtel. And he enriched his own possessions by returning with a small, rusty steel pen which he found on Beethoven's grave in the Währing cemetery, where both Beethoven and Schubert were buried.

On his way back to Leipzig Schumann had news of his brother Eduard's illness. It was not a complete surprise to him, because towards the end of March, while absorbed in a new composition, he had been haunted by a strange presentiment of death, and his mind was flooded with visions of funerals, coffins and despairing faces as he worked. His immediate choice of title was *Leichenfantasie*, but this was eventually changed to *Nachtstücke* (Op. 23). At the moment of his brother's death on 6th April Schumann told Clara that he distinctly heard a chorale played by trombones. His temperament, so finely attuned to the remoter waves of human experience, had little difficulty in accepting the mystical and supernatural. It was a grievous blow, as from Eduard he had received not only sympathy but also practical help at any time of trouble. But the experience of death was becoming less strange to him: both his friend Ludwig Schunke and his mother had died in the last few years, and Clara's fears for a return of his 1833 breakdown proved needless. At the same time his life was far from settled or happy. Clara was away in Paris, oppressed with business worries pertaining to her concerts, because for the first time Wieck, in a final effort to make her realize her dependence on him, had remained behind at home. The ruse almost succeeded,

[1] Such as Hirschbach, who came to Schumann's notice in 1838.

for Clara, in a suddenly renewed outburst of filial affection, suggested to Schumann that their marriage should be postponed until their financial future was more assured, and that in the meantime she should continue her career with her father at her side. Schumann was bitterly hurt, though he never for a moment doubted her love. Even though Clara's name was a household word, whereas his was comparatively obscure and unknown, he had complete confidence in his musical future, and the thought that Clara would sacrifice anything in marrying him never occurred to him. Whenever she worried about any lack in the appreciation accorded to him he replied, with remarkable fore-sight, that she would live to see the day when his compositions would come into notice and be much talked about. Furthermore, since October, 1837, he had kept a *Haushaltbuch* in which to record factual details of his daily life, with special reference to every penny earned or spent. And reviewing his financial situation anew, he realized they had means to live adequately, even if not grandly. His only doubts concerned his temperament, as he confesses in a letter of 3rd June, 1839:

> In years to come you will often worry about me, so much is still needed to make a man of me; I am often too restless, too childish, too yielding; and I often abandon myself to whatever gives me pleasure without considering other people; in short, I have my bad days on which there is nothing to be done with me.

Loyal as Clara was to her father despite all, the significance of Schumann's early nickname for him, Meister Allesgeld, began to sink in when he now drew up conditions for the marriage only allowing her a small interest on her past earnings, which he was to retain, besides cutting her out of his will and insisting that Schumann should settle two-thirds of his own capital on her and allow a solicitor of Wieck's choosing to examine his accounts. Furthermore they were to live outside Saxony, to make no attempt to contact him, and to be married by Michaelmas. After the next affront, a refusal to correspond with Schumann at all except through Clementine Wieck, his wife, by September 1839 Clara was more than ready to sign an affidavit seeking legal permission to marry without her father's consent. In court Wieck had to be called to order for his violent outbursts against Schumann as musician, potential wage-earner and man – notably as regards inconstancy with women (in this Wieck even un-successfully sought support from the jilted Ernestine) and addiction to drink. Only the drinking charge was accepted. But their appeal against it gave Wieck time to circulate a document, signed under the fictitious name of Lehmann, slandering Schumann in more personal ways. Though ready to admit to 'a certain amount of dissipation before I met Clara', Schumann was totally unprepared for such ruthless public defamation of his character. In his anguish he would have started proceedings for libel but for the persuasion of his lawyer friend, Töpken.

Meanwhile Clara, between concert tours, found some comfort in the home of her mother, Frau Bargiel,[1] in Berlin. And Schumann at Leipzig attempted to pick up the threads of his old life there. He had the satisfaction of hearing the first performance at the Gewandhaus of Schubert's 'Great' C major Symphony, which he had discovered in manuscript in Vienna and sent to Mendelssohn. His confidence in the work was renewed and he pronounced it as 'the greatest achievement in instrumental music since Beethoven, not excepting even Spohr and Mendelssohn', and confesses 'it has made me tingle to be at work on a symphony, too, and I believe something will come of it, once I am happily married to Clara. . . .'[2] Liszt's visit in March 1840 gave him the long-awaited opportunity of meeting perhaps the most lionized artist of the day, but in spite of spontaneous affection and admiration for Liszt, he writes: 'But his world is not mine, Clärchen. Art, as we know it – you when you play, I when I compose – has an intimate charm that is worth more to me than all Liszt's splendour and tinsel.' His own piano compositions were growing apace. Vienna had inspired *Faschingsschwank aus Wien* (Op. 26), and during 1839 he had also written *Blumenstück* (Op. 19), *Humoreske* (Op. 20) and *Three Romances* (Op. 28) as well as the *Nachtstücke* already mentioned. In October that year he discovered from his publishers that between two hundred and fifty and three hundred copies of *Carnaval* and *Phantasiestücke* had already been sold, and between three hundred and three hundred and fifty of the *Kinderscenen*, though published only six months. In 1840 the piano no longer seemed an adequate medium

---

[1] She had left Wieck in 1824, and married the Berlin piano teacher Adolf Bargiel shortly afterwards.

[2] In a letter to E. A. Becker, 11th December 1839.

for his ideas, and he began a great outpouring of song, selecting the verses of Heine and fellow Romantics who said in words all that he wanted to express in music. In May he writes to Clara: 'I have been composing so much that it really seems quite uncanny at times. I cannot help it, and should like to sing myself to death, like a nightingale.' In spite of his complete confidence in his powers as a composer, he still felt that he lacked an official position, and for Clara's sake resumed inquiries about obtaining a doctor's degree, now addressing them to his friend Keferstein, who had some influence at Jena University. He was prepared to write a thesis on Shakespeare and his relation to music, but wondered if it were possible for the honour to come in recognition of his past services as composer and critic, and whether it could be a Doctorate of Music. Though this last wish was not gratified, since there is no such degree in Germany, he was soon made a Doctor of Philosophy *honoris causa* by the University of Jena, which caused him pleasure in the delight he knew it would give Clara. In July he presented her with a more tangible token of love – a Härtel grand piano, delivered in her rooms, as a complete surprise, while he took her for a walk.

On 12th August the Court of Appeal gave its decision in their favour. Throughout the four long years of frustration they had felt in their hearts that 'fate always intended us for one another', and the legal sanction only confirmed a decision they made long ago and knew to be wholly and unquestionably right. They were married the day before Clara's twenty-first birthday, 12th September 1840.

'What can I write about this day?' writes Clara in her diary.

> We were married at Schönefeld at ten o'clock. First came a chorale, and after that a short address by Wildenhahn, the preacher, a friend of Robert's youth. His words were simple, but heartfelt. My whole self was filled with gratitude to Him who had brought us safely over so many rocks and precipices to meet at last. I prayed fervently that He would preserve my Robert to me for many, many years. Indeed, the thought that I might one day lose him is enough to send me out of my mind. Heaven avert this calamity! I could not bear it.
>
> Emilie and Elise List took me by surprise after the wedding. We spent the morning in company with Reuter, Wenzel, Herrmann, Becker, Mother and the Lists, at the Carls', the afternoon at Zweinaundorf and the evening at the Carls' again, when Madame List came too.

There was a little dancing, no excessive gaiety, but every face shone with real satisfaction. The weather was lovely. Even the sun, which had hidden his face for many days, shed his warm beams upon us as we drove to church, as if to bless our union. It was a day without a jar, and I may thus enter it in this book as the fairest and most momentous of my life.

3

1840–1856

The years immediately following Schumann's marriage were the happiest he had ever known, or was to know, for the fulfilment of his love brought with it the fulfilment of his artistic powers. It was as if all his pent-up emotion, now transmuted into sheer gladness and delight, surged up within him and broke loose in a flood of musical images which he could hardly fasten down on paper before they dissolved into feeling again. Even more valuable than happiness was the deep content which now took the place of all the restless, spiritual striving of his youth. In Clara he found himself; and though she was ten years his junior, her love and her encouragement gave him the harbourage he had so long sought. And in that harbourage he was satisfied to turn his back on the outside world, and live and work within himself and the walls of their lodgings at No. 5 Inselstrasse. At first Clara, likewise, found her chief joy in losing herself in her husband. If at times she cast longing looks at her own silent piano while her husband in another room composed at his (the 'evils of thin walls' was a mutual complaint) or while engrossed in household duties, she felt that what her fingers lost in agility her mind gained in understanding and experience. In their spare time they would sometimes study literature together: Jean Paul, Shakespeare and Goethe; at other times the literature of music, often with special relation to what Schumann himself was composing at the time. They had started their married life with Bach's *Well-tempered Clavier*, and 1841, Schumann's symphonic year, began with a study of Beethoven's orchestral scores. During 1842, the year of chamber music, they perused the quartets of Haydn and Mozart. So that in the diary of their married life which they would write in turn, week by week, the following entry, made by Schumann in August 1841, is typical:

Clara is studying a great deal of Beethoven (together with much

48

wifely attention to Schumann) with right good will; she has helped me much in arranging my symphony, and in the intervals she is reading Goethe's life, and she chops beans when necessary! Music she cares for more than anything, and that gives me great pleasure.

The only conflict in an otherwise perfectly harmonious relationship was when Clara went away to give concerts. Schumann found separation from his wife as unbearable as touring with her – at neither time could he compose, and the ignominy of his position when she turned wage-earner was distasteful to his sensitive temperament.

The year of 1840 was largely devoted to sets and cycles of songs, including Opp. 24, 25, 27, 29–31, 33–6, 39, 40, 42, 43, 45, 48, 49 and 53, for Schumann found a continuous source of inspiration in the subjective sentiments of the romantic poets. He could identify their emotions with his own, so that his music never failed to capture the essential overtones of the verse. Hitherto his ideas had always taken shape at the piano, through the medium of the keyboard – now they travelled straight from his head on to manuscript paper, and on 28th September 1840 he writes to Stamaty: 'My own work has become gayer, gentler and more melodious in character.' But in spite of the many exquisite miniatures that came from his pen with Schubertian spontaneity and ease, his first hearing of Schubert's C major symphony the previous year, coupled with constant urgings from Clara to spread his wings, was gradually beginning to make the lure of the orchestra irresistible. Already on October 13, a month and a day after his wedding, the diary records the first of several symphonic forays. By January, 1841, his imagination was fully alight. 'It was born in a fiery hour' was his comment on what very soon emerged as his Symphony No. 1 in B flat major, a work growing from his own personal feelings of rebirth no less than a spring poem by his slightly younger contemporary, Adolph Böttger. As he put it in a subsequent letter to Spohr:

> It was inspired, if I may say so, by the spirit of spring which seems to possess us all anew every year, irrespective of age. The music is not intended to describe or paint anything definite, but I believe the season did much to shape the particular form it took.

The work was sketched between 23rd and 26th January, and the orchestration completed by 20th February, though such intense concentration cost Schumann many a sleepless night, and exhaustion was the natural outcome. On 31st March it was given its first performance under Mendelssohn at the Gewandhaus, in a concert at which Clara played part of Chopin's F minor Concerto as well as solos by Schumann. The occasion was an overwhelming success for both husband and wife, and of the Symphony Schumann writes:

> How much I enjoyed hearing it performed! and so did other people; for it was received with an amount of sympathy, such as I don't think has been accorded to any modern symphony since Beethoven.

His faith in it was complete, and a cool press notice in the *Leipziger Zeitung* provoked him to write indignantly to the critic, E. F. Wenzel:

> Was that your essay . . . ? I was so much hurt by it! I had been in such good spirits. To point to the *future*, after a work performed with so much enthusiasm – and in such cool words! And yet it *surprised* you? I hate those expressions like poison. I have been too industrious all my life to be spoken of as a possible future light, and to surprise people – I know that much.

As his self-confidence increased, he more frequently lost patience with his adverse critics, and in May 1841 he protests to another musicologist, C. Kossmaly:

> I was a little disappointed to find myself relegated to the second rank in your essay on song-writers. It is not that I claim a place in the first, but that I feel I deserve a place apart. I am anything but pleased to see myself classed with Reissiger, Curschmann, etc. My aims and my abilities are, I know, far higher, and I hope you will admit this without accusing me of vanity, which is far from me.

As 1840 had been devoted to song and the preceding years to piano music, so 1841 was the year of orchestral music. An *Overture, Scherzo and Finale* (Op. 52), sketched and scored in April and May, followed hard on the heels of the 'Spring' Symphony. Then came a *Phantasie* in A minor, afterwards transformed into the first movement of the piano Concerto, Op. 54, and a second Symphony, in D minor was Schumann's birthday surprise for Clara on 13th September. In the early part of November a 'little Symphony in C minor' was sketched but never completed.[1] The first performances of the second Symphony and the *Overture, Scherzo and Finale* were given at the Gewandhaus on 6th December 1841 in a concert at which both Liszt and Clara appeared as soloists; but the two works were not so well received as the first. Schumann was disappointed, but not deterred. 'It was almost too much at once, I think, and then we missed Mendelssohn as conductor,' he writes to Kossmaly on 8th January 1842. 'But all that matters nothing. I know the things are not a whit behind the first, and sooner or later will assert themselves in their own way' – an estimate as right in the case of the revised version of the D minor Symphony, which appeared in 1851, as it was wrong for the *Overture, Scherzo and Finale*.

On 1st September 1841 a daughter was born to Clara. She was christened Marie, and Mendelssohn was among the god-parents. Both parents were delighted, but for Clara the claims of motherhood on top of those of wife and artist brought new problems. Her inner conflict is frequently revealed in such entries in the diary as these: 'I also owe it to my reputation not to retire completely. It is a feeling of duty towards you and towards myself which speaks in me. And again: 'I shall be quite forgotten, and in a few years' time, when perhaps we shall want to make a tour, who knows what other things in art people may be interested in.' However, in February 1842 an invitation from Bremen and Hamburg, which embraced the desire to hear both Clara's playing and Schumann's B flat Symphony, made it possible for them to go away together. In each place the Symphony was well received, but Clara's playing inevitably met with the greater applause; and at Oldenburg an invitation to the court for Clara only was typical of the public's valuation of their respective powers. It was at this moment that having more or less agreed to accompany her to Copenhagen where she had further engagements, Schumann abruptly decided to return to Leipzig under the pretext of no longer being able to neglect his paper or his own creative work. Loneliness and dejection in Clara's absence nevertheless not only made all serious composition impossible, but also led to heavy drinking to drown his sorrows, as the word 'Katzenjammer' and other such admissions in the *Haushaltbuch* so often reveal. Not until after

[1] The Scherzo was subsequently salvaged as a piano piece, Op. 99, No. 13.

her return on 26th April was he able to start writing the chamber works that for some time he had recognized as his next major challenge. By the end of July he had completed three string Quartets, in A minor, F major and A major (Op. 41, Nos. 1, 2 and 3). The Quintet for piano and strings in E flat (Op. 44) followed in October, after an August holiday visit to Bohemian spas including Marienbad and Königswart (where they were very kindly received by Prince Metternich). In November he wrote the Quartet for piano and strings in E flat major (Op. 47), and soon after, the *Phantasiestücke* for piano, violin and cello (Op. 88).[1] Schumann wrote of these works that 'they seemed to please players and listeners alike, in particular Mendelssohn', and it is interesting to discover how they caused various hitherto doubtful critics to revise their estimate of the composer's worth. The distinguished Hauptmann wrote to Spohr:

> At David's I heard three quartets of Schumann's: his first, which pleased me greatly indeed, made me marvel at his talent, which I thought by no means so remarkable, judging from his previous pianoforte pieces – that were so aphoristic and fragmentary, sheer revellings in strangeness. Here, too, there is no lack of the unusual in content and form, but it is cleverly conceived and held together, and a great deal of it very lovely.

Until the end of 1840 Schumann's entire output, though as valuable as anything he wrote subsequently, had been mainly comprised of miniatures – intimate, revealing pictures of his emotional life. But now for the first time he was composing extended works, which, though undoubtedly conceived as the result of some extra-musical stimulus, had to generate their own musical driving-power to keep them going. This weaving of music out of notes rather than ideas, and the consideration of formal requirements above those of content, became ideals towards which Schumann, no doubt in emulation of Mendelssohn, was continually striving from this time onwards. Such an attitude was foreign to his natural, subjective temperament, and the deficiencies of his early training made it the harder for him to reason in terms of pure music. It was not surprising that the cumulative effect of the two years' intensive work should be an illness, described by Schumann as 'weakness of the nerves'. Throughout the winter of 1842–3 composition became impossible, and his

[1] Revised in 1850.

disturbed mental condition was aggravated by the realization that he had a family to support, and that no work meant no money. In a letter to Kossmaly, dated 5th May 1843, he gives some indication of his change of attitude towards the material aspects of his labours:

> Times have changed with me too. I used to be indifferent to the amount of notice I received, but a wife and children put a different complexion upon everything. It becomes imperative to think of the future, desirable to see the fruits of one's labour – not the artistic, but the prosaic fruits necessary to life.

His appointment as professor of piano, composition and score reading at the Leipzig Music School, opened in April under Mendelssohn's direction, was valuable in augmenting his income and giving him an official position in the musical world, and even more so in providing him with an interest beyond himself. His increasing withdrawal from the outside world since his marriage had tended to increase his old shyness when with strangers, and his inability to express himself fluently in their company led to certain embarrassments in his teaching. Wasielewski,[1] who was a student at the music school at that time, quotes an incident from his own experience when called upon to play the violin part in Schubert's B flat piano Trio (Op. 99), which one of Schumann's piano pupils was studying. 'The lesson was given with hardly a word from Schumann; although, as I well remember, there was abundant occasion,' was his comment. But whatever Schumann's pupils may have lost in factual knowledge, they gained in understanding of the spiritual significance of music through coming into contact with his refreshingly unacademic mind.

Various other incidents served as diversions in the early part of 1843. At the end of January Schumann was able to meet the much discussed and criticized Berlioz, who was on a visit to Leipzig. Though not in complete sympathy with his 'programme' eccentricities, Schumann had always upheld Berlioz in print; and Berlioz in his turn, though normally critical of German music of that period, expressed his approval of Schumann's piano Quintet at its first performance. During that same month Wieck attempted to make amends for his past conduct by expressing a desire to see Clara again and to hear some of her husband's music. Schumann was relieved in the satisfaction this reconciliation afforded Clara

[1] In *Life and Letters of Schumann*.

– her entries in the diary revealed that the strained relations had long been worrying her – though he himself had no dealings with Wieck till the end of the year. And in April the normal routine of No. 5 Inselstrasse was disturbed by the arrival of a second daughter, Elise, on the 25th of the month.

As early as January Schumann had returned to composition, though the first fruits of his labours, including the *Andante and Variations* for two pianos, two cellos and horn, did not really please him. 'I have only heard the variations for two pianos, etc. once,' he writes to his Dutch conductor-composer friend Verhulst in June, 'but they did not go particularly well. That sort of thing wants to be studied. It has something of the spirit of an clegy; I think I was rather melancholy when I composed it.' The greater part of his energies that year was devoted to the production of a big choral work, *Paradise and the Peri*. His old school friend, Emil Flechsig, had sent him a translation of the poem, taken from Thomas Moore's *Lalla Rookh*, in 1841. But though he at once invited the help of Adolph Böttger (the poet of his 'Spring' Symphony) in adapting the text, it was not until the early spring of 1843 that musical ideas began to take definite shape on paper. His letters reveal that he considered it his most ambitious undertaking to date, an oratorio 'not for the conventicle, but for bright, happy people', as he once put it. As Mendelssohn was away, Schumann conducted all the rehearsals as well as the performances. It was his début on the rostrum, and though he himself felt 'quite inspired', Livia Frege, who was singing the part of the Peri, felt moved to write to Clara: 'If only you could persuade your dear husband to scold a little and to insist on greater attention, all would go well at once.' Perhaps Clara did, for the first performance at Leipzig on 4th December was such a success that it had to be repeated on the 11th, and yet again in Dresden on the 15th. Whatever mistrust had still lingered in the public mind concerning Schumann's ability – and collectively the public had a cautious, suspicious mind – was now cleared away; and perhaps of greater significance than anything else was the fact that Wieck, either out of genuine appreciation, or from the baser realization that his daughter's husband might after all prove an asset to the family, swallowed his pride and extended the hand of friendship to Schumann. Christmas 1843 witnessed the first family reunion at Wieck's Dresden home for seven years.

Before his marriage Schumann had given Clara a 'sacred promise' that he would one day accompany her to St Petersburg, and the early part of 1844 seemed as propitious a time as any for undertaking a Russian tour. Whereas in younger days he relished every opportunity for widening his horizon, now the prospect of travel seemed only to disturb that inner tranquillity he found essential for composition. At this moment he would certainly have preferred to remain at home and meditate on the subject of an opera. But he had promised, and as Clara frequently reminded him, the tour would help to fill the family purse. Their Leipzig expenditure had been bigger than his income. So entrusting their two children to the care of Schumann's brother Carl and his wife, they left Leipzig on 25th January and did not return until the end of May. Clara gave concerts at Königsberg, Mittau, Riga, Dorpat, St Petersburg and Moscow, always arousing real enthusiasm. As Schumann wrote to his father-in-law, whereas interest in Liszt had gradually waned, with Clara it increased whenever she played more than once in any place. In private life they were warmly welcomed by musicians, including their old friend, Henselt, and Romberg, as well as by many aristocratic patrons of the arts, even the Emperor and Empress themselves in St Petersburg. Though never as fêted as Clara, and often frustrated because unable to work, Schumann was nevertheless rewarded with performances of his Piano Quintet and Variations for two pianos at various soirées, and Count Vielhorsky even had an orchestra at his own reception so that Schumann could conduct his B flat Symphony. Seeing the Kremlin (which inspired him to write several poems as well as to draw it), hearing Glinka's *A Life for the Tsar*, and visiting an old uncle who had migrated to Russia, were among his other most lasting memories.

The real anxiety throughout the journey had been his indifferent health, and back at Leipzig it became quite clear that he would have to conserve his energy as much as possible. Consequently his first move was to hand over the editorship of the *Neue Zeitschrift* to Lorenz. The paper was now ten years old and had made its mark thanks to Schumann's rigid adherence to original policy, but the more his powers of composition had asserted themselves in the last four years, the more he felt that editorial duties only trespassed on his time. Relieved of this big responsibility, he returned to the contemplation of an opera.

Letters to his friends reveal that the establishment of a national German Opera had been one of his long-cherished dreams, but the only subject which actually inspired some musical sketches was Byron's *Corsair*, and these got no further than an aria and a chorus. But while searching for subjects he had been struck again by the power of Goethe's *Faust* and soon became possessed with the alternative idea of composing a concert version of the final scene of the second part for chorus and orchestra. Unfortunately his enthusiasm overstepped the bounds of discretion, and once again his health broke down under the intensive strain. A short journey to the Harz mountains in September failed to improve matters, and it became increasingly clear that a complete change of environment would be the only salvation. So both he and Clara abandoned their work at the music school[1] and took a flat in Dresden. Dr Helbig, to whom Schumann went immediately for medical advice, found him in a morbid condition, with a strange fear of death and a dread of high hills or tall houses. At this point it is pertinent to remember his breakdown in 1833, when he occupied fourth-floor lodgings at No. 21 Burgstrasse and was terrified lest in a moment of distraction he might jump out of a window, and how in August 1838, when contemplating a stay with his friend Fischof in Vienna, he had written to inquire how high up it would be, as sickness and giddiness made it impossible for him to stay long in an upper storey. Dr Helbig also mentioned a fear of infection, and this too had been manifest as early as 1831, when there had been a serious cholera epidemic near Leipzig. His mental condition was accompanied by physical disturbances including headaches, shivering, faintness and cold feet as well as insomnia and aural delusions in the night. He was a difficult patient, and in his diagnosis[2] Dr Helbig wrote:

> As he studied every prescription until he found some reason for not taking it, I ordered him cold plunge baths, which so far improved his health that he was able to return to his usual (only) occupation, composition. As I had made a study of similar cases, especially among men who worked immoderately at one thing (for instance, accounts, etc.), I was led to advise that he should employ himself and distract his mind with something else than music. He first chose natural history, then natural philosophy, but

[1] Clara had started giving piano lessons in August.
[2] Quoted in full in Wasielewski's *Life and Letters of Robert Schumann*.

abandoned them after a few days and gave himself up, wherever he might be, to his musical thoughts.

By December the change of air, surroundings and friends had brought enough alleviation to persuade both Clara and Schumann to make Dresden their home. Leipzig was Clara's native city, it had witnessed Schumann's early endeavour and later achievement, and it was the pivot of all German music. But the vacant Gewandhaus conductorship for the winter 1844–5 had been offered to Gade, not Schumann; and most important, Mendelssohn had gone, and for Schumann Leipzig in consequence was a city without a heart which he could leave with few regrets.

Schumann's reaction to the comparative scarcity of music in Dresden was at first favourable: 'Here one can get back the old lost longing for music, there is so little to hear!' he writes to Ferdinand David. But it was not long before he realized that provincial conditions in the Saxon capital left much to be desired. Artistic life centred in the court, and the general atmosphere was one of easy-going dilettantism, the pursuit of pleasure being deemed of more consequence than the cultivation of high standards of taste. The professional musicians were on the whole unenterprising, happy in their strict observance of traditions and suspicious of any new ideas. Ferdinand Hiller was the only one to extend a welcoming hand to Schumann and his wife, and it was not long before Hiller and Schumann together were attempting to introduce new life into Dresden by organizing a series of subscription concerts. Some idea of their difficulties is to be gained from Schumann's letter to Mendelssohn of 24th September 1845:

> There is nothing to be done with the orchestra, and nothing without it. Convention is all-powerful here. Thus the band will never play a Beethoven symphony at an extra concert for fear of injuring the concert on Palm Sunday and the pension fund.

And again on 22nd October:

> I am in hope that the subscription concerts will be carried out. I believe the band can hardly realize it yet; indeed, it will be an unheard-of thing. For our part, we have acted with perfect openness, but yet they cannot believe the thing to be possible.

One other musician in Dresden was wrestling with convention

in his own sphere – no less a person than Richard Wagner, employed as *Kapellmeister* at the bureaucratic court theatre. It was unfortunate that incompatibility of temperament prevented Schumann and Wagner from becoming greater friends, since both in their different ways were ardent pioneers in the cause of romanticism. Had they met in Leipzig ten years earlier their relationship might have been very different, for Schumann as an impulsive young man would not have found Wagner's dynamic personality and volubility quite so tiresome. But as the years passed after Schumann's marriage, not only did the Florestan in him gradually give way to the retiring Eusebius, but even his music became the more conservative as it grew from himself rather than the outside world. Wagner's music, on the other hand, was continually striving away from abstraction and purity to realism and richness of emotion, and the methods by which he brought his meaning home seemed at times to Schumann to overstep the limits of good taste. Thus on 22nd October he writes to Mendelssohn of *Tannhäuser*:

> But of course, what does the world (including many musicians) know of pure harmony? There is Wagner, who has just finished another opera, undoubtedly a clever fellow, full of crazy ideas and bold to a degree. The aristocracy is raving about *Rienzi*, but I declare he cannot write or imagine four consecutive bars that are melodious, or *even correct*. That is what they all lack – pure harmony and capacity for four-part choral composition. What permanent good can come of such a state of things? And now the full score lies beautifully printed before us, and its fifths and octaves into the bargain; and now he would like to make corrections and erasures. Too late! Well, enough! The music is not a shade better than *Rienzi*; in fact, rather weaker and more strained. But if one says anything of that kind people say directly 'Oh, what envy!' so I only say it to you, as I am sure that you have known it for a long time.

As soon as Schumann heard and saw the work on the stage he realized that it had great persuasive power, and he did not mind retracting his original criticism. But even though he subsequently wrote of Wagner's works in May 1853 to van Bruyck that they were deeply moving and possessed of 'a mysterious magic that overpowers our senses', he always remained slightly suspicious of the musical means by which Wagner achieved his dramatic ends. Wagner was one of a company of friends whom Schumann would meet regularly once a week for discussion and debate, but on the whole he preferred the others, Bendemann, Rietschel, Hübner and Reinick, who were artists and poets, and also Hiller, to the excitable little man from the opera house.

From Schumann's correspondence during 1845 it is quite clear that no one in Dresden occupied the same place in his affections as his old friend Mendelssohn, who was once again back at Leipzig at the Gewandhaus for the winter of 1845–6. Not only has nearly every letter some warm-hearted praise either for Mendelssohn's latest composition or achievement, but also there is evidence of a deep personal regard. Thus on 18th November Schumann writes:

> Well, my best love to you. I shall soon write to you again – indeed, could we not write to one another from time to time without any special reason? If our friendship were a wine, this would be a good year for it (today, ten years ago Rosenthal). Perhaps you think as I do, and will soon write to me again.

Rumours have arisen to suggest that Mendelssohn did not reciprocate these feelings – and as early as 1838 one of Schumann's letters to Clara reveals that Schumann himself had heard things not to his liking:

> I have not gone often to Mendelssohn, he has come more often to me. After all, he is the most eminent man I have met so far. I am told that he is not sincere with regard to me. That would pain me, as I am consciously loyal to him, and have proved it. But tell me sometime what you know. . . . I know exactly how I compare with him as a musician, and for years to come I could learn from him. But he could also learn something from me. If I had grown up in circumstances such as his, destined to music from childhood, I should outsoar you one and all – the energy of my ideas makes me feel it.

These suspicions proved only a passing shadow, and Schumann's faith in his friend remained complete even though he knew there were things about his own music which Mendelssohn found awkward and not always to his liking. One of the factors which drew them together was their common admiration for Bach. Both deplored the fact that numerous Bach manuscripts were stored away in the library of the Berlin *Singakademie*, and they not only made it their business to supervise the publication of a complete edition of Bach's music, but also to provide the indifferent public with as many opportunities as possible for hearing it.

Schumann's intensive study of Bach resulted in 1845 in an outpouring of contrapuntal music, including Studies for pedal-piano (Op. 56), Sketches for pedal-piano (Op. 58), six Fugues on B.A.C.H. for organ or pedal-piano (Op. 60) and four Fugues for piano (Op. 72). The only other music composed during that first year in Dresden was an *Intermezzo and Finale* to follow the *Phantasie* for piano and orchestra of 1841, thus transforming the whole into the A minor piano Concerto (Op. 54), also some sketches for the Symphony in C major (Op. 61). In spite of the restful loveliness of the surrounding countryside, which for a little while had given Schumann new life, his health still stood between himself and any intensive work. His letters continuously mention exhaustion and despair, and that to Mendelssohn of 22nd October is particularly revealing:

> Unfortunately I have not recovered my usual strength. Any sort of disturbance of the simple order of my life throws me off my balance and into a nervous, irritable state. That is why I preferred staying at home when my wife was with you – much to my regret. Wherever there is fun and enjoyment I must still keep out of the way. The only thing to be done is hope, hope – and so I will.

The year 1846 was hardly more fruitful. The C major Symphony, with its 'doleful bassoon' (as he once put it) in the *Adagio*, was completed with difficulty, for an irritation of the aural nerve caused a frequent singing in his ear. Apart from this work, he wrote only the ten unaccompanied part-songs of Op. 55 and Op. 59. A stay with friends in the nearby village of Maxen that May merely increased his hypochondria, at one point even driving him to consult a local phrenologist. From his bedroom window he could see Sonnenstein, a lunatic asylum, which in some strangely prophetic way constantly haunted him.

An unfailing source of comfort throughout this difficult time was his wife and family. Two children had already been born in Dresden, Julie, on 11 March 1845, and Emil, on 8th February 1846, making four in all.[1] For Clara, all too soon pregnant again, there was nevertheless an element of secret relief when sea-

[1] Having always recorded the start of Clara's every pregnancy in the *Haushaltbuch*, likewise the date of each child's birth and of his subsequent resumption of sexual relations with Clara, from April 13th, 1846 onwards Schumann also entered a small sign in the margin on every night that he and Clara made love.

bathing, medically prescribed for Schumann at Norderney that summer, induced a miscarriage. A diary entry of May, 1847, when she realized yet another child was on the way, reveals her continuing personal conflict despite unswerving devotion to her husband: 'What will become of my work? But Robert says: "Children are blessings", and he is right, for there is no happiness without children, and therefore I have determined to face the difficult time that is coming with as cheery a spirit as possible. Whether I shall always be able to do so or not I do not know'.

But just as she had managed to give several concerts during the winter of 1845–6, including the first performance of her husband's piano concerto in Dresden on 4th December, 1845, followed by a second performance at Leipzig's Gewandhaus on 1st January, 1846, so the winter of 1846–7 seemed as good a time as any for a return visit to Vienna. Taking their two eldest children, they set out on 24th November, 1846. Many disappointments awaited them. Since her marriage Clara had no further use for the empty bravura pieces with which she took Vienna by storm nine years earlier, and Vienna in its turn had little understanding of the romantic music of Chopin, Schumann and Mendelssohn which now filled her recital programmes. At her third concert Schumann's piano Concerto and B flat Symphony met with such a cool reception that she could no longer contain her indignation, and afterwards, in the company of a few friends, gave vent to her feelings so bitterly that Schumann had to remonstrate gently with the words: 'Calm yourself, dear Clara; in ten years' time all this will have changed.' Only the last concert was a success, and that primarily because their friend, Jenny Lind, was kind enough to sing in the same programme. From Vienna they went to Brno and then to Prague, where an enthusiastic reception compensated for all recent disappointment, and after a few days in Dresden they arrived in Berlin on 11th February 1847. Schumann had received an invitation from the *Singakademie* to conduct a performance of his *Paradise and the Peri*, and he immediately threw himself into the difficult business of rehearsing a choir whose conservative tendencies had permitted them no previous experience of 'modern' music. After endless difficulties, arising from the caprices of soloists, the performance was given on 17th February, but not with its earlier success. The rest of their stay in Berlin was sheer enjoyment, and leaving their many sympathetic friends on 24th March to return to the uneventful life of Dresden was a wrench for them both.

For Schumann the experiences of the last few months, though bitter-sweet, were invaluable. His thoughts had been forcibly diverted from himself and his mind stimulated by contact with other minds; as a result he could turn to composition again with new energy and a profusion of ideas. He resumed work on *Faust* and also completed two piano Trios, in D minor (Op. 63) and F major (Op. 80). But most important was his discovery of a suitable subject for an opera – the legend of St Geneviève. Preferring Hebbel's stronger treatment of the tragedy to Tieck's, he asked his poet friend, Robert Reinick, to compile a libretto primarily from that source. As the result verged on the sentimental, Schumann then wrote to Hebbel himself for help. But though Hebbel briefly visited Schumann when passing through Dresden, he found him too withdrawn and taciturn to make co-operation possible. So Schumann was driven to preparing his own libretto, and it was this labour, together with sketches for the overture, which preoccupied him for much of 1847.

A pleasant interruption occurred in July when Zwickau prepared a musical festival in Schumann's honour – an occasion which entirely disproved the saying that a prophet is without honour in his own country. For a fortnight Schumann experienced the appreciation which rarely falls to a creative artist in his lifetime, and Clara, who so often deplored her husband's struggle for recognition more than he did himself, was deeply content too.

It seemed as if the year which began in shadow was to end in brightness, but Mendelssohn's sudden death on 4th November cast a dark cloud over the whole musical world and enveloped Schumann in a gloom even more intense than that from which he had recently emerged. Once again outside events saved him from himself, for when Hiller left Dresden shortly after Mendelssohn's funeral to become director of music at Düsseldorf, Schumann took over his position as conductor of the *Liedertafel*, or men's choral society, in Dresden. A letter to Nottebohm in July 1847, inquiring about the vacant directorship of the Vienna Conservatory, reveals that Schumann at times felt he ought to hold some official position in the musical world, if only to gratify his wife's relentless ambitions for him, and so he began the new work in Dresden with great enthusiasm. He fully realized its salutary effect on his health, and in subsequent letters to Hiller mentions how the task had increased his confidence in his own powers, especially in his powers of conducting, which in his nervous, hypochondriacal state he thought he had quite lost. Not content with male voices, he also formed a 'Choral Union' for mixed voices in the early part of January 1848, and it was this new society of his own which gave him the most pleasure and the most scope.

> My choral association is a great delight to me. It consists of sixty to seventy members, and enables me to arrange and adapt any sort of music I like, according to my own sweet will,

he writes to Hiller in April 1849, but in the same letter explains:

> On the other hand, I have given up the men's choral association. I found too little genuine musical feeling, and did not feel equal to it, nice people though they were.

As Schumann's critics frequently reproached him for lack of energy in his conducting at public concerts, it is interesting to have the views of a certain Fräulein Marie von Lindemann, who was a pupil of Clara's and a regular attender at the weekly choir practices. Both she and the choir in general felt that Schumann's influence as conductor was highly inspiring.

> True he had neither the commanding voice nor the commanding eye that enforces immediate obedience [quotes Niecks[1]]. His voice was soft, a pleasant tenor; his movements were quiet; but his whole being showed the nobility of a great artist and bore the stamp of genius, and unconsciously he thereby raised the whole company to a high level of intelligence. Everybody felt that this was a question of serious artistic endeavour and that each must do his best for the good of the whole.

It was natural that Schumann should write several small part-songs for the choir, but the general improvement of his health made 1848 productive in many ways. *Genoveva* (Op. 81) was completed by August, the music to Byron's *Manfred* (Op. 115) started immediately afterwards, also a setting of Rückert's *Adventlied* (Op. 71) for solo voices, chorus and orchestra. And he returned to the piano again, to write a collection of small, easy

---

[1] In his biography *Robert Schumann*.

pieces, *Album für die Jugend* (Op. 68), also some duets, *Bilder aus Osten* (Op. 66).

Even the revolutionary storm-clouds which gathered during 1848 and broke over Dresden in the spring of 1849 could not stem the flow of Schumann's music. Wagner was actively supporting the insurrectionists until a warrant was issued for his arrest, causing him to flee from Germany and concentrate all his energies on the writing of revolutionary pamphlets. Schumann, on the other hand, in spite of his liberal views and sympathy with the people, wanted only to escape from painful realities, notably compulsory enlistment, and early in May fled with Clara and their eldest daughter, Marie, to a friend's house at Maxen. It was Clara who, though again pregnant, risked the street firing when returning to collect the younger children and who again took the initiative when it was necessary to fetch further possessions for their longer stay in the little village of Kreischa. Shortly before the insurrection Schumann attempted to explain his state of mind to Hiller: 'I have been very busy all this time; it has been my most fruitful year. It is just as if outward storms drove one more into oneself, for only in my work did I find any compensation for the terrible storm which burst upon me from without.'

Apart from three revolutionary choruses for male-voice choir and military band which he wrote in 1848 but was fearful of publishing, and the 'barricade' Marches for piano, Op. 76, dating from his return to Dresden in June 1849 (eventually published without the large '1849' he originally included to proclaim his republican sympathies) his music reflects nothing of the stirring spirit abroad. At Maxen and Kreischa he wrote songs and partsongs untroubled enough for Clara to observe in the diary:

> It seems to me extraordinary how the terrible events without have awakened his poetic feeling in so entirely contrary a manner. All the songs breathe the spirit of perfect peace, they seem to me like spring, and laugh like blossoming flowers.

Whereas previously it had been his practice to concentrate on one particular form of music at a time, now he ranged over many different varieties of music from piano solos – the *Waldscenen* (Op. 82) – to pieces for other instruments with piano, including oboe, clarinet and horn, as well as completing *Manfred*, adding even more scenes to his *Faust* music and composing the *Requiem für Mignon* for choir and orchestra and several other Goethe settings for solo voice in honour of this poet's centenary. During the actual centenary celebrations in August he had the satisfaction of having as much of the *Faust* music as was then completed performed at Dresden, Weimar and Leipzig. At Leipzig alone it was not completely successful, and that, he felt, was because of the bad arrangement of the programme. He had sometimes wondered if he had been presumptuous in setting such perfect poetry to music, and was particularly gratified to learn that some people in Dresden confessed that his music made the meaning of the poem clear to them for the first time.

On the whole he was well satisfied with his position in the public eye during 1849. Only one thing troubled him, and that was the endless delay over the production of *Genoveva* at Leipzig. He had started negotiating with Rietz, conductor of the Leipzig Opera, as early as November 1848, and the first performance was arranged for February 1849. It did not actually take place till June 1850, and Schumann was secretly distressed by rumours that the many postponements were due to the intrigues of the local musicians. He had always considered Leipzig above pettiness. Both Schumann and Clara were delighted with what appeared to be growing enthusiasm in the audience as the opera was repeated a second and third night, but the excitement was short-lived, and they soon realized in their hearts that rather more had been expected from the composer of *Paradise and the Peri*.

A concert tour to Bremen, Hamburg and Altona with Clara in the early part of 1850 had temporarily interrupted Schumann's composition. The production of *Genoveva* had brought further disturbances, and throughout the summer of that year his mind was much preoccupied with plans for the immediate future. His desire for some regular work had grown. Not only had he written about the directorship of the Vienna Conservatory in 1847, but in 1849 he also made discreet inquiries about the Gewandhaus conductorship – as well as considering the possibility of becoming second *Kapellmeister* at the Dresden theatre. Then in the autumn of 1849 his friend Hiller, about to move to Cologne, had written to offer him the Düsseldorf music directorship. At first Schumann was doubtful of accepting. It was a long, expensive journey and as he was now the father of five children,[1] money had to be

---

[1] Ludwig and Ferdinand had been born in January 1848 and July 1849, but his first son, Emil, had died in 1847.

considered. He had always remembered Mendelssohn's unfavourable opinion of Düsseldorf; he feared there might be no
openings for Clara and no opportunities for them to get away
together. But most important of all was a secret fear which he
discloses to Hiller in December 1849:

> The other day I looked for some notices of Düsseldorf in an old
> geography book, and among the places of note in that town I found
> mentioned three convents and a mad-house. I have no objection to
> the former, but it made me quite uncomfortable to read about the
> latter. I will tell you how that is: a few years ago, as you will
> remember, we lived at Maxen. I there discovered that the principal
> view from my windows was on to the Sonnenstein. At last I
> perfectly hated the sight of it, and it entirely spoilt my stay there. So
> I thought the same thing might happen at Düsseldorf. But possibly
> the notice is altogether incorrect, and the institution may be merely
> a hospital, such as one finds in every town. I have to be very careful
> in guarding against all melancholy impressions of that kind. And
> though, as you are aware, we musicians often dwell in sunny
> heights, yet when the unhappiness of life comes before our eyes in
> all its naked ugliness, it hurts us all the more. At least, that is my
> case, with my fervid imagination.

Clara, on the other hand, had no doubts. She disliked the close,
conservative atmosphere of Dresden, and ever since 1840, just
before their marriage,[1] had been very eager for her husband to
assert himself in the eyes of the world by holding some official
musical position. Accordingly they set out for Düsseldorf on 1st
September 1850.

No welcome could have been more auspicious than that which
the local musicians and notable townsfolk offered to Schumann
and Clara during their first week at Düsseldorf. On the evening of
arrival, they found laurel trees placed outside their hotel and
their rooms decorated with flowers, while a few hours later the
choral society arrived to serenade them. Two evenings later the
strains of Mozart's *Don Giovanni* overture reached their ears as
they sat at dinner, and this time it was the local orchestra
serenading them. The biggest celebration of all was a concert,
supper and ball in their honour at the end of the week, when
Schumann was greeted with a flourish of trumpets as he entered

---

[1] In a letter dated 31st May 1840 Schumann warned her not to be too
ambitious for him, fearing she would never be a *Kapellmeisterin*.

the hall and then entertained by a programme of his own music. So many new faces and four days of unsuccessful house-hunting following hard on the heels of a strenuous journey had tired them so much that they were unable to stay for the final ball, nor were they able to take part in an excursion the following day, organized by Hiller and some other artists, designed to introduce them to the beauties of the neighbourhood.

Ever since his student days Schumann had loved the Rhineland and its wines, and to live on the river's banks brought a sense of fulfilment of its own. Furthermore the Lower Rhenish Festival held periodically at Düsseldorf had served to foster a widespread interest in music throughout the town, there was plenty of scope for Clara both as teacher and performer, and most important, with an orchestra and choir at his disposal Schumann could try out every new work at once. Though not notable for any outstanding individual talent, the orchestra had been very well trained under such recent musical directors as Mendelssohn, Rietz and Hiller: Schumann himself lost no time in bringing in Joseph von Wasielewski as a strong new leader. Official duties involved rehearsing orchestra and choir and conducting the regular subscription concerts; there were also occasional extra performances connected with the Roman Catholic Church. Despite difficulties in finding a quiet and congenial enough home, and Clara's constant diary complaints about lack of earnestness amongst the music-lovers and insufficient respect from the lower classes ('who think they are our equals'), Schumann's letters during these early days suggest he was happy in the new routine, and still found plenty of time to compose. The year 1850 saw the completion of his *Faust* music (excepting the overture), the songs Opp. 77, 83, 87, 89, 90 and 96, the cello Concerto in A minor (Op. 129), also the 'Rhenish' Symphony in E flat major (Op. 97), directly inspired by a visit to Cologne early that autumn. 1851 was equally fruitful. In the realms of pure instrumental music he rescored and revised his D minor Symphony of 1841[1] and also wrote a third piano Trio, in G minor (Op. 110), and two violin Sonatas, in A minor (Op. 105) and D minor (Op. 121). But his main inspiration that year was literature, for he composed overtures to Schiller's *Braut von Messina* (Op. 100), Shake-

[1] Published as No. 4, Op. 120.

speare's *Julius Caesar* (Op. 128) and Goethe's *Hermann und Dorothea* (Op. 136), as well as two secular cantatas, *Der Rose Pilgerfahrt* (Op. 112) with words by a young poet, Moritz Horn, and *Der Königssohn* (Op. 116) by Uhland. It was also during 1851 that Schumann began to contemplate an oratorio on the life of Luther. His librettist was Richard Pohl, a young critic and writer on musical subjects, and their correspondence reveals what definite and original ideas Schumann had in mind for the character and form of the work, even though it was finally abandoned.

It was therefore something of an unpleasant shock for Schumann when in March 1851, towards the end of his first season, an anonymous article appeared in the *Düsseldorfer Zeitung* objecting to the way in which concerts had been directed. Admittedly, minor conflicts with the choir had arisen in the early part of the year, but otherwise Schumann was unaware of the shadow of doubt forming on the horizon about his suitability for his appointment. Clara's indignation was sufficient to prevent her husband from pondering the matter in his private mind. Her lifelong ambition was satisfied – Schumann held a publicly recognized position, and in her blind veneration for his genius she failed to realize the difficulties which his increasingly retiring personality experienced in making contact with the outside world. An idyllic summer holiday in Switzerland (via Heidelberg), followed by a visit to Belgium, where Schumann was on the jury of a male voice choir contest in Antwerp, provided welcome distraction – as did a visit from the Liszt–Wittgenstein *ménage* soon after their return. But back in harness for the new season of 1851–2 they could see only too plainly that the critical article had represented rather more than a solitary opinion. First signs of recalcitrance came from the choir. Its members were mainly amateurs, responsive enough to systematic and vigorous leadership, but wholly perplexed by a gentle, ruminative conductor whose vision of the music as it should be and the practical means of achieving his ends were just as remote from each other as he, personally, was from them, as people. At one rehearsal the sopranos, finding themselves in trouble, stopped singing. The other voices did the same, but Schumann, immersed in his mental conception of the music, continued to conduct as if nothing was wrong. Tausch, the accompanist, eventually decided that it was time he stopped playing alone, whereupon Schumann called him over to the rostrum. Instead of showing any signs of annoyance, Schumann merely pointed to a certain passage in the score, saying: 'Look, this bar is beautiful!' In gesture as in speech he had become restrained and shy, and not even the fullest flood of music could break down the barrier which held back his feelings from any outward manifestation. In consequence he was incapable of inspiring others, and out of sheer boredom rather than deliberate malice, members gradually stayed away, while the standard of those remaining fell low enough to disgrace the traditions of Düsseldorf.

The strain of the season caused Schumann a further breakdown during the summer of 1852, with nervous tension and hypochondria now exacerbated by intermittent rheumatic pains, insomnia and other passing physical disorders. Cold-water bathing was again medically prescribed, now by a new doctor, and after an unsuccessful course of eighteen daily bathes in the Rhine at Godesberg Clara took him and their eldest daughter, Marie, to the sea at Scheveningen – incidentally causing brief but acute alarm when the cold water (as at Norderney in 1846) terminated her latest unwanted pregnancy.

It was during the stresses of the same year that Schumann's thoughts began to centre on religious music. His own beliefs had always been ethical rather than spiritual, which is to say 'he regarded the religion of humanity as the only authorized standard for conduct', as Wasielewski once put it. His own words had been: 'If a man knows the Bible, Shakespeare and Goethe and has taken them unto himself, he needs no more.' Until this time his only essays in the realm of sacred music had been fairly recent settings of three poems by Rückert – Christ through the poet's eyes. But in a letter of January 1851 to Strackerjan, a Dutch singer, he had gone on to say:

> It must always remain an artist's highest aim to direct his efforts to sacred music. In youth we are all so firmly rooted to earth, with its joys and sorrows, though as we grow older our branches do aspire to higher things. I hope this will be my case before long.

And so it proved. A setting of the Mass (Op. 147) and then a Requiem (Op. 148) loomed large over all other undertakings of 1852, including two secular cantatas, *Des Sängers Fluch* (Op. 139) and *Vom Pagen und der Königstochter* (Op. 140). Amidst

the secret fears and dreads of his own imagination his personal
search for assuagement was nevertheless increasingly inclining
towards the mystical and occult. Most ominous was his enthusiasm for the currently fashionable pastime of table-turning, which
reached a climax in the spring of 1853. In a letter to Hiller that
April he writes:

> Yesterday we had *table-turning* for the first time. A wonderful
> power! Just fancy, I asked what was the rhythm of the first two
> bars of the C minor Symphony! There was more hesitation than
> usual about the answer. At last it came: ♪ ♪ ♪ ♪ | ♩ |– but rather
> slowly at first, and when I said, 'But the tempo ought to be rather
> faster, dear table', it was promptly rapped out in the right time. I
> also asked whether it could tell the number *I had thought of*, and it
> gave *three* quite correctly. We were all of us lost in amazement and
> felt as though surrounded by wonders. Well enough! I am too full
> of it today to be able to keep it to myself!

The 'sad weakening of my energies' which Schumann had
noted in the *Haushaltbuch* in August, 1852, after impulsively
taking over the baton from his deputy, Julius Tausch, for the
première of his own *Julius Caesar* overture, in fact kept him off
the rostrum until that December, by which time he had begun to
complain of 'strange afflictions of hearing'. Few words of
welcome greeted him on his return; instead, three members of the
committee of the choir requested his resignation. They were soon
forced to apologize and resign themselves. But their action made it
quite clear that during Schumann's absence Tausch had obtained
results from both choir and orchestra which far surpassed those of
the musical director himself. Tausch had come to Düsseldorf in
1846 on Mendelssohn's recommendation, after two years' study
at the Leipzig music school. And though Clara, prejudiced against
him from the start, was always ready to suspect him of intrigue,
dispassionate observers knew that his loyalty was unshakeable
even though he had cause to deplore the spectacle of Schumann in
such a miscast rôle. The Lower Rhine Festival in the spring of
1853 brought diverting interests of its own, but the lion's share of
the conducting fell to Hiller, invited for the purpose, and though
Schumann scored a big success with the revised version of his D
minor Symphony the press made no secret of its preference for
Düsseldorf's former musical director. In the autumn fresh

troubles arose with the orchestra: the players were beginning to lose patience with their apathetic conductor. At times he would stand ready with baton in hand and yet not begin, till the orchestra, tired of waiting, would start itself off. At other times he would go over and over a certain passage without telling the players what he was attempting to correct. On one occasion he did explain that the trombone had missed its cue and after a repeat said to the player: 'It is all right now, and sounds very well.' But the trombone had been silent as before. Added to this, all tempos seemed too fast to him. Finally, after a disgraceful concert in October 1853, the committee asked him to rest awhile from conducting anything but his own works. There was no malice and no personal intrigue in their request, but they could no longer ignore honest and just criticism from all sides of Schumann's total unfitness for this most regrettable appointment. Again this was beyond Clara's understanding, and her renewed indignation contributed to a breach with the committee which was not repaired. Schumann never conducted at Düsseldorf again.

Throughout these difficulties and the moments of panic caused by his health, such as at Bonn on 30th July 1853, when a doctor was hurriedly summoned after some strange paralytic seizure, Schumann was sustained by the love of his family,[1] his own ceaseless composing, and as much as anything by the friendship of the young Joachim and Brahms. His strong affection for Joachim dated from the spring festival when he was profoundly moved by Joachim's performance of Beethoven's violin concerto. And it was Joachim's introduction which brought Brahms to the Schumanns' house on 30th September 1853. With remarkable perception Schumann at once realized that the compositions[2] of this youth of twenty gave promise of real genius, and as well as writing enthusiastically to Dr Härtel, the Leipzig publisher, he also contributed an article, 'Neue Bahnen', to the *Neue Zeitschrift*, after a period of nine years away from that paper, to 'assist the young eagle in his first flight through the world'.[3] Brahms, shy and

---

[1] Clara's birthday on 13th September 1853 was a particularly happy day when returning from an excursion together she found a new Klems grand piano waiting for her, and on it flowers and a setting of some poems written when he gave her a Härtel grand in 1840.

[2] Including the piano sonatas, Opp. 1 and 2, and the Scherzo in E flat minor, Op. 4.

[3] From a letter to Joachim, 13th October 1853.

uncouth, responded to the older man with affectionate respect, and his devotion to Clara still smouldered in his heart when he died. With the co-operation of Brahms and Albert Dietrich,[1] Schumann composed a violin Sonata for Joachim in the early autumn of 1853, and it was Joachim again who inspired Schumann's *Phantasie* for violin and orchestra (Op. 131) and violin Concerto. If Schumann's ideas now reflected a certain mental tiredness and emotional apathy, there was no hesitation in their flow. Other compositions of 1853 included an *Introduction and Allegro* for piano and orchestra (Op. 134), a secular cantata *Das Glück von Edenhall* (Op. 143), a Festal Overture on the *Rheinweinlied* (Op. 123), an Overture, at last, to the *Scenes from Faust*, several pieces for piano, and piano accompaniments for Bach's unaccompanied violin and cello sonatas and Paganini's violin caprices. The year also saw his third and last independent experiment with melodrama, Hebbel's *Ballade vom Heideknaben* (Op. 122, No. 1), in succession to earlier Hebbel and Shelley essays in this form which he had first explored in *Manfred*.

A natural desire to run away from the unpleasantness of Düsseldorf caused Schumann and Clara to contemplate Vienna as a future home – in spite of their varied fortunes in that city, the magic of its musical past always haunted them. Meanwhile a tour of Holland satisfied their immediate need of escape, and both Schumann's music and Clara's playing were greeted at Utrecht, The Hague, Rotterdam and Amsterdam with an enthusiasm surpassing anything they had previously experienced. A visit to Hanover in the new year of 1854 was equally successful, and there a reunion with Brahms and Joachim added to their joy. Conflicts and difficulties there had always been in Schumann's life, but at this particular time their dark colours served only to emphasize the glow of his achievement, and he could review his life-work with the sudden realization that his ultimate goal was reached. Towards the end of 1853 he writes to van Bruyck:

> My music is spreading more and more, and in other countries too, especially in Holland and England, and it always delights the artist to see that – for it is not praise that causes his exultation, but joy that what he has felt himself finds harmonious echoes in men's hearts.

[1] A young Düsseldorf musician who became Schumann's pupil in 1851.

Back at Düsseldorf in February, Schumann worked unceasingly at his *Dichtergarten*, a collection of quotations from poets old and new on the subject of music. On 7th February he explains to Joachim:

> Meanwhile I have been working at my garden, which is growing more and more imposing. I have added some signposts to keep people from straying – i.e. an explanatory text. I am at present occupied with the ancients, Homer and the Greeks. In Plato especially I have found some splendid passages.

But the opening of the letter sounded an ominous note: 'We have been away a whole week without sending you or your companions a sign,' he writes. 'But I have often written to you in spirit, and there is an invisible writing, to be revealed later, underlying this letter. . . . I will close now. It is growing dark. . . .'

On the night of 10th February the darkness arrived. For a week Schumann's tired mind had no peace: from a solitary note which thrummed through his head there grew strange music 'more wonderful and played by more exquisite instruments than ever sounded on earth'.[1] During the night of the 17th he jumped out of bed to write down a theme which the angels had sent him.[2] Then the heavenly voices changed into voices of demons, and it was not long before he knew that his fears had turned to hideous reality. He begged to be taken to an asylum, but the next day was calm enough to work on the variations of his mystical theme. Of that day, 27th February 1854, Clara writes in her diary:

> Robert got up, but he was more profoundly melancholy than words can say. If I so much as touched him, he said: 'Ah! Clara, I am not worthy of your love.' He said this, he whom I always look up to with the greatest, the most profound reverence . . . ah! and all that I could say was of no use. He made a fair copy of the variations, and as he was at the last he suddenly left the room and went sighing into his bedroom – I had left the room only for a few minutes, in order to say something to Dr Hasenclever in the next room, and had left Mariechen sitting with him (for ten days I had never left him alone for a minute). Marie thought he would come back in a minute, but he did not come, but ran out into the most dreadful rain, in nothing but his coat, with no boots and no waistcoat. Bertha suddenly burst in and told me that he had gone

[1] Schumann's own description, quoted by Clara in the diary.
[2] In reality the theme of the slow movement of his recently composed violin Concerto.

— no words can describe my feelings, only I knew that I felt as if my heart had ceased to beat. Dietrich, Hasenclever and in fact all who were there ran out to look for him, but could not find him; an hour later two strangers brought him back; where and how they had found him I could not learn. . . .

On 4th March he was taken by two male nurses to Dr Richarz's private asylum at Endenich, near Bonn. Clara was not allowed to see him, nor at the start did Schumann seem aware of broken links. Sometimes he would pace his room, or kneel down and wring his hands, or argue with imaginary voices accusing him of plagiarism in his music. Otherwise he was placid enough to be allowed considerable freedom in the asylum ground, and to be taken for walks – he liked going to Bonn to see the Beethoven monument and the view of the Siebengebirge. The wedding anniversary and Clara's birthday in September brought their first exchange of letters. 'Oh if I could see you and speak to you again, but the way is too far' he wrote in reply to Clara's greeting, questioning her about the children, her new piano and her playing, his manuscripts and much else, besides tenderly recalling the love-poems he sent her in Paris from Vienna in 1839 and some of their happiest recent travels. The next affectionate note included a request for money to give to poor beggars encountered on his walks. Towards the end of 1854 he was writing lucid appraisals of Brahms's recently completed Variations, Op. 9 (on his own No. 4 from *Bunte Blätter*, Op. 99) and Ballades, Op. 10, and he even resumed work on his piano accompaniments for Paganini's Caprices.

But hopes of recovery cherished by Clara, increasingly accepting concert engagements to support their seven children[1] and keep her own heart from breaking, were not shared by Dr Richarz, who, as he subsequently revealed in an appendix for Wasielewski's biography, had diagnosed a progressive organic disease which 'first took root in early youth, gradually increasing with the growth of the man, and not resulting in madness for a long time'. His eventual autopsy revealed distended blood vessels, ossification of the base of the brain and degeneration of covering tissues, which, with considerable atrophy of the whole brain itself, he guardedly attributed to the stress of overwork impairing

[1] Two more children had been born at Düsseldorf: Eugenie in December 1851 and Felix in June 1854, when Schumann was already at Endenich.

the nutrition and metabolism of the brain. Certain later researchers, notably Eliot Slater, Alfred Meyer and Eric Sams, have nevertheless dismissed this, along with every subsequent psychotic diagnosis, in favour of tertiary syphilis, or general paresis, contracted, albeit treated and ostensibly cured, during what Schumann himself once referred to as 'a certain amount of dissipation' in student days. Others, in their awareness of the limitations of nineteenth-century pathology, have preferred to leave the door wider open – not excluding generalized arteriosclerosis as a possible alternative interpretation of Dr Richarz's 'progressive organic disease'.

Whatever the cause (and it will always remain contentious), by the late summer of 1855 Dr Richarz gave warning that there was no more hope. Besides increasing difficulties of enunciation, hallucinations, once primarily aural, now spread to taste and smell. There was not even the relief of euphoria commonly associated with insanity, but rather a deepening, debilitating melancholy. Wasielewski, who had sent Schumann a piano, listened unseen one day as he extemporized 'like a machine whose springs are broken, but which still tries to work, jerking convulsively'. When Brahms paid Schumann a birthday visit in June, 1856, he found him emaciated and oblivious to almost all but picking out names from an atlas to arrange in alphabetical order. Towards the end of July Clara received a telegram warning her that the end was near. Her diary tells all that remains to be said.

I saw him between 6 and 7 in the evening (27th July 1856). He smiled, and put his arms round me with a great effort, for he can no longer control his limbs. I shall never forget it.

Not all the treasures in the world could equal this embrace. My Robert, it was thus that we had to see each other again, how painfully I had to trace out your beloved features! What a sorrowful sight it was!

Two and a half years ago you were torn from me without any farewell, though your heart must have been full, and now I lay silent at your feet hardly daring to breathe; only now and then I received a look clouded as it were, but unspeakably gentle. . . .

On Monday, the 28th, Johannes and I spent the whole day out there, going in and out of his room, but often only looking at him through the little window in the wall. He suffered dreadfully and he often spoke vehemently. Ah! I could only pray to God to release him, because I loved him so dearly. . . .

On Tuesday, the 29th, he was to be released from his suffering. At 4 o'clock in the afternoon he fell peacefully asleep. His last hours were quiet, and he passed away in his sleep without its being noticed; no one was with him at the moment. I did not see him till half an hour later. . . . All my feelings were absorbed in thankfulness to God that he was at last set free, and as I knelt by his bed I was filled with awe, it was as if his holy spirit was hovering over me – Ah! if only he had taken me with him. . . .

The funeral was at 7 o'clock on Thursday, the 31st [at Bonn]. I was in the little chapel at the churchyard. I heard the funeral music. Now he was lowered into the grave. Yet I had a clear sense that it was not he, but his body only – his spirit was with me – I never prayed more fervently than at that hour. God give me strength to live without him.

Johannes and Joachim went before the coffin, which was carried as a mark of respect by members of the *Concordiagesellschaft* who once serenaded him at Düsseldorf. The mayors went with them, and Hiller came from Cologne, but there were no other friends. I had not let it be known, because I did not want a number of strangers to come. His dearest friends were in front, and I came (unnoticed) behind, and it was best thus; he would have liked it so. And so, with his departure, all my happiness is over. A new life is beginning for me.

4

Approach to the Music

There is a story told of Mallarmé and a young poet in the early days of this present century. The poet was in great distress, and when Mallarmé inquired what was the matter the poet replied that he had no ideas with which to finish the sonnet he was writing. Whereupon Mallarmé replied: 'Poetry is not made with ideas but with words.' Had he been speaking to a composer in a similar plight he would undoubtedly have said that music was not made with ideas but with notes.

The composer who would have most disagreed with this point of view, had it been suggested to him as a young man, is surely Schumann. It must be emphasized as a young man, since it is quite clear that Schumann's whole personality and outlook changed as he grew older. But the most lovable Schumann is the Schumann of the piano music, the Schumann of the songs, the Schumann of the piano Quintet and Concerto – all composed before he was thirty-five. So it can safely be said that the young Schumann is the essential Schumann, and as a young man he was perhaps the most romantic of all the nineteenth-century romantic composers in Germany.

The meaning of romanticism is made abundantly clear in so short a piece for the piano as *Bittendes Kind* from *Kinderscenen*, but it is a quality less easy to describe in words. Goethe, while discussing his *Walpurgisnacht* with Eckermann, remarked:

> The distinction between classical and romantic poetry, which is now spread over the whole world and occasions so many quarrels and divisions, came originally from Schiller and myself. I laid down the maxim of objective treatment in poetry, and would allow no other; but Schiller, who worked quite in the subjective way, deemed his own fashion right. . . . The Schlegels took up this idea and carried it further, so that it has now been diffused over the whole world; and everybody talks about classicism and romanticism – of which nobody thought fifty years ago.

In this he suggests that romanticism is a quality antithetic to classicism, signifying the personal approach to his subject on the part of the creative artist, whose gamut, in consequence, will in the first place be determined by the extent of his own emotional experience. It follows that in the true romanticist life and work are so closely intermingled that understanding of one, in the fullest sense, is dependent on understanding of the other. Schumann himself admitted that in his youth 'the man and the musician in me were always trying to speak at once', so that in spite of the spontaneously attractive qualities of his music, it cannot be divorced from its background, nor fully appreciated in terms of pure notes. The approach must first be made through the composer's own medium of ideas.

As a young man of twenty-two Schumann had written to his mother: 'I still consider that music is the ideal language of the soul: but some think it is only meant to tickle the ear, others treat it like a sum in arithmetic and act accordingly.' But it was six years later, in a letter to Clara, that he provided the most valuable clue to the workings of his musical mind:

> I am affected by everything that goes on in the world and think it all over in my own way, politics, literature and people, and then I long to express my feelings and find an outlet for them in music. That is why my compositions are sometimes difficult to understand, because they are connected with distant interests; and sometimes striking, because everything extraordinary that happens impresses me, and impels me to express it in music.

In spite of this definitive pointer towards politics, literature and people as incentives to composition it does not follow that Schumann's music is blatant programme music. His letters to his friends betray his love of veiled allusions, symbolism and mystery in general, and his musical thinking is no less fantastic or subtle.

It would be hard to find a work more characteristic of Schumann's highly individual youthful romanticism than *Carnaval*. In the first place the whole work grew from what was to him a discovery of no mean significance: that the letters constituting Asch, his Ernestine's birthplace, were (in German) musical letters, and that they corresponded to the four musical letters in his own surname. He describes this in a letter to Henriette Voigt, and ends with a musical postscript:

Ex. 1

But in *Carnaval* itself it is not till the mysterious insertion *Sphinxes* halfway through the work, written but not played, that he reveals that the music is a set of variations on three of the possible musical translations of the four letters. Though in the variations themselves Chopin and Paganini appear under their own names, the remaining 'dancers' are cunningly disguised, some by the masks of the old *commedia dell'arte*, but Ernestine von Fricken, Clara and Schumann himself under their Davids-bund titles of Estrella, Chiarina and Eusebius and Florestan. All these musical portraits are nevertheless far too lifelike to make it easy to believe Schumann's remark two years later, in a letter to Moscheles, that 'the titles of the various pieces came after their composition' – though admittedly this claim is true of that very small part of the background music of the ball quarried from his own earlier rejected variations on Schubert's *Sehnsuchtswaltzer*. In the same letter to Moscheles Schumann actually refers to the work as *Maskentanz*, thereby admitting that his mind was still working on the same masked ball wavelength of *Papillons*. This is clinched in the music itself by two quotations from *Papillons*. In *Florestan* he even goes so far as to write 'Papillons?' above the phrase borrowed from *Papillons* No. 1 – perhaps a quizzical allusion to his own butterfly nature in the company of Estrella and Chiarina. And in the concluding *Marche des Davidsbündler contre les Philistins* the Philistines are caricatured by the old *Grossvatertanz* tune already introduced into the finale of *Papillons*.

Of the people behind his music, inevitably no one played a larger part than Clara. When she was only thirteen he had written Impromptus on a Romance of her own composition. Two years later she not only had her portrait in *Carnaval* but was also the proud possessor of a sonata in F sharp minor inscribed 'To Clara, from Florestan and Eusebius'. In the following year his F minor sonata appeared with a slow movement in the form of variations on an Andantino of Clara Wieck. Throughout the unhappy months when Wieck kept them apart, almost every note from Schumann's pen enshrined her image. 'A deep lament for you' he confessed of the first movement of the C major *Phantasie*, and of the *Davidsbündlertänze* 'there are many bridal thoughts in the dances . . . the whole story is a *Polterabend*'. Of *Kreisleriana* he wrote 'you and one of your ideas are the principal subject', and of the *Novelletten* 'you, my bride, appear in every possible setting and circumstance'. The *Phantasiestücke, Kinderscenen* and other works of the later 1830s also contain plenty to suggest that she was never far from his thoughts.

Once or twice Schumann provided overt clues in the printed score, as in the first two bars of the *Davidsbündlertänze* inscribed *Motto von C. W.* But increasingly he resorted to secret thematic allusions that only she would understand. Nothing would seem to have meant more to them both than a falling five-note figure like a musical embodiment of Clara's name. It haunts not only his works (and never more passionately and poignantly than in the

Ex. 2A

Ex. 2B

Clara
Andante con moto

first movement of the C major *Phantasie*) but hers too, as in the F
minor Andantino. Its intimate, mutual significance is indisputably
clinched in the second trio of Schumann's last *Novellette* (Ex. 2A).
Marked *Stimme aus der Ferne* this is a direct quotation (with
identical harmonies though key and notation are different) of the
first ten bars of a *Notturno* written by Clara in 1836–7 (Ex. 2B).

Though no other motif is quite so omnipresent, several
(especially a phrase curling around a B minor tonic and leading
note, much in evidence in the F sharp minor sonata and the
Davidsbündlertänze) recur too often to be without some special
reason for being there. Occasionally the message is conveyed by
allusions of a different kind, notably the subtle reference to
Beethoven's *An die ferne Geliebte* cycle in the first movement of
the C major *Phantasie*. Perhaps many other secrets still remain to
be discovered and de-coded. Eric Sams, a tireless researcher in this
field, has already come up with a host of ingenious suggestions,
such as that the bare E B E bass in the song 'Mondnacht', written
during an idyllic fortnight with Clara in Berlin in the spring of
1840, conceals the German word for marriage, *Ehe*. Certainly in a

letter to Clara in 1838 Schumann remarked on the musical potential (the German nomenclature for B natural is H) of that word.

Beside Asch, with its Ernestine connotations, Schumann also made music out of the names of Abegg, Bach and Gade. The Danish composer, Gade, sparked off not just the *Northern Song* (in *Album für die Jugend*, Op. 68) but also a fanciful farewell when he left Leipzig, in the early 1840s, which Schumann wrote in his autograph book.

Ex. 3.

Three other people are openly linked with Schumann's music. The theme of the *Études symphoniques* came originally (though Schumann revised it) from Baron von Fricken, while the finale contains a salute to Schumann's English friend, Sterndale Bennett (the dedicatee) through a quotation of the phrase 'Du stolzes England, freue dich' ('Proud England, rejoice') from Marschner's Ivanhoe opera, *Der Templer und die Jüdin*, as its main theme. And as he wrote his *Nachtstücke* Schumann claimed that he was haunted by a strange presentiment and saw 'funerals, coffins and unhappy despairing faces'. Soon afterwards came the news of his brother Eduard's death.

Admissions of direct literary inspiration in the early piano music are plentiful, though very often Schumann preferred to keep the sources secret.[1] The earliest example is *Papillons*, closely linked to Jean Paul, though in the many attempts to describe the

---

[1] The relationship of the *Waldscenen* to Laube's 'Jagdbrevier' and of the *Gesänge der Frühe* to Hölderlin's 'Diotima' poems has only recently come to light, and probably many more such connections exist unknown.

actual workings of his mind Schumann was sometimes ambiguous and contradictory in assessing just how much he owed to the masquerade near the end of *Flegeljahre*. Certainly the last number contains the most tangible evidence of extra-musical inspiration, with its chiming clock and the gradual dying away of the strains of revelry (the *Grossvatertanz* theme); the other numbers, it has frequently been suggested, owe more to Schubert than to Jean Paul. The waltz and polonaise rhythms are unmistakably Schubertian in style, but Schubert and Jean Paul were not incompatible to Schumann. In 1829, when several of the *Papillons* were first composed, he had written to Wieck: 'Schubert is still "my only Schubert", especially as he has everything in common with "my only Jean Paul". When I play Schubert I feel as if I were reading a romance of Jean Paul's set to music. . . .' Possibly in *Papillons* he deliberately reversed the process and reproduced Jean Paul in Schubert's similarly aphoristic dance-music style.

In the second of the *Intermezzi*, Op. 4, the underlying agitation of the main substance of the piece is explained in the words written over the melody in the quieter middle section 'Meine Ruh' ist hin'. It is interesting to discover this early reference to Goethe's *Faust*, a work which could be said to have fired his imagination more continuously than any other in the German language – in fact right up to within a year of his last fatal breakdown. The Intermezzo in the D major *Novellette*, Op. 21, No. 3, had originally the words of Shakespeare's witches in Macbeth inscribed above it 'When shall we three meet again?' to explain what in later editions is hidden in the indication 'Rasch und wild'.

Though *Kreisleriana* was as much inspired by Clara as by literature, Schumann here chose to hide personal feeling under a literary cloak. The Kapellmeister Kreisler[1] is a character from E. T. A. Hoffmann with whom Schumann could easily identify himself at this time in thwarted hopes and dreams. Wasielewski suggests that the work could equally well have been called *Wertheriana* after Goethe's tale of heartache, but Kreisler was chosen because 'we always think of him at his piano'. Life and literature grew still closer in the years of Schumann's marriage when feeling overflowed into song. It was not second-hand

[1] See p. 112

emotion that he dissolved into music, but sentiment as much as his own as that of Heine, Rückert, Chamisso, Eichendorff and his other chosen Romantics. All he needed was the impact of their magical words on his heart to release what in 1840 was nothing less than a torrent of musical inspiration – again, as thematic allusions often make clear, much of it addressed to Clara.

In placing politics alongside people and literature, in his letter of 1838, Schumann was perhaps overestimating the part they played in his youthful mental and musical life. His letters – even those written a few months later from Vienna – are entirely void of political references. As for his music, admittedly the 'jest' of *Faschingsschwank aus Wien* lies in his introduction of the *Marseillaise*, a tune forbidden in Vienna at the time for its political associations, and the same tune also serves as the climax of the song *Die beiden Grenadiere*. But neither is more than a light-hearted, daredevil allusion.

It was not till the upheavals of 1848, which ultimately forced the Schumanns to leave their Dresden home and take refuge in the village of Kreischa, that his attention was forcibly drawn to the state of the outside world. By this time he had eschewed all extra-musical stimulus, otherwise the greater part of his work at this time might not have been of the peaceful nature which surprised even Clara. But that he was momentarily excited politically, and wanted to say so in terms of music, can be seen by his settings of three revolutionary poems by three revolutionary poets: Titus Ulrich's *Zu den Waffen!* (*To Arms!*), Ferdinand Freiligrath's *Schwarz-Rot-Gold* (*Black-Red-Gold*, the old Imperial colours adopted by the democrats) and J. Fürst's *Freiheitssang* (*Song of Freedom*). The three were arranged for male-voice choir with military band accompaniment and were intended as his Op. 65. But Schumann cautiously refrained from publishing them. His excitement is shown again in the Marches,[1] Op. 76, of which the last includes a further passing reference to the *Marseillaise*. As he wrote to his publisher:

> You receive herewith some marches – not the old Dessauer type – but rather, republican. It was the best way I could find to express my excitement – they have been written with real fiery enthusiasm.

[1] 'Composed on 12th June 1849, on the way from Kreischa to Dresden' is written at the bottom of the first.

THE BIRTHPLACE, HAUPTMARKT, ZWICKAU

CLARA WIECK, 1832

By courtesy of Macmillan & Co.

ROBERT AND CLARA SCHUMANN
After a Daguerreotype taken in Hamburg in 1850

CLARA SCHUMANN
From a Painting by Sohn, 1853
By courtesy of Macmillan & Co.

PORTRAIT OF SCHUMANN
*From a Reproduction in Lithography by G. Feckert
of a Drawing by A. Menzel*

ALBUM

FOR THE

YOUNG

DESIGN BY LUDWIG RICHTER FOR THE TITLE PAGE OF
'ALBUM FOR THE YOUNG'

FACSIMILE OF SCORING (FROM THE B FLAT MAJOR SYMPHONY)

ROBERT SCHUMANN

Again, in a letter to Liszt:

> I enclose a novelty – IV Marches – I shall be pleased if they are to your taste. The date they bear has a meaning this time, as you will easily see. O time – O princes – O people!

One more instance calls for comment: the reappearance of the *Marseillaise*, this time in the *Hermann und Dorothea* Overture of 1851. Dr Gerald Abraham[1] produced the ingenious theory that this work, written and orchestrated between 19th and 23rd December, owes its existence not so much to Goethe as to the '*coup d'état* of 2nd December 1851, by which Louis Napoleon overthrew the Second Republic, and the events that followed – when liberty was being crushed to the ground in France'. In support of this argument he suggests that the French soldiers are unimportant in Goethe, 'whose story is pure idyll', and continues: 'The only element of dramatic conflict in it is the opposition between Hermann and his father, not the opposition of French Republicans and patriotic Germans.' On the other hand the composer, in a footnote to the score, writes: 'By way of explanation of the introduction of the *Marseillaise* into the overture, it may be remarked that the latter was intended for the opening of a *Singspiel* based on Goethe's poem, the first scene of which represented the retreat of soldiers of the French Republic.' And a diary entry confirms that it was as far back as March, 1846, that the idea of a 'Singspiel am Clavier nach Goethes Gedicht' first occurred. As literature lay behind so much of Schumann's music in 1851 and 1852, not forgetting other overtures written for his Düsseldorf orchestra, everything in fact suggests that the *Hermann und Dorothea* overture was something bound to come – regardless of Louis Napoleon. But such was Schumann's relationship with the *Marseillaise* that this one last surreptitious fling with it must have been irresistible.

Interesting as these later political references may be as sidelights on the composer's mind, they are nevertheless insufficient in number and significance to prove any intrinsic connection between life and work in the adult Schumann. But before proceeding to the extraordinary change which took place in him as he grew older, we must examine the extent to which his

[1] 'On a Dull Overture by Schumann', *Monthly Musical Record*, December 1946.

youthful style was influenced by his attitude to music. In the first place it resulted in ten years of little but miniatures, obviously because his themes were musical embodiments of definite subject-ive moods,[1] ideas or mental pictures, complete in themselves, written down, as he admitted, 'on the impulse of the moment'. They were not malleable sequences of abstract notes, and therefore not suitable for development in the classical manner. A perfect example is the four-bar phrase from which the entire piece *Warum?* (from Op. 12) is built:

Ex. 4.

In the first place it is a lyrical melody, not a 'motif', and secondly it is so very clearly an embodiment of the mood implied in the title of the piece that to invert it or play any other tricks on it would only destroy its character. Schumann retains the phrase in its original shape for the most part, just occasionally permitting small variations in the ending, and he treats it in the manner of a dialogue between Eusebius and Florestan. To gain extra length he indicates that the second section should be repeated just as it stands rather than developed.

A study of the form of the *Novelletten* is equally revealing. Each one is composed of short episodes of very definite individual character. If extra length is required, repetition is invariably preferred to development.

It must also be remembered that Schumann's youthful artistic sensibility far outreached his technique as a craftsman. He was impatient with Wieck's academic tuition, and hardly less so with Dorn. His counterpoint he claimed to have learnt from Jean Paul and naïvely wrote to Clara of his method of working: 'It is most extraordinary how I write almost everything in canon, and then

---

[1] Often he would label them with words, such as '29 April 38, since no letter came from you'.

only detect the imitation afterwards, and often find inversions, rhythms in contrary motion, etc.' In the first movements of the F sharp minor and G minor Sonatas his actual material is well suited to the demands of sonata form, but it can be seen that he lacked the sheer technical skill required to make the development sections really develop. Certainly he realized this himself by choosing variation form – in which the journey can be made in shorter laps – for so many of his large-scale piano works.

There are numerous expression marks throughout Schumann's early music, with many detailed indications of *rubato* among them. This again testifies to his romantic attitude to music, the whole time pulling away from impersonal, classical rigidity towards the greater freedom of personal expression. It is equal testimony to his own wayward temperament, and it is significant that the self-portrait, *Florestan* (in *Carnaval*), should provide the most extreme example of constantly changing tempo. At times these indications give rise to serious problems in interpretation. The *prestissimo* coda at the very end of the G minor Sonata which then has to be played *immer schneller und schneller* is merely a problem of prestidigitation. But in the *Marche des Davids-bündler contre les Philistins* (in *Carnaval*) the tempo changes from *non allegro* to *molto più vivo* (with an *accelerando*), *animato* (with a *stringendo*), *vivo* (with *sempre brillante*), *animato molto* (with *stringendo sempre più e più*) and finally *piu stretto* (with two *stringendi*), and in consequence might produce some curious results if observed to the letter in performance. In the first movement of the C major *Phantasie* there are admittedly occasional *a tempo* markings to restore the balance, but even so the interpreter is faced with many problems arising from the over-frequent appearance of the indication *ritenuto*, and even such simple pieces as the *Kinderscenen* are at times perplexing for the same reason.

Another characteristic of his early music is its love of un-expected changes of key. Hummel in 1832 complained to Schumann of his 'too sudden changes of harmony', and the eminent critic Hauptmann also found far too many 'sheer revellings in strangeness' in the aphoristic and fragmentary piano music. This can be attributed in part to that aspect of romanticism to which Walter Pater referred when commenting that 'the essence of romanticism is the blending of strangeness with the beautiful'. Schumann himself admitted in the letter quoted at the beginning of this chapter that 'everything extraordinary that happens impresses me and impels me to express it in music'. Extraordinary things can only be expressed by extraordinary means, and it is obvious that whenever Schumann wished to reveal his own youthful delight in the element of strangeness or surprise to be found in everyday experience he relied on key-change to achieve his end, not the gradual process of modulation through the orthodox circle of fifths, but rather by short cuts – breath-taking chromaticism, enharmonic changes or plunges without any preliminary preparation. Of these methods his plunges are invariably the most effective, particularly the plunges from keys a major third apart, of which many of the early piano pieces and the songs[1] provide numerous instances. The device at its best can be found in the slow movement of the F sharp minor piano Sonata where F major follows A major with a solitary C natural as the only link (Ex. 5). The lovely chord progression which opens the last movement of the *Phantasie*, Op. 17, is built in the same way (Ex. 6). The change from F minor to the chord of

Ex. 5

[1] See Chapter 6, pp. 126–7

Ex. 6

A major in *In der Nacht* from Op. 12 (see pp. 111–12) is equally beautiful in effect.

Sometimes there is an enharmonic link between his seemingly unrelated keys. In the *Allegro*, Op. 8, the note E flat – that is the dominant of the key of A flat major – is turned in imagination into D sharp, the leading-note of E major, to achieve this delightful three-bar episode in a new tonal world:

Ex. 7

It is probable that both Schubert and Marschner were his models for this device.

An excellent example of his chromatic modulation is that found in the fourth of the *Intermezzi*, Op. 4:

Ex. 8

The passage is heralded by an effective change from a chord of C major to A flat major, and then by exploiting the semitonal drop in the melody he sideslips through E major, E flat major, A flat major and back to C major all in the space of four bars. Some of these hasty chromatic modulations betray all too clearly his lack of a proper grounding in harmony and are both clumsy and ineffective – such as his method of getting from B major back to his home key of B flat major in the *alternativo* section of the fifth *Intermezzo* from Op. 4:

Ex. 9

The return from B major to A flat major in *Reconnaissance* (*Carnaval*) is equally lacking in subtlety, and is effective in performance only when a substantial *ritardando* gives the listener time to adjust himself to the tonal hairpin bend.

Schumann's experiments with rhythm can also be attributed to this same romantic and temperamental love of strangeness and surprise. He makes an early attempt to confuse duple and triple time in the fifth *Intermezzo*, Op. 4:

Ex. 10

Further examples occur in the first movement of *Faschingsschwank aus Wien* (quoted on p. 113) and somewhat later in the last movement of the piano Concerto (see p. 146), but in both cases the device defeats its own ends after a certain length of time. In *Faschingsschwank aus Wien* the ear eventually imagines the third beat to be the first, and in the Concerto it soon translates the intricate syncopation into a simple

It would be wrong to describe Schumann's eloquent melodies as classical, yet formally, in their square-cut, sectional construction, they have more in common with the discrete melody typical of Haydn and Mozart than the continuous type of melody which was a by-product of the romantic movement. But, paradoxically enough, romantic verse can be held responsible for this, particularly the four-line stanza frequently used by Heine and many others. Literature was food and drink to Schumann, and whereas its substance frequently provided the content of his music, so its metre even more often conditioned his form. So many of the piano pieces are songs without words, for the melodies could take words as they stand, without alteration of a single note. How well would the first verse of Lenau's *An die Entfernte*,

> Diese Rose pflück ich hier
> In der fremden Ferne.
> Liebes Mädchen, dir, ach dir
> Brächt' ich sie so gerne!

fit to the melody of the trio from the *Novellette* in F major:

Ex.11

The melodies of the eleventh *Davidsbündlertänz* and the F sharp major *Romanze*, Op. 28, provide further excellent examples, and there are enough others to suggest that words coursed through Schumann's mind as he composed far more frequently than he ever admitted.

So much for Schumann's youth. But a study of both his life and his music in the years following 1840 reveals that a very striking change took place in him as he grew older. In his life the change can be attributed to his marriage and his health. Marriage brought him the deep content that he had never previously experienced in his intensely susceptible youth – one moment on top of the world and the next in suicidal despair. It stabilized his wayward character, temporarily resolved the conflicting Florestan and Eusebius elements in his temperament, and was so complete a fulfilment that it made him feel the whole world had nothing richer to offer than life in his own home. His happiness was marred only by increasingly bad health, and because of this and his own secret fears of the truth he withdrew even more into himself, shrinking from the strain of travel, casual conversation and all other things which might disturb the routine of his life. Admittedly for Clara's sake – and Clara for all her art had inherited more than a streak of her father's worldliness – he accepted several appointments which drew him forcibly into public life. But his experiences with his various choirs and orchestras, particularly at Düsseldorf, reveal that his mind by this time had turned in on itself to an extent which made it quite incapable of dealing adequately with outside administrative problems.

Since life and music are perhaps more closely interrelated in Schumann than in any other composer, it was inevitable that his music should reflect a similar change. When only twenty-two he had written to Dorn: 'My whole nature seems to rebel against any instigation from the outer world, and I feel as if my ideas ought to come to me quite independently, to be then worked out and put in the proper place.' But he had written those words because he felt that was what a music-master would wish him to write – in exactly the same way that as a law student he would tell his guardian he was attending lectures regularly whenever he wanted an increased allowance. It was Mendelssohn's elegant craftmanship which eventually made him aware of some of his own technical shortcomings and, moreover, opened his eyes to the cause of them – his preoccupation with ideas rather than notes. And so in the seclusion of his new home he resolved to turn his back on 'people, literature and politics' and all his youthful romantic ways and apply himself to the task of reasoning in terms of pure music.

The 'Spring' Symphony of 1841 is the best example of the

beginning of the change of style. Schumann admitted that the work was inspired by a spring poem by Adolph Böttger – he clearly saw some symbolic connection between the idea of spring and his own newly awakened married happiness; moreover he disclosed that the four movements were originally to have been called 'Spring's Awakening', 'Evening', 'Merry Playmates' and 'Spring's Farewell'. But in spite of this romantic background, an analysis of the work reveals that the composer was just as concerned with the problem of how to evolve a large-scale work out of the minimum of material as with the idea of spring. Nor was it an isolated experiment. For the most part he rigidly eschewed all descriptive miniatures throughout the rest of 1841 and 1842 and devoted himself to full-grown orchestral and chamber music of an entirely abstract kind. The D minor Symphony (original version) and the piano Quintet are outstanding achievements of this period, for in them his imagination lacked none of its youthful spontaneity, but was disciplined by a mind at the height of its powers.

Unfortunately this happy balance between the romantic and classical elements in Schumann's make-up was not preserved consistently throughout the remaining twelve years of his composing life. Whenever a touch of romantic inspiration was permitted to rekindle his imagination in these later years, the result was invariably a masterpiece, such for example as the 'Rhenish' Symphony of 1850, the two violin Sonatas of 1851 or even the less ambitious *Waldscenen* for piano of 1849. But on other occasions his mind – and often a tired mind – would labour to manipulate abstract sound-material in such a way as he thought befitted a would-be orthodox 'classical' composer, with the result that his most valuable attribute – his spontaneous imagination – was gradually smothered and destroyed. The choral ballads which occupied him during the 1850s are excellent examples. Each is a conscientious enough setting of the words, but with the exception of a few instances, such as some of the solo songs from *The Minstrel's Curse*, the spirit of the words is invariably sacrificed to the academic demands of the music. By leaving these scores covered in dust on the highest library shelves posterity has judged correctly. Without romance Schumann is not Schumann, and it is Schumann that posterity wishes to remember.

With regard to his later 'classical' style, it is very obvious that his mind played as large a part in fashioning it as did his heart his youthful romanticism. Whereas his early miniatures were characterized by a lavish use of new material in preference to development of the old, the most interesting feature of his later and larger instrumental music is the preoccupation with unity and compression in symphonic and similar forms by means of economy of material and inter-thematic relationship of the movements. Again his example was Mendelssohn and even Beethoven in the fifth Symphony, but Schumann went far beyond their most extravagant dreams in this respect and in so doing contributed more to the development of classical symphonic form, as opposed to the romantic type of symphony culminating in the symphonic poem, than any other composer in his generation.

The outstanding examples of unity can be found in the 'Spring' Symphony, in which the introductory motto is made to serve as the main material of the first two movements, while the second and third movements are also related; in the C major Symphony, where a motto pervades the whole work, as well as the second and fourth movements being related; in the string Quartets, where first and second subjects are closely connected in each opening movement, as well as there being occasional thematic links between the other movements; in the piano Quartet, where the third and fourth movements are linked; in the piano Quintet where the opening theme recurs at the very end of the work; in the piano Concerto, in which the first movement is almost monothematic and the remaining two movements are directly related to this same dominating theme; in the D minor violin Sonata, in which the two middle movements are organically linked; and, most important of all, in the D minor Symphony, where each movement derives from the two short themes announced in the introduction. Occasionally Schumann would expand his scherzo movements by the addition of a second trio, and in the 'Rhenish' Symphony there is an expansion by means of an additional slow movement. But for the most part his experiments with unity lead to compression. Of this the best example is the cello Concerto, where all three movements are condensed and embraced in one collective whole.

In his transitional middle period Schumann's harmony retained much of the same youthful delight in adventure off the beaten track, but was guided by a new logic. He no longer somersaulted into new keys for the sheer delight of turning somersaults, but travelled with a definite destination in mind, such as can be seen in the examples from the second and third string Quartets quoted on pp. 156–7. But in his later music he abandoned much of his originality in this respect and was content to accept the more predictable harmonies used by his lesser, academic contemporaries. Neither is there enough rhythmic vitality in the later music, which too often settles down into a repetitive patterning. But it must be admitted that the 'Rhenish' Symphony of 1850 opens with the most subtle of all his rhythmic experiments. The main theme by itself could equally well be barred in 2–4 time, but by retaining an accompaniment suggestive of 3–4 the rhythmic tug-of-war is discernible by the ear as well as the eye.[1] In his earlier experiments with syncopation Schumann had frequently overlooked the fact that the abnormal can be appreciated only when heard against the norm.

His later instrumental melody is nearly always as square-cut as in youth, but far more often continuous as opposed to discrete – suggesting that he applied his mind to its continuation instead of writing it down impulsively. The symphonies provide good examples, especially the slow movement of the C major, in which the second phrase deliberately inverts the rising intervals of the first (Ex. 12).

Ex. 12

Sometimes in his later choral works he attempted to set prose in a possibly Wagner-inspired type of *arioso*, but in spite of the many hours spent in evolving sinuous, self-determining, instrumental fugue themes during his belated effort to improve his counter-

[1] See p. 142.

point, he often found it difficult to give his melody strong impulse or sense of direction when cut adrift from four-square structural support.

Among his possessions Schumann had an old steel pen which he had found on Beethoven's grave in Vienna. He kept it as a kind of talisman and used it only on very special occasions. It was almost inevitable that he should use this pen to write his 'Spring' Symphony, as if invoking Beethoven's blessing on his first-born symphonic child. But it would be wrong to expect to find Beethovenian strength or ethical grandeur in this work, or – except for parts of the *Scenes from Faust* and perhaps the fourth movement of the 'Rhenish' symphony – in anything described in the following chapters. Schumann was never a lonely, questing philosopher wrestling with life's insoluble problems, not even in later days. His world was essentially the world of his own experience, a world as rich in personal emotional response as in fancy, yet basically centred in hearth and home. Like Wordsworth, he found delight in life's more simple things – butterflies, rainbows, daffodils and the whimsical fancies of children, and like Wordsworth he could say:

> Thanks to the human heart by which we live,
> Thanks to its tenderness, its joys, and fears,
> To me the meanest flower that blows can give
> Thoughts that do often lie too deep for tears.

5

Piano music

Schumann's piano music must come first, for the piano was his first love. He spent the first ten years of his life as a composer writing almost exclusively for this instrument, for even after his own ruined hopes of a soloist's career, inspiration still came from Clara. All his best known and most fanciful works derive from the prolific output of that first decade. In later life he would occasionally relax from more ambitious undertakings by returning to the keyboard. But though age and experience undoubtedly brought him greater facility, never again did his imagination catch fire with quite the same spontaneity as in his twenties.

The reason is perhaps best explained by his youthful remark: 'the man and the musician in me are always trying to speak at once'. In other words, his early piano music was a diary of his emotional experience, and it was when inspired by some extra-musical idea that he was at his best. What mattered to him was the delineation of feeling: at this time he found little motivation in a purely musical challenge, and indeed had a struggle to keep afloat if lured into extended abstract seas. 'I believe I have *Phantasie*, and no-one denies it me' he once confessed (albeit of early literary rather than musical aspirations) in his first *Tagebuch*, continuing 'I'm not a deep thinker: I can never logically continue the threads I have perhaps tied well.' It is his subjective attitude which places him, as a young man, in the vanguard of the nineteenth century romanticists. And just as Heine, Eichendorff or Rückert could crystallize an emotion in four lines of lyric poetry, so could Schumann say most in the short 'character' piece. Though Beethoven in his *Bagatelles* and Schubert in his *Moments Musicaux* and his *Impromptus* had already made use of the miniature, it was Schumann who realized its richest potential, and it is often through the miniature that his own greatness is revealed.

As a result of his early training as a pianist, Schumann knew well what the human hand could and could not do. And as his ideas nearly always took shape through his own fingers at the keyboard, his piano music literally 'plays into the hands' of all pianists. He was one of the first composers to realize what enormous possibilities lay in the sustaining pedal. Not all his effects come off in the degree he intended, yet the most cursory glance through his compositions reveals that the pedal was as integral a part of his thought as the marks of expression and the crotchets and quavers themselves. And he could also achieve strange effects by deliberately refraining from the use of the pedal, as in the finales of the 'Abegg' *Variations* and *Papillons*:

Ex. 13

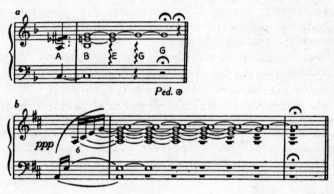

The texture of his music, particularly his favourite arpeggio figuration, is quite unlike anything that had been written for the piano before, yet he did not exploit the instrument's technical and tonal possibilities in the same degree as his notable contemporaries, Chopin and Liszt. The explanation of this may lie in the fact that Schumann, though a good pianist, was prevented from developing into a virtuoso pianist. It is a great tribute to the fertility of his imagination that he could write such a rich variety of music without straying far from the middle registers of the piano, or without in any way sacrificing his artistic integrity to mere sensuous sound.

Schumann's first prolific trying-out period lasted until 1835, when Florestan and Eusebius assumed control. Though evidence survives of one or two sonata and concerto experiments, the greater part of his unpublished juvenilia consists of variations, including solo variations on a theme of his own in G, on Schubert's *Sehnsuchtswalzer*, on the *Allegretto* from Beethoven's seventh Symphony and on Chopin's G minor Nocturne, Op. 15, No. 3, besides four-handed variations on a theme of Prince Louis Ferdinand, and a few for piano and orchestra on the 'Rondeau à la clochette' theme from Paganini's B minor Concerto. Not only was it easier for him, as one who composed at the keyboard, to vary his themes than develop them, but also variation form was the prevalent fashion of the day. Nevertheless his diary entries for 1831 and 1832 reveal that Bach, Mozart, Beethoven and Schubert were already his gods, opening his eyes to the superficialities of the bravura style exploited by composers like Hummel and Moscheles, which explains why he was often able to salvage extracts from these works for subsequent use.

The first group of published works comprises the *'Abegg' Variations* (Op. 1), *Papillons* (Op. 2), *Paganini Caprices* (Op. 3 and 10), *Six Intermezzi* (Op. 4), *Impromptus on a Theme by Clara Wieck* (Op. 5), *Toccata* (Op. 7) and *Allegro* (Op. 8). It is highly significant that for his official Opus 1 Schumann should have chosen the *'Abegg' Variations* of 1830, a work originating from his personal life in that he is known to have had friends with the surname Abegg, from which the theme is derived.

Ex. 14.

The fictitious 'Mademoiselle Pauline Comtesse d'Abegg' of the dedication has long been thought to conceal the identity of one of the family called Meta, an attractive dancing partner at a Mannheim ball. But in spite of much ingeniously fanciful figuration in the ensuing variations, the bias in this work is still towards the note-spinning virtuoso school. The *Allegro* of the rejected 'Rondeau à la clochette' variation material is even closer to the style of Hummel and Moscheles; he himself frequently referred to it as an 'Allegro di bravura', and showed his wisdom in not carrying out his original intention of making it the first movement (it is in sonata form) of a complete sonata.

Papillons, also completed in 1831, belongs to a new world, his own world of romance. He admitted that the work was much influenced by Jean Paul, though in a letter to Henriette Voigt he qualified this claim by adding that he 'adapted the text to the music and not vice versa', except in the case of the finale, which was a direct musical account of the masked ball described near the end of *Flegeljahre*, complete with a striking clock to denote the end of the festivities. The finale makes use of the *Grossvatertanz*:

Ex. 15

an old tune, traditionally played at the end of a ball, with which Schumann subsequently routed the Philistines in *Carnaval*. The title *Papillons* could not have been better chosen, since nearly all of the twelve pieces underwent an elaborate metamorphosis, like larvae, before emerging in their full butterfly grace and charm. This was due to the fact that much of the material derived originally from a set of two-handed waltzes and another of four-handed polonaises dating from 1828 to 1830, and that old and new ideas had to be welded into some kind of basic musical unity before qualifying for adoption by Jean Paul. Had Schumann been strictly honest he would have admitted that the work was as much influenced by Schubert as Jean Paul, for his own four-handed polonaises grew direct from Schubert's four-handed polonaises (Op. 75) which as a student he often played with his friend Töpken. His waltzes, too, were so closely modelled on those of Schubert that in the case of *Papillons* No. 8, with its typically Schubertian key-change at the double-bar, he was once able to pass the music off on Töpken, for a joke, as an original Schubert waltz.

The *Intermezzi* (Op. 4) of 1832 Schumann described as 'longer Papillons', but it can be seen from their figuration that he was rapidly discovering his own peculiar keyboard idiom by this time. With the exception of the fourth of the six, each has a contrasting 'alternativo' middle section, after which the opening material is recapitulated with certain modifications or extensions. The third, fourth and fifth contain interesting examples of some of his unacademic and unorthodox short-cut modulations such as are to be found in all his early works, and the fourth has the additional interest of being based on the opening melody of his setting of Ekert's poem *Hirtenknabe* (composed in 1828, and published in the supplementary volume of the Breitkopf *Gesamtausgabe*), also incorporating a phrase from his youthful C minor piano quartet (1828–9). The second of the set, in E minor, is of the greatest artistic value. The mood of the opening is one of disturbed agitation, and in the contrasting middle section Schumann deliberately reveals the music's meaning by writing Gretchen's words 'Meine Ruh' ist hin' in the score. Like many other composers of his time he could not escape from the fascination of *Faust*.

There is evidence of close relationship between life and music in the *Impromptus* on Clara Wieck's theme, the music testifying to the extraordinarily happy summer of 1833 spent in the company of Friedrich Wieck and his daughter. Clara had written her *Romanze* on a bass which was originally Robert's, and had herself composed a set of bravura variations on the theme which she dedicated to Robert. Schumann's *Impromptus* appeared as a birthday surprise for Wieck that same August. In spite of the title the work is in fact a set of variations with the spotlight as much on the bass as the melody, no doubt in emulation of Beethoven's 'Prometheus' variations. The whole composition abounds in poetry – though the imperfect expression of his ideas led Schumann to revise the work in 1850. These small alterations give proof of more able craftmanship and in no way rob the music of its freshness, so that the second edition is to be recommended for study of the work. Paganini's playing made such an impression on Schumann in 1830 that he arranged two sets of that composer's violin caprices as studies for the piano, published as Opp. 3 and 10 in 1832 and 1833 respectively. The first set is prefaced by a general account of the purpose of these studies, and each one has its own particular explanation and a few preliminary exercises to meet the forthcoming difficulties. In this first set he adheres to Paganini's text as closely as possible, but in the second set his aim is 'to give the impression of an original pianoforte composition, which, without separating itself from the original poetic idea, had forgotten its violin origin'. He describes how this was achieved in a detailed article on the work in *Music and Musicians*, and when comparing his result with Liszt's he stresses the point that whereas Liszt's are bravura studies for the purpose of display, his set out to reveal the poetry of Paganini's original music. The final version of the C major *Toccata* (Op. 7), originally sketched as an *Étude fantastique* in D in 1829, also dates from 1833. It adheres to orthodox sonata form to the last degree, but is of greater value to the performer as a study in double notes than to the listener.

It was in the early part of 1834 that the first number of the *Neue Zeitschrift für Musik* appeared, and throughout that year Schumann devoted most of his time and energy to literary work. But during the next three years he returned to the piano with a new lease of musical life, and though still a young man composed those works by which he will always first and foremost be remembered: *Carnaval*, Op. 9, *Davidsbündlertänze*, Op. 6, *Études symphoniques*, Op. 13, *Phantasie* in C major, Op. 17, and, of slightly lesser significance, the three Sonatas, in F sharp minor, F minor and G minor, Opp. 11, 14 and 22 respectively. It is an interesting period. Not only does his music take on a deeper autobiographical significance in such works as *Carnaval*, *Davidsbündlertänze* and the *Phantasie*, but at the same time in the *Études symphoniques* and sonatas he embarks on his first important adventures with purely musical thought.

Not many composers have had the good fortune to win their popularity by means of one of their best works, but such is the case with Schumann and *Carnaval*, completed in 1835. Its extra-musical story reveals one of the most attractive flights of fancy of which the composer was capable, while its form, a collection of short related sections, was at that time the most comfortable medium in which he could express his ideas. The work grew from the discovery that the letters which formed the name of his Ernestine's birthplace, A S C H, were also the musical letters in his own surname – hence the subtitle 'Scènes mignonnes sur quatre notes'. A mysterious insertion, *Sphinxes* half way through the work (not intended to be played) sheds further light on the three possible musical translations of those letters:

Ex. 16

and it is from these three thematic snippets that the whole work, with the exception of the opening *Préambule*, is built. But rather than listening to *Carnaval* as a set of quasi-variations, the imaginative listener will prefer to think of it as an account of some masked ball at which Florestan and Eusebius, Chiarina (Clara Wieck), Estrella (Ernestine herself) and Chopin and Paginini appear, together with Pierrot, Harlequin, Pantalon and Columbine of the ancient *commedia dell' arte*. Various dance movements mark the progress of the ball, and in the finale Schumann's friends of the Davidsbund, who so often attacked their ancient enemies, the Philistines, in print, now for the first time wage war on them in music. In writing this march in 3–4 time Schumann undoubtedly challenges convention on behalf of the Davidsbund while he caricatures the Philistines by means of the traditional *Grossvatertanz* tune first heard in *Papillons*. As in *Papillons*, so in *Carnaval* Schumann made extensive revisions before the work emerged in its final form, some of its material having originated in some variations he had sketched on Schubert's *Sehnsuchtswalzer*.

In spite of the earlier opus number, the *Davidsbündlertänze* were not completed until two years after *Carnaval*. By this time the Davidsbund was well established in the *Neue Zeitschrift*, and now Schumann reintroduces his mysterious society to the public in terms of music, crediting the composition of the more excitable of the eighteen numbers to Florestan and most of the dreamy remainder to Eusebius, while at times an 'F. and E.' signature denotes the collaboration of the two. In the second edition Schumann not only removed these initials but also the revealing remarks written above certain numbers in the score (such as over the ninth: 'Here Florestan kept silent, but his lips were quivering with emotion'), and even more important, the old German proverb at the beginning:

In all' und jeder Zeit   Along the way we go
Verknüpft sich Lust und Leid, Are mingled weal and woe,
Bleibt fromm in Lust und seid In weal, though glad, be grave,
Beim Leid mit Mut bereit.   In woe, though sad, be brave.

as if in later life he was ashamed of his youthful, romantic extravagances. Though the work is dedicated to Walter von Goethe, the great writer's grandson, its inner musical message was for Clara Wieck alone, for whom Schumann had by this time openly declared his love. He uses a motto composed by her for the first phrase:

Ex. 17

and in a letter once confessed: 'My Clara will find out for me what is in the dances: they are more her own than anything else of mine . . . the whole story is of a *Polterabend*.' Though there is no declared thematic connection as in the 'sphinxes' of *Carnaval*, the seeds from which most of the dances grow are the falling seconds of Clara's motto, and, equally important, a B minor motif plainly of some special secret significance to them both since it recurs frequently in various forms in Schumann's music.[1]

It is not surprising that Clara so frequently included the work in her later recital programmes. In the second edition Schumann removed the 'Tänze' from the title, no doubt used in the first place to relate the work to *Carnaval*, in which the Davidsbund had routed the Philistines – there are one or two brief thematic references to *Carnaval*.

The great C major *Phantasie* is perhaps the most personal and deeply felt of all Schumann's piano works. Again he supplied a clue in a letter to Clara: 'I have finished a fantasia in three movements that I sketched in all but the detail in June 1836. The first movement is, I think, the most passionate thing I have ever composed – a deep lament for you.' There were also other emotions astir in the composer at the time. Towards the end of 1835 Liszt had started a scheme for a monument to Beethoven at

[1] See p. 81.

Bonn, and Schumann, by composing a 'Grand Sonata for the Pianoforte', felt he could give assistance by devoting proceeds from the sale of the work to the subscription fund. It was eventually published under the title *Phantasie*, with a dedication to Liszt. The original titles of the three movements: 'Ruins', 'Triumphal Arch' and 'Starry Crown', were removed, and an enigmatic quotation from Schlegel was affixed to the head of the score: 'Through all the tones that sound in earth's fitful dream, one gentle note is there for the secret listener.' In the first movement the Clara and Beethoven strands are cunningly interwoven. The first subject begins as the most impassioned version of the falling-five-note motif,[1] of deep personal significance for both young lovers, that Schumann had yet devised. This merges into a phrase of dedication from the sixth of Beethoven's *An die ferne Geliebte* songs (Ex. 18A), though the allusion is not made fully explicit until the very beautiful coda (Ex. 18B). Whereas so often at this time Schumann had difficulty in hiding his seams in larger canvases, such was his ardour in this rhapsodic first movement that exposition, development and re-capitulation, like the themes themselves, flow into each other. Moreover, despite the lyrical nature of the subject matter, the central section brings true, organic development, notably when the second subject's initial uprising fourth grows into a grave C minor episode headed *Im Legendenton*. The proud, march-like middle movement in E flat (Beethoven's most heroic key) is cast as a sonata-rondo, an easy solution to the problem of large-scale architecture. The slow movement, a deep, introspective meditation, comes last. The five-note falling motto is cunningly concealed in the bass of the first subject; a surprise switch from C to A flat brings a new theme, first noted in Schumann's sketch-book on 30th November 1836, to the words 'dabei selig geschwärmt' (was in blissful rapture). Recapitulation follows without development. The coda, derived from the second theme, brings one last fervent surge of emotion before sinking to rest in a profoundly tranquil C major.[2]

---

[1] See p. 80.

[2] A manuscript of the *Fantasia* (recently discovered in the National Széchényi Library in Budapest), carrying Schumann's signature and the date 19 December 1838, reveals that he originally intended to end the work by recalling the *An die ferne Geliebte* quotation – with a small but significant change of one melody note and its harmonization.

Ex. 18A

Ex. 18B

The three sonatas came to a head between 1835 and 1836 (though the first three movements of the G minor had been sketched earlier, and its new, definitive finale was not added until 1838). Schumann knew these works were not wholly satisfactory from a structural viewpoint. Despite an underlying allegiance to classical sonata principles, in the strongly motivated *Phantasie* the ideas themselves seem to generate their own form. But in the three sonatas Schumann too patently manipulates his argument in accordance with procrustean textbook demands. The F sharp minor sonata, after an introduction of great beauty, introduces an admirable first subject because of its two pregnant motifs (*a*) and (*b*):

Ex. 19

But after a satisfactory exposition, the first movement[1] falls flat because of Schumann's inability to develop his material: he

[1] Originally sketched as an independent Fandango in 1832.

merely resorts to such devices as sequence, decoration and mere repetition (expressed in thick, matted texture) in a brave endeavour to keep going for the required length of time. The first movement of the G minor Sonata is much more concise and to the point – here canon and sequential repetition of the first subject in varying keys carry him through the development. The F minor Sonata is the least satisfactory of the three. It is written in such an extravagantly grand manner that the publisher suggested it should be called 'Concert sans orchestre', and in agreeing to this Schumann removed the two scherzos and revised the first movement. In the second edition of the work in 1853 he restored the first movement to its original, slightly simpler form and put back one of the scherzos. There is a wealth of beautiful material in the first movement, but its weakness lies in the recapitulation of its already tedious development section – a curious extended form which Schumann not only employs again in the finale of this work but had already used in the two other finales as well. Beethoven's codas were frequently not unlike a second development, but Schumann goes a stage further in repeating his development sections after the normal recapitulation and then adding a coda. This is well illustrated in the definitive finale of the G minor Sonata, substituted in 1838 for the more flightily virtuosic original finale of 1835, and described as a rondo. After the rousing main theme in G minor there is a restful second subject of thirty-two bars in B flat major (in which one little tune is repeated seven times). Then follows a pseudo-development section of seventy-two bars, of which the first thirty-two are sequential repetitions of a four-bar phrase derived from the first subject, while the last forty treat the first subject in canon in flatter keys. At this point, first and second subjects return in G minor and E flat major, respectively, as if this were the recapitulation. But then Schumann courts disaster with a complete recall of the seventy-two-bar development section, identical in matter though different in key, before a final return of the first subject and a brilliant coda. This 'padding' is to be found in four movements of the three sonatas, and demands exceptional tact and imagination from every interpreter. The scherzos are excessively symmetrical – only in an Intermezzo occurring in the middle section of the F sharp minor scherzo does Schumann break loose and indulge in a little burlesque at the expense of his musical enemies, the academics. In each sonata the most shapely and eloquent movement is the slow one, where Schumann's innate lyricism carries him along on its own tide. Two of the three have the special interest of being transcriptions of early songs from the set sent to Wiedebein for criticism in 1828. That of the F sharp minor Sonata is a fairly straightforward A major version of his Kerner setting, *An Anna* (the first movement's introduction is derived from the same source). For the G minor Sonata he turned to his setting of the same poet's *Im Herbste*, this time not so much merely transcribing as recomposing it. The F minor's slow movement is a sequence of variations on an Andantino of Clara Wieck: its kernel is the falling five-note motto not only haunting this sonata but the two others too, as in the motif (*b*) from Ex. 19.

A more successful large-scale abstract work is the *Études symphoniques*, published, after considerable revision, in 1837. The theme was composed by Baron von Fricken, but apart from that spurious connection with life, the music is 'pure' music. In a later edition[1] Schumann changed the title to *Études en forme de variations*, since most of the numbers are in fact variations of the theme. And as Schumann had already discovered, variation form was one of the happiest ways in which any romantic composer not endowed with the gift of development in the classical sense could achieve a unified work of some size. Quite frequently the descending arpeggio from the first bar of the theme is introduced without any attempt at disguise, but more often he prefers to work with new shoots which have germinated from the theme, so that though structurally most of the variations divide into the two balanced sections suggested by the theme, each is music of such powerful originality that its parentage is not immediately discernible. The new motif which opens the finale is derived from a phrase in Marschner's opera *Der Templer und die Jüdin* to the words 'Du stolzes England, freue dich' – a compliment to Sterndale Bennett, to whom the work is dedicated. Only in the finale does Schumann indulge in unnecessary repetition – the rest of the work gains much of its power from concentration and economy of means.

[1] Of 1852. The five variations which Schumann rejected (because stemming from his discarded 'pathetic' conception of the work) in both editions were published by Brahms in the supplementary volume of Schumann's Complete Works in 1893.

In the three years preceding his marriage Schumann brought his first big spate of piano music to an end with a series of smaller pieces gathered into collections under the names of *Phantasiestücke*, Op. 12, *Kinderscenen*, Op. 15, *Kreisleriana*, Op. 16, *Arabeske*, Op. 18, *Blumenstück*, Op. 19, *Humoreske*, Op. 20, *Novelletten*, Op. 21, *Nachtstücke*, Op. 23, *Faschingsschwank aus Wien*, Op. 26, *Romanzen*, Op. 28, and *Clavierstücke*, Op. 32, again with Clara never far from his thoughts.

Schumann affixed titles at the head of each piece of the *Phantasiestücke* and *Kinderscenen* only; for the rest he was content to let the music speak for itself. He explained that the latter were not meant for children, but were an adult's recollections of youth for adults to play, and hastened to add that the music itself suggested the titles afterwards. Whichever came first, the title is an invaluable clue to interpretation in both collections. From a purely musical viewpoint the *Kinderscenen* need little explanation, since each is evolved from a single idea into a simple example of binary or ternary form. The *Phantasiestücke* are slightly more complex in structure – the popular *Aufschwung* and *Grillen*, for example, make use of a kind of miniature sonata-rondo form. The first, *Des Abends*, is a typical example of the composer's style. It employs his favourite figuration – a melody worked into an arpeggio accompaniment. The two-against-three cross-rhythms and the off-beat melody which appears in the twenty-first bar:

Ex. 20

are good examples of his rhythmic experimentation – a feature even more prominent in his later work. And the unexpected plunges to and from unrelated keys such as in the twenty-fifth bar:

Ex. 21

are typical of his substitutes for the logical system of modulation through the circle of fifths. A similar example of this is to be found in *In der Nacht*:

Ex. 22

when a sudden shaft of light is thrown by the unexpected chord on A, suggesting D major, after F minor.

The *Kreisleriana* and *Novelletten*, both composed in 1838, comprise considerably more extended pieces. Some are in simple ternary form, though the majority use a kind of rondo form in which the contrasting episodes (sometimes called Intermezzi) are held together by frequent recurrences of the main theme. The title *Kreisleriana* was suggested by Hoffmann's Kapellmeister Kreisler, a character Schumann believed to have been based on Ludwig Böhner (1787–1860), a once celebrated eccentric genius of unlimited potential against whom the tables had turned. In his own chequered courtship Schumann saw himself in a similar rôle. All eight pieces are as introspectively expressive as anything he ever wrote, and at times the chromaticism, usually achieved by means of anticipated or suspended notes in his chords, must have sounded exceedingly strange to contemporary ears. Example 23 from the second piece makes it easy to understand Clara's plea that he should be more lucid, as it hurt her when people could not understand him.

Ex. 23

The *Novelletten* are less tortured and tortuous. 'I have composed a shocking amount for you, jests, Egmont stories, family scenes with fathers, a wedding – and called the whole *Novelletten*' he wrote to Clara, while to another friend he explained them as closely connected and written with great enjoyment, on the whole light and superficial 'excepting one or two sections where I go deeper'. Nowhere is there greater depth than in the *Stimme aus der Ferne* episode in the last, a true wedding of true minds in its embrace of the opening of Clara's Notturno[1] as his own. As for the *Nachtstücke*, associated with a strange presentiment of his brother Eduard's death, Schumann's original intention was to call the four pieces Funeral March, Strange Company, Nocturnal Feast, and Round with Solo Voices. In their sectional construction they are not unlike shorter *Novelletten*. Of the *Drei Romanzen*, also dating from 1839, the gem is the second, a song-without-words for whose beautiful melody Schumann resorts to the then unusual device of a third stave.

In spite of its suggestive title, *Faschingsschwank aus Wien* is as nearly an abstract suite of pieces as the Scherzo, Gigue, Romanze and Fughetta of the *Clavierstücke*, also completed in 1839 soon after Schumann's return from Vienna. The actual 'jest' occurs in the first of its five movements, an *allegro* in extended rondo form, where in one of the episodes Schumann introduces the *Marseillaise*, a tune forbidden in Vienna at that time for obvious political reasons. From this same movement the second episode provides an example of one of Schumann's less successful experiments with syncopation. As he destroys all vestiges of the first beat in each bar, the ear eventually comes to accept the third beat as the first beat, and the tied notes are of no more significance than ordinary minims:

Ex. 24

[1] See pp. 80–1.

The similarity between the last episode:

Ex. 25.

and the trio of the minuet in Beethoven's E flat major Sonata, Op. 31, No. 3, could hardly have been a coincidence, especially if one remembers the opening of Schumann's A major string Quartet, which makes equally striking reference to the first motif of this same Sonata. The other Suite, Op. 32, seems to belong in spirit to Schumann's next phase of piano writing, for in spite of the romantic qualities with which he invests the old forms of gigue and fughetta (the subject of the latter being accompanied even on first appearance), notes rather than feelings are his main preoccupation. The *Arabeske*, *Blumenstück* and *Humoreske* of 1839 are not a group of three pieces; each stands alone with its own opus number. Delicate and pianistic as is the main idea of the *Arabeske*, its recall in full between each contrasting minor episode is apt to detract from its aerial charm. In the *Blumenstück* the second section is overworked in the same way, and the piece as a whole lacks rhythmic variety. The *Humoreske*, on the other hand, is a more successful experiment in extended form. Each of the five main sections is a self-contained piece of fairly elaborate ternary form, yet the work as a whole is continuous and should be played without any suggestion of division into five movements. The subject-matter is imaginative to a degree,[1] even including a mysterious 'inner voice', written but not played, in the second main section.

Perhaps Schumann realized that for the moment he had said all he had to say in keyboard terms only, for in 1840 he turned to song-writing and his prodigious output for that year shows how

---

[1] Of this Schumann wrote to Clara: 'I have been all the week at the piano, composing, writing, laughing and crying, all at once. You will find this state of affairs nicely described in my Op. 20, the *Grosse Humoreske*.'

his imagination was rekindled by the efflorescence of romantic poetry around him. The year 1841 saw him launching out into more ambitious orchestral music; in 1842 chamber music was his main preoccupation; and in the next two years, amid crises of nervous exhaustion, he turned to extended choral writing. It may have been for temporary relaxation that he came back to the piano in 1845, but the music he wrote is more interesting as evidence of his belated determination to improve his counterpoint than as actual music for performance. The *Six Studies* (Op. 56) and *Four Sketches* (Op. 58) for pedal piano were written as a result of the appearance of an instrument of that kind in the Leipzig Music School for the organ scholars' practice, prompting him to hire a pedal-board to attach to his own piano at home. The six of the first set are in the nature of exercises in canon, whereas the four of the second are more harmonic in texture. His admiration for Bach led him to make an extensive study of the '48' shortly after his marriage, so that it is not surprising to find that the first of his own fugal experiments in 1845 took the form of a set of six, Op. 60, for organ or pedal piano, on the name B A C H, which like 'Abegg' and 'Asch', is easily translatable into musical nomenclature. In each case the four notes:

Ex. 26

provide only the starting-point of the subjects, yet his six variants of just these four notes are ingenious in themselves. In the fourth he is so pleased with his discovery that the theme can be worked against its retrograde form that he writes 'Tema retrograda' in the score each time the miracle is performed. In the fifth 'per moto contrario' also appears on the one occasion that the subject is inverted. The second set of Four Fugues, Op. 72, written the same year, is for ordinary piano, and like the earlier set departs from strict classical tradition in the absence of permanent counter-subjects, and in the grand endings where counterpoint is abandoned in favour of good strong chords. It is also interesting to note that the subject of the third of the set has a romantic flavour which owes more to Chopin's F minor Study (of *Trois Nouvelles Études*) than to Bach:

Ex. 27

(a) SCHUMANN *Nicht schnell und sehr ausdrucksvoll*

(b) CHOPIN

Schumann's delight in the child mind dates from the time when he was the young Clara's 'moonstruck maker of charades'. His *Kinderscenen* had described a children's world, and in the *Album for the Young*, Op. 68, of 1848, he writes music especially for children to play. Most of the forty-three pieces have some small technical problem, but it is cleverly concealed by an imaginative title. And with great understanding of children Schumann insisted on having an attractive cover design by Ludwig Richter – famous for his fairy-tale illustrations. *Erinnerung* (No. 28), in the style of a song without words, has the sub-title '4. November 1847. Todestag Mendelssohns', and in No. 41, *Nordisches Lied*, Schumann reverts to his old habit of making themes out of names – this time the name of Gade, his Danish composer-friend. In all of them Schumann manages to recapture his own youthful spontaneity, so that he could write: 'I felt as though I were beginning to compose again at the very beginning. And you will come upon traces of the old humour here and there.' The three *Sonatas for the Young* (Op. 118, *a*, *b* and *c*) which he wrote in 1853 for his daughters: Julie, aged eight; Elise, aged ten; Marie, aged twelve, are longer, though not much more difficult, pieces of music, and his introduction of unorthodox movements such as a *Gypsy Dance* and a *Doll's Cradle Song* makes the title 'Sonata' less forbidding to any child.

Some of the remaining works of Schumann's last period of piano writing are as slight and as whimsical as his early *Papillons*. In the *Waldscenen*, Op. 82, of 1849, a suite of nine miniatures linked by German forest romanticism, he again allowed his

imagination to catch fire from simple poetic images; beyond their
titles the pieces were also originally inscribed with mottos from
Laube's *Jagdbrevier*, though these were subsequently removed.
The trifles which make up *Bunte Blätter*, Op. 99 and *Albumblätter*, Op. 124, were composed at different times between 1832
and 1849 and owe their late opus numbers only to the fact that
Schumann did not decide to salvage them for publication until
1851 and 1854 respectively. Amongst the *Bunte Blätter* (originally planned for separate issue each in a different colour) No. 6 is
interesting as a rejected waltz from *Carnaval*, No. 11 as a rejected
March from the 'Barricade' set, Op. 76, and No. 13 as the Scherzo
of the unfinished C minor Symphony of 1841. Moreover Brahms
selected No. 4 in F sharp minor as the theme of his Op. 9 piano
Variations and incorporated some of No. 5 in his own ninth
variation. As for the *Albumblätter*, Schumann salvaged No. 2
from his early unpublished variations on the *Allegretto* from
Beethoven's seventh Symphony,[1] No. 3 is a rejected *Papillon*, and
Nos. 4, 11, 15 and 17 were all rejections from *Carnaval*.

Finally, there are four sets of untitled pieces: *Four Marches*, Op.
76, of 1849, *Phantasiestücke*, Op. 111, *Sieben Clavierstücke in
Fughettenform*, Op. 126, and *Gesänge der Frühe*, Op. 133. The
Marches are of greater extra-musical significance than musical
value, but credit is due to Schumann for his many varieties of
rhythm within the standard 4–4 march measure. The *Phantasiestücke* date from 1851, the year of the two violin Sonatas, when
his creative powers seemed to take on a new lease of life. It would
seem from the indication *attacca* at the end of the second that the
three pieces were meant to be played consecutively, and from that
viewpoint the idyllic and almost Schubertian middle number
provides ideal contrast between the turbulent first number (in
which chromaticism is used as effectively as in Chopin's 'Revolutionary' Study) and the vigorous finale in march rhythm –a much
more virile march than any of the 1849 collection. The *Gesänge
der Frühe* were among Schumann's last compositions of 1853,
and are curiously unequal. It would be hard to find among all his
piano music anything of greater serenity than the first, or anything
more poignantly lovely than the final section of the fourth. Yet the
second lacks all sense of direction, and the third is frankly dull

---

[1] The complete work was published for the first time in 1976 (Henle Verlag).

with its one overworked rhythmic figure. He himself described them as 'characteristic pieces which depict the emotions on the approach and advance of morning, but more as expression of feeling than painting', and recent research has revealed Hölderlin's 'Diotima' poems as a further source of inspiration. The *Sieben Clavierstücke in Fughettenform* of 1853 and the undated canon on F. H. Himmel's song, *An Alexis*, are transparent, lightweight continuations of the fugal experiments of 1845.

The *Andante and Variations* in B flat major (Op. 46) for two pianos was originally written for two pianos, two cellos and horn, but so sufficient were the pianos in themselves that Schumann eventually removed the other instruments, omitting one of the later variations in which they were prominent, as well as the brief *sostenuto* introduction and that interlude between the fifth and sixth variations in which he quoted the opening theme of his *Frauenliebe und -leben* song-cycle – a quotation suggesting some purely domestic celebration as explanation of the unusual original scoring. As a set of variations on a warm, romantic theme the work is thoroughly successful, but viewed as an example of two-piano writing it is far from satisfactory. Admittedly Schumann shares his subject-matter between the two instruments, yet all the way through one piano is redundant, merely reinforcing the harmony with octaves or simple chords, or worse still, as at one point in the third variation, doubling the other part note for note, while awaiting its turn for the theme. The four sets of duets for one piano: *Bilder aus Osten* (Op. 66) of 1848, *Zwölf vierhändige Clavierstücke für kleine und grosse Kinder* (Op. 85) of 1849, *Ballscenen* (Op. 109) of 1851 and *Kinderball* (Op. 130) of 1853, all show a much more skilful grasp of this medium, and though Schumann says nothing very new or important in them, they are extraordinarily virile for such late works.

Schumann's very last work for the piano, the Variations on a Theme in E flat, stands apart from the rest of the music surveyed in this chapter as a tragic postscript. The theme itself came to him 'from the angels', so he thought, on the night of 17th February 1854, though other people quickly identified it as a reminiscence of the slow movement of his recently composed violin concerto. He worked on the variations in the days immediately preceding and following his attempted suicide, just before removal to the private asylum at Endenich. In their alternating naïvety and crudity these variations leave no doubt of a mind strained to breaking point. But at least Schumann's chosen member of the younger generation, Johannes Brahms, brought the theme to the glory Schumann himself was striving for when choosing it in 1861 for a set of variations of his own for piano duet, Op. 23.

6

Songs

In view of Schumann's literary background and keen interest in poetry, it is surprising that he was content to write piano music for such a long time before turning to the new medium of song. It is doubly surprising when we recall that of his several youthful compositions written at Leipzig while a student of law, he selected songs to send to Wiedebein, and that Wiedebein's criticism was the all-important turning-point in his career. Ten of these eleven manuscript songs, dedicated to Schumann's sisters-in-law, Therese, Rosalie and Emilie, have since been published: three by Brahms in the supplementary volume of the Breitkopf *Gesamtausgabe*, six by Karl Geiringer in 1933 for Universal Edition, and Goethe's *Der Fischer* as a supplement to the *Zeitschrift für Musik* in 1933. Kerner's *An Anna*[1] and *Im Herbste* and Ekert's *Hirtenknabe* were the three selected by Brahms for the excellent reason that Schumann had salvaged them himself and made the first two serve as the substance of the slow movements of his piano sonatas, Opp. 11 and 22 respectively, while the third appears as the main theme of the fourth *Intermezzo*, in C major, for piano, Op. 4.

However, it was not till 1840, having for the time said all there was to say in terms of the piano, that he selected the new medium of song and wrote nothing else but songs. 'Oh, Clara, what bliss to write songs! Too long have I been a stranger to it,' were his words in the spring of the year, and a few weeks later: 'I have again composed so much that it sometimes seems quite uncanny. Oh, I can't help it. I should like to sing myself to death like a nightingale.' The song-cycles Opp. 24, 25, 27, 29–31, 33–6, 39, 40, 42, 43, 45, 48, 49 and 53 as well as many individual songs were all written in 1840, and though he frequently returned to the medium of song as an older and more skilful craftsman, none of

---

[1] The second of the two Kerner settings of this title.

his later work surpasses or even equals these first spontaneous settings when his romanticism was in full flood. 'I dare not promise better things than I have already accomplished – I mean in song,' were his own, prescient words in 1842.[1]

Schubert, Schumann's great predecessor in the school of German song-writers, turned first and foremost to Goethe and Schiller, the fathers of lyric poetry in Germany, and also to such older romantics as Klopstock and F. Schlegel for his words. Wilhelm Müller was the only one of the younger poets he used extensively. Schumann, on the other hand, went direct to the later romantics – Heine, Eichendorff, Rückert, Mörike, Lenau, Chamisso and others, all of them poets whose subjective attitude to their art was akin to his own. His admiration for Goethe was unbounded – *Faust* was a continuous source of inspiration to him all his life. Yet Schumann used only nineteen of his poems for solo songs (though several others for partsongs) as compared with Schubert's seventy-two, and Schiller he used only three times as against Schubert's fifty-four. The reason is not hard to explain. Schubert, Goethe and Schiller all had one foot firmly planted in the eighteenth century, whereas Schumann belonged whole-heartedly to the nineteenth. And whereas in the eighteenth century emotion was only a by-product of craftsmanship, in the nineteenth it was the sole justification for the act of creating. Poetry to the younger romantics was a means of crystallizing personal emotional experience, of photographing in words spontaneous individual reactions to moonlight, spring and twilight – or using these things as symbols of love and longing, hope and despair. Winds, trees, birds and streams were for ever in secret communication with them, whispering messages of comfort or sorrow to their lovelorn hearts. And this, too, was the world in which Schumann loved to live in imagination.

In all, Schumann wrote thirty-three sets of solo songs and two independent ballads, totalling well over two hundred. Many of the sets are cycles devoted to poems by a single poet: from Heine come the *Liederkreis*, Op. 24, and *Dichterliebe*, Op. 48, from Chamisso *Frauenliebe und-leben*, Op. 42, and there are other Eichendorff, Kerner, Reinick, Geibel, Lenau, Wilfried von der Neun, Byron, Goethe, Elisabeth Kulmann and Pfarrius cycles.

[1] Letter to Kahlert.

Others, such as *Myrthen*, Op. 25, or the several volumes of *Lieder und Gesänge* and *Romanzen und Balladen*, are made up of poems chosen arbitrarily from various different poets. The *Romanzen und Balladen* are frequently short narrative poems set in the German *Volkslied* style, otherwise there is no unifying, underlying idea in these miscellaneous sets.

There was never a song-writer with a greater intuitive understanding of poetry than Schumann, so that his musical treatment of each poem is entirely conditioned by its character. And in view of the immense variety of his material, it is not surprising to discover equal variety in the style of his settings. From a structural viewpoint they can be divided into two main categories: those written in strophic style, i.e. the same melody and accompaniment used for the different words of each verse, and those in which the poet's sentiments ask for detailed interpretation in a through-composed form. Most of the simple folk poems are treated in strophic style, outstanding examples being *Es fiel ein Reif*, the second of Heine's miniature trilogy *Tragödie* (from Op. 64), which is a genuine national song collected by the poet in the Rhineland, also *Hee Balou*, which as a gentle Scottish lullaby (by Burns) cries out for this naïve treatment. Often Schumann uses the strophic style for more complex poems too, such as the well-known *Im wunderschönen Monat Mai* which opens the *Dichterliebe* cycle, or *Berg' und Burgen* (Op. 24), perhaps in the latter to suggest the everlasting flow of the Rhine, or *Stille Liebe* (Op. 23), in which subtle variation is introduced by the change of key for the second verse and the new piano accompaniment in the third. One of the very loveliest of all Schumann's strophic songs is *Mondnacht* (Op. 39), which is almost entirely built from one eight-bar phrase repeated twice to form each verse:

Ex. 28

except the last, which begins with eight bars of new melody. There are also numerous varieties of the strophic style, such as *Schöne Wiege meiner Leiden* (from Op. 24), in which the melody of the first verse predominates even though there are two substantial vocal episodes of entirely new material.

Schiller's ballad *Der Handschuh* (Op. 87) is an admirable example of the other, through-composed type of song in its most obvious form, the melody adapting itself in key, time, rhythm and general shape to the changing situations of the poem. But it is not only in these longer dramatic or narrative poems that Schumann adopts this style; he frequently uses it to shed light on the meaning of personal and intimate poetry such as Neun's *Röselein, Röselein* (from Op. 89), where every minute shade of the poet's sleeping and waking thoughts and feelings is faithfully reflected in the music. *Nun hast du mir*, which ends the *Frauenliebe und -leben* cycle, is another excellent example.

It is frequently in the strophic songs that Schumann's vocal lines correspond more to the popular idea of good tunes, tunes such as *Wanderlust* (from Op. 35), which can stand on their own feet, as it were, and explain their own significance without the harmonic background. In the other type of song the melody is quite often (but not always) merely the surface of the harmony, in itself uncertain in its sense of direction and curiously incomplete in effect. This is more often to be observed in the later songs, such for example as *An die Königin Elisabeth* (from Op. 135). But it is safe to say that in both types of song the setting of words according to 'just note and accent' was not so much Schumann's concern as dissolving the poem and re-creating its essence in musical terms. It was the general atmospheric effect which mattered to him more than the creation of beautiful melody *per se*, and following the example of Schubert, it was invariably on the piano that he relied most to achieve this.

There are numerous instances among the songs, particularly the early songs of 1840, where Schumann allowed the piano to take too much on its own shoulders. In *Die Nonne* (from Op. 49) the voice is entirely redundant, all the melody – except for the last two notes – is there in the piano part. *Liebesbotschaft* (from Op. 36) could equally well discard the voice and stand by itself without a single alteration as a Romance in F for piano solo – similarly *Wehmuth* (from Op. 39). Many of the *Dichterliebe* songs have so much of the melody incorporated in the accompaniment that only a few alterations would be necessary to transform them into typically Schumannesque piano pieces. In *Im wunder-*

123

schönen Monat Mai Schumann doubles voice and piano for the first four bars and then makes a gallant effort to break away, though he does not succeed in getting very far:

Ex. 29

Apart from this one weakness – a natural enough mistake for a pianist-composer to make, and one which he continued to make in his chamber music where the piano frequently doubles the string parts – his piano accompaniments are all sheer genius. At times, like Schubert, he makes use of descriptive figuration, such as in *Mein Wagen rollet langsam* (from Op. 142), where the piano paints in sound the slow, regular roll of the carriage wheels:

Ex. 30

Some of the songs inspired by the Rhine preserve some definite flowing figure in the accompaniment, either slow and stately as in *Im Rhein* (from the *Dichterliebe* cycle):

Ex. 31

or suggestive of more rapid current as in *Berg' und Burgen* (from Op. 24). A spinning-wheel is evoked in *Die Spinnerin* (from Op. 107), though Schumann's semiquavers are not quite so suggestive of the up-and-down rhythm of the foot as Schubert's in *Gretchen*. On the other hand, the motion of rowing – action and respite – is most subtly portrayed in the first of the *Zwei Venetianische Lieder* (from Op. 25):

Ex. 32

In *Lieb' Liebchen* (from Op. 24) the scanty but regular quaver chords depict the carpenter's ominous hammer strokes.

Atmosphere of a less pictorial and more abstract kind is equally effectively realized. For outstanding examples there is the airy delicacy and grace of early spring in the light semiquaver lilt of *Jasminenstrauch* (from Op. 27), the rapt wonder of love in the rich harmonies of *Du bist wie eine Blume* (from Op. 25), the mystery of twilight in the stealthy counterpoint of *Zwielicht* (from Op. 39):

Ex. 33

and complete despair in the bleak, bare chords of *Nun hast du mir* (from Op. 42; *see* Ex. 35, p. 128).

Like Schubert before him, Schumann realized the enormous power of key-change as a means of expression. In *Ich wandelte unter den Bäumen* (from Op. 24) the difference between the man and the birds is emphasized by the use of a warm B major for the man's question and a more ethereal G major for the reply of the birds. The conversation between the man and Loreley, the spirit of the woods, is similarly depicted in *Waldesgespräch* (from Op. 39) by E major and C major (though Schumann sacrifices this element of realism in the second verse so that the song may end in the home-key of E major). In *Widmung* (from Op. 25) there is a further example of a plunge (rather than a modulation) into a key a major third below, when A flat major changes to E major for the description of the peace brought to the heart through mutual love; similarly in *Meine Rose* (from Op. 90) the poet's vision of his rose revived is expressed in G major as against the music for the drooping rose in B major in the first and third verses. The repeated use of these keys a major third distant is a stylistic idiosyncrasy rather than a mere coincidence, for it occurs frequently throughout the piano music. In *Röselein, Röselein* (from Op. 89) the use of A minor and its relative major for the poet awake and A major (the tonic major) for the poet asleep and the voice of the brooklet is extraordinarily effective.

Detailed word-painting is frequently carried out by a momentary change of key without change of key-signature. In *Die Lotosblume* (from Op. 25) there is a most beautiful plunge from C major into A flat major (again the major third) for the words 'Der Mond, der ist ihr Buhle':

Ex. 34

and in *Dein Angesicht* (from Op. 127) an equally effective plunge from warm flats into cold sharps at the mention of death's kisses. Chromaticism is used with great poignancy in *Nun hast du mir* (from Op. 42) to harmonize the falling vocal line speaking of emptiness and despair:

Ex. 35

Twice, when asking a question, Schumann uses a chord of the diminished seventh as a musical symbol of interrogation. It can be found in *Rätsel*:

Ex. 36

and in the second *Lied der Braut*:

Ex. 37

(both from Op. 25).

The intimate interconnection of voice and piano parts can be seen in the way in which the piano is sometimes left to complete the vocal line, as in the second of the *Dichterliebe* cycle, *Aus meinen Tränen spriessen*:

Ex. 38

or in *Der Nussbaum* (from Op. 25), where the piano supplies the second half of the first vocal phrase wherever it occurs. At the end of each verse of *Lieb' Liebchen* (from Op. 24) the voice, not to be outdone, adds its last three notes after the piano has already come to the rescue (see Ex. 39 below). There are numerous instances where the two are inseparable, such as in the later song *Weh, wie zornig* (from Op. 138), which reveals most subtle and intimate give and take. Often the voice-part ends on a note of the dominant chord, as in *Im Rhein* and *Am leuchtenden Sommermorgen* in the *Dichterliebe* cycle, or *Kommen und Scheiden* (from Op. 90), and the piano is left to bring the music back to the tonic key.

Ex. 39

These final piano epilogues play an important part in most of Schumann's songs. Their function is normally to summarize the particular song in question, but at the end of the *Dichterliebe* and *Frauenliebe und -leben* cycles the epilogue is of such length and quality as to summarize the complete cycle rather than just the last song of each. The recall of the melody of the first song in *Frauenliebe und -leben* in the piano epilogue after the grief-stricken widow of the last song has reflected on departed joys is particularly effective when the cycle is performed complete.

It must be noticed that Schumann's wide literary interests led him to set translations of Spanish, Scottish, English, Danish and Greek poems as well as those of his own country. The most ambitious of the Spanish efforts is undoubtedly the set of *Spanische Liebeslieder*, Op. 138, taken from a collection of Spanish folksongs and romances translated by Geibel, comprising five solo songs for various voices, two duets, two quartets and a prelude and intermezzo for piano duet. The prelude is written 'Im Bolero Tempo', the intermezzo has as a subtitle *Nationaltanz* (type unspecified), and the fifth number, a *Romanze* for baritone solo, has an arpeggio accompaniment with the indication 'Gleichsam Guitarre' above it, showing that Schumann tried to introduce a little local colour, though the result in each case is a very Germanic picture of Spain. With Scotland and Burns he was very much more successful, managing in many of his settings (such as those in the *Myrthen* cycle) to catch the lightly plaintive spirit of the verse by cultivating a quasi-Celtic emotional reserve and making use of simple strophic form in preference to romantic through-composed melody. Of Byron, Shelley, Moore and Shakespeare it was unquestionably the first with whom he was most in sympathy, particularly as a younger man. The introspective melancholy of *Mein Herz ist schwer* is perfectly matched in his setting of this poem in the *Myrthen* cycle of 1840, and it is more convincing than his Byron cycle, Op. 95, composed ten years later in the grand, declamatory, impersonal style which he often seemed to favour in later life. The whimsical gaiety of Catherine Fanshawe's *Rätsel* is also delightfully caught in *Myrthen*. The Danish poems are translations of Hans Andersen and are included in the *Fünf Lieder*, Op. 40, along with Schumann's solitary Greek setting, translated by Chamisso.

Naturally enough, it was from the younger German romantics that Schumann derived the most spontaneous inspiration all his life. Listeners today may be embarrassed by the naïve sentimentality of some of the verse he selected, such, for example, as Chamisso's *Frauenliebe und -leben*, just as they may be puzzled by his enthusiasm for the immature banalities of Elisabeth Kulmann, whom he saved from oblivion in his *Sieben Lieder*, Op. 104, of 1851. On occasions such as these Schumann was greater than his poets, and in the former case managed to transform the commonplace into the sublime by avoiding detailed interpretation of the poet's subjective emotion and instilling into his music a strain of strengthening, classical objectivity. But on the whole his choice of poems did credit to his literary taste as well as to his understanding of what lay within his own particular experience. And by frequently turning to Heine in 1840 he could have had no doubt in his mind that this was the poet to whom he was initially most finely attuned. Willoughby has described Heine's early *Buch der Lieder*, from which most of Schumann's lyrics are taken, as 'a mixture of pathos, irony, earnestness and frivolity', and it would be hard to find a more apt description of Schumann's own curiously contradictory youthful nature. Hence the effortless mating, the perfect union of words and music in the *Liederkreis*, Op. 24, and *Dichterliebe*, Op. 48, cycles, placing them among the finest of all German songs ever written. Needless to say they and so many other love-songs of this *annus mirabilis* were exclusively addressed to Clara – in fact he even gave her the *Myrthen* cycle as a wedding present. Consequently motto themes (not least the falling five-note motif) familiar from the piano music are never hard to find.

This chapter would be incomplete without reference to the many duets, trios and accompanied and unaccompanied quartets and partsongs for male, female and mixed voices which Schumann wrote, as well as to his three declamations with piano accompaniment. Most of the partsongs were written at Dresden where there were male and mixed choral societies to be catered for, both when Hiller was in charge and later when Schumann himself took over the conductorship. In size they extend from miniatures such as the five Burns settings of Op. 55, to longer works for double choir, such as the four settings of Op. 141 – 'für grössere Gesangvereine'. The *Jagdlieder*, Op. 137, of 1849, for male voices, are interesting for their accompaniment of four horns, since in the same year Schumann had written the *Concertstück* for four horns and orchestra, Op. 86, as well as an *Adagio and Allegro* for horn and piano, Op. 70, and was obviously eager to experiment with the tone-colour of this instrument in many ways.[1] Only the last two of the five songs are successful, where he achieves an independent accompaniment instead of doubling the voice-parts. As regards the vocal writing in all his partsongs, Schumann invariably shows greater interest in harmony than in counterpoint, and if explanation had to be found for the present-day neglect of these works, it might well be the lack of melodic interest in all but the top part.

For his three declamations with piano accompaniment Schumann used three ballads, Hebbel's *Schön Hedwig* and *Ballade vom Heideknaben* and a Shelley translation, *Die Flüchtlinge*, setting the first, Op. 106, in 1849 and the last two, Op. 122, in 1852–3. Often in his later songs as well as in the later choral music Schumann seemed anxious to escape from strictly metrical settings of words, yet found it difficult to write melodies with a sense of direction in prose rhythm; so that melodrama was the perfect compromise for him, enabling him to gain his verbal freedom without sacrificing the impulse of the music. The background music in these three declamations is not so fully worked out as it was in *Manfred*, consisting mainly of short descriptive phrases and a few tremolos, rushing scales, sudden pauses and other mildly theatrical devices for creating atmosphere. Yet all three works are considerably more vivid in conception that many of Schumann's more ambitious ballad settings in later life, whether for solo voice or chorus.

[1] See p. 147.

7

Orchestral Music

The first indications of Schumann's desire to spread his wings came in letters to Dorn and Becker towards the end of 1839. To Dorn he admitted that the piano was becoming 'too narrow' for his thoughts, and to Becker he confessed that hearing Schubert's C major Symphony for the first time had made him 'tingle to be at work on a symphony'. Nevertheless, it was not till 1841 that he embarked on his first serious adventures with the orchestra and large-scale symphonic form.[1] A 'Spring' Symphony, in B flat major, Op. 38, written in the first two months of that year, was soon followed by the *Overture, Scherzo and Finale*, Op. 52, also a second Symphony, in D minor, Op. 120, as well as sketches for a little C minor Symphony (never completed) and the first movement of a work which in 1845 became the piano Concerto. Towards the end of that same first year (1845) in Dresden he began his third Symphony, in C major, Op. 61, not completed till October 1846, and his move to Düsseldorf in 1850 was marked by yet another Symphony, in E flat major, Op. 97. His cello Concerto, two works for piano and orchestra, two works for violin and orchestra, the *Concertstück* for four horns and orchestra and several orchestral overtures were all written between 1849 and 1853.

Of the symphonies Schumann admitted that the first was inspired by a spring poem by Adolph Böttger. Writing to a conductor before a subsequent performance, he said:

> Try to inspire the orchestra with some of the spring longing which chiefly possessed me when I wrote the Symphony in February 1841. At the very beginning I should like the trumpets to sound as if from on high, like a call to awaken. In what follows of

[1] The G minor symphony of 1832–3, saluting Mozart, Schubert and Beethoven, as well as including some bold individual strokes, was just a student flash-in-the-pan, with only the first two movements complete enough for Marc Andreae to edit and publish in 1972 (Peters).

the introduction there might be a suggestion of the growing green of everything, even of a butterfly flying up, and in the following *allegro* of the gradual assembling of all that belongs to spring. But these are fancies which came to me after the completion of the work.

Other 'fancies' included descriptive titles for the four movements: 'Spring's Awakening' for the opening *allegro*, 'Evening' for the slow movement, 'Merry Playmates' for the scherzo and 'Spring's Farewell' for the finale – all of which were abandoned before the work was published. Often in his early piano music Schumann claimed that the music itself suggested the titles afterwards – a claim which is more than difficult to believe. This Symphony, on the other hand, though glowing with romantic feeling, is sufficiently cunning in form to suggest that he was much more preoccupied with the disposition of his actual musical material than with a programme of any kind. And his removal of the titles of the movements was as good as admitting that he now felt that 'fancies', even if afterthoughts, were obstacles which might obscure appreciation of the actual music. In youth his exuberant imagination invariably resulted in great lavishness of new material: new ideas came more easily to him than development of the old. But maturity brought with it a change of style, and his main preoccupation in this first Symphony, as indeed in all four, may well be said to be economy of means – making a little go a long way, and thereby compressing and unifying the symphony as an art-form in the process.

In the first Symphony it is the horn and trumpet 'call to awaken' at the opening of the slow introduction which holds the work together:

Ex. 40

It serves as the first subject of the following *allegro* and provides the main substance of the so-called development section (even though Schumann's development is little else than sequential repetition), sometimes appearing in the bass and sometimes just as a rhythm stripped of all melodic clothing. In fact its rhythm is so prominent all the way through the movement that Schumann introduces a new smoothly flowing hymn-like passage for the sake of contrast in the coda. The same 'call to awaken' generates the main theme of the slow movement, the clue to the relationship being the three ascending notes, a:

Ex. 41

By transforming what appears to be an extravagant last-minute appearance of a new theme at the end of the slow movement:

Ex. 42

into the main theme of the scherzo:

Ex. 43

Schumann links these two middle movements together rather cleverly. Most of the material in the finale is new, including the delightfully aerial first subject, but in the development section trombones make one very strident reference to the rhythm of the 'call' as if to bring this seemingly independent movement back into the fold.

Both Beethoven and Mendelssohn had occasionally attempted to unify their symphonies by interquotation, and sometimes, as in Mendelssohn's A minor Symphony, by indicating that the movements should be played without a break. But Schumann, in his next Symphony, in D minor, Op. 120,[1] surpasses both their efforts and his own. Whether it is the 'Clara' symphony, which a diary entry in March 1841 reveals he intended to write ('and in it I will paint her picture with flutes and oboes and harps'), or whether that impulse found expression in the piano concerto, remains his secret: certainly the first motif of the introduction is not unlike the B minor motif so prominent in the Clara-inspired *Davidsbündlertänze*. Outwardly, however, his entire energy is given to evolving a large-scale work out of two short motto themes, both announced in the slow introduction:

Ex. 44

Ex. 45

B constitutes not only the first subject of the ensuing *allegro*, but the second also – the only clue to the latter's arrival being the change of key from D minor to the relative major, F major. This same theme provides the main substance of the development section which follows after the conventional double bar and repeat. The development is at first typical of Schumann's inability to develop, and is mere sequential repetition of B in an arbitrary choice of keys, but very soon B does in fact give birth to a new,

Ex. 46

---

[1] The late opus number is explained by the fact that Schumann revised the Symphony in 1851 and published it as the fourth – as which it is now generally known.

bold chordal theme in D flat major: (Ex. 46). There is no denying the origin of this new theme, for B, like a good protective parent, hovers round it in the accompaniment. Very soon the violins introduce what appears to be a completely unrelated *cantabile* tune in F major:

Ex. 47

But the original version of the Symphony proves that this was intended as a sister theme to Ex. 46, since in the original version the same parent theme, B, remained in the accompaniment. The insipid broken chord accompaniment in the 1851 version is a textual revision which cannot be considered an improvement. This much of the development section is then repeated in sharper keys to restore the work to an even keel after its lurch into flats, but there is no attempt at formal recapitulation. The development leads straight into the coda, which recalls old material in a triumphant D major. The *Romanze*, which follows after only a crotchet's pause, begins with a new, plaintive oboe tune, but after only eleven bars this gives way to A from the introduction of the work, which remains until the formal recall of the short oboe tune at the very end of the movement. One of the happiest of Schumann's thematic metamorphoses is that at the twenty-sixth bar when the key changes from A minor to D major for a solo violin to dance in semiquaver triplets above the one-time ominous quavers:

Ex. 48

After a short pause on a dominant pedal the scherzo follows in D minor. Its first few notes are an inversion of A:

Ex. 49

and the melody of the trio is no other than the triplet figuration introduced by the solo violin in the slow movement, this time appearing in even quavers in simple 3–4 time:

Ex. 50

The link between this movement and the finale is derived from B and its offspring, Ex. 46, from the first movement, and is as striking a transition as the corresponding passage in Beethoven's fifth Symphony. It must not be forgotten that Schumann made an intensive study of Beethoven before embarking on his own symphonies – in fact it is pertinent at this point to wonder if the delightful cadenza-like passage for horns and flute heralding the recapitulation in the last movement of the 'Spring' Symphony was suggested by Beethoven's oboe cadenza at the same place in the first movement of the fifth Symphony. The finale in D major, which again follows after only a short pause on the dominant pedal, has B's triumphant offspring, Ex. 46, as its main subject, and in the 1851 version of the Symphony it is punctuated (as in the opening movement) with B itself. Owing to the persistence of its abrupt dotted rhythm in the development section, this subject is not recapitulated, and further relief is afforded by the appearance of a bold new tune to bring the work to a rousing finish.

Schumann discarded his original title, *Symphonic Fantasia*, in favour of the subtitle *Introduction, Allegro, Romanze, Scherzo und Finale in einem Satze*, as in the revised version all movements follow each other without a break instead of just the last two. With the exception of the one example mentioned in the first movement, the small textual revisions in the 1851 version are generally considered to be steps in the right direction, notably the substitution of the motto theme B in the last few bars of the slow introduction in place of an ordinary chromatic scale *stringendo*, and also the inclusion of that same motto theme as an accompaniment to its offspring in the opening bars of the finale. Yet, where scoring is concerned, the first version is preferable for its greater clarity. This at first seems surprising in view of Schumann's experiences with orchestras in the intervening years. But Tovey[1] has advanced the ingenious theory that his poor conductorship and inability to help instruments to come in at the right moment in unfamiliar works led him to make 'all entries fool-proof by doubling them in other parts and filling up the rests'.

Whereas the 'Spring' Symphony spoke only of all that was young and fresh and free, this second work, in D minor, is infinitely more mature in its depth and scope of feeling, ranging from the shadows of the opening to the triumphant finale. Apart from the opening of the *Romanze* and the trio of the scherzo, the tonal centre is D in each movement, but the interplay of minor and major succeeds in relieving the monotony which might have resulted from such a stay-at-home key-scheme in a large-scale work. Structurally it is perhaps Schumann's most enterprising achievement; and its importance, at a time when all the possibilities of symphonic form appeared to have been exhausted by Beethoven's ninth, cannot be overestimated.

The next Symphony, in C major, Op. 61 (known as the second), has a motto theme announced at the outset of the work by horns, trumpets and trombones:

Ex. 51

Though several times recalled it does not grow, nor does the symphony as a whole derive the unity from it found in Schumann's earlier experiments with this device. Far more subtle is the way an ascending four-note quaver motif from the first movement's second subject generates the darting semiquaver theme of the Scherzo. The finale in its turn brings a striking major key transformation of the nostalgic opening theme of the slow movement:

[1] *Essays in Musical Analysis*, vol. ii.

Ex. 52

into its own confident second subject:

Ex. 53

In a letter Schumann admitted that the Symphony was conceived during a serious breakdown, and that the 'capricious and refractory' first movement reflected his struggle for ascendancy over weakness and depression. In consequence the work has sometimes, unjustly, been dismissed as the laboured product of a sick mind. Lavish use of new material in the exposition of this opening movement might at first suggest that he had tired of economy. But the development section quickly disproves that. As well as first and second subjects, every subsidiary fragment is turned to good account, such as scraps of arpeggios:

Ex. 54

and 'asides':

Ex. 55

With its two contrasted trios, the spirited Scherzo is unconventionally placed second. In the heart-felt *Adagio espressivo* in C minor, the yearningly nostalgic opening theme, with its assuaging secondary episode in the major, returns in yet richer scoring after a brief, contrapuntally motivated quasi development section. No music in Schumann's entire orchestral output combines deeper personal sentiment with more ravishing sonority. The finale is memorable for Schumann's merging of the development into an extended coda generated by the same quotation from Beethoven's *An die ferne Geliebte* song-cycle through which in both his C major *Phantasie* for piano and F major string quartet he had already reaffirmed love for Clara:

Ex. 56

Here, underpinned by recalls of the symphony's opening motto, this theme joyously salutes her as the true source of his own Beethovenian victory over fate.

In his last Symphony, in E flat major, Op. 97, Schumann was concerned with evoking atmosphere as much as with problems of symphonic form. Early in September 1850 he had moved to Düsseldorf in his beloved Rhineland, and it was after a visit to Cologne at the end of the same month that the idea of writing a 'Rhenish' symphony occurred to him. The scherzo, with its swinging, Ländler-like main theme, was originally called 'Morning on the Rhine', and the awe-inspiring fourth movement, suggested by Cologne Cathedral itself in a state of readiness for Archbishop von Geissel's enthronement as Cardinal, was headed 'In the style of an accompaniment to a solemn ceremony'. But both these titles were removed before the work was published. There is no conventional double bar and repeat in the first movement, and there is a second slow movement (before the cathedral movement), making a total of five in all. Otherwise this Symphony – in spite of being scene-painting – is more orthodox in construction than any of the other three and reveals a most happy reconciliation between the opposing romantic and classical elements in the composer's make-up.

The fine first movement dispenses with a slow introduction and plunges headlong into a first subject which dominates the movement:

Ex. 57

Its invigorating stride immediately evokes the atmosphere of the landscape which inspired it, while the tug-of-war between triple and duple time – one of Schumann's most subtle experiments with syncopation – gives the movement an extraordinary rhythmic virility. The unobtrusive second subject is linked to the first by an important staccato figure:

Ex. 58

and from this material Schumann evolves one of his most powerful development sections, remarkable for its directness, absence of padding of any kind, and continuous organic growth. Of the remaining movements the delightfully lyrical scherzo and the 'cathedral' slow movement are the most distinguished. The melody of the latter is characterized by rising fourths, but seems rather more the result of a particularly expressive chromatic chord-sequence than a melody *per se*. It is later decorated in turn by a flowing quaver and semiquaver background in the manner of sixteenth-century variations – possibly it is this which gives the music its feeling of Gothic antiquity and austerity in contrast to the romantic 'Innigkeit' of so many of Schumann's slow movements.

Though Schumann subsequently revised the last movement of his *Overture, Scherzo and Finale*, Op. 52, composed between the 'Spring' and D minor Symphonies, he never added a slow movement, and in consequence the work does not enjoy symphonic status. Academically, the finale is the most interesting in its attempt to combine fugue with sonata form: a quasi-fugal exposition takes the place of the customary first subject. The Overture follows the lines of a traditional symphonic first movement preceded by a slow introduction; and as Schumann was much preoccupied with interquotation at that time, it is not surprising to discover that the main subject of the slow introduction reappears in quick tempo in the second-subject group, and that the first *allegro* subject of this movement recurs in the coda of the scherzo. On paper the work seems to consist of painstaking workmanship applied to indifferent material – though, as so often with Schumann's later works, a little special pleading in performance can help quite a lot.

The most frequently criticized feature of Schumann's symphonies is the scoring. As a young man of twenty-two, after the not very successful first performance of his 'student' Symphony in G minor, he admitted that he often 'put in yellow instead of blue', and described orchestration as an art which would take long years of study. Whether or not he did make it a study during the many years in which he wrote nothing but piano music is not known, but his symphonies would suggest that neither were they conceived, in the first place, in terms of instrumental colour, nor was the subsequent orchestration the work of a man imaginatively inflamed by timbre *per se*. The most obvious example is the very opening of the first Symphony. The *fortissimo* 'call to awaken' was originally written at this pitch:

Ex. 59

as it occurs at the beginning of the *allegro*. It was not till the first rehearsal that Schumann discovered that the horns and trumpets in the orchestra, without valves, were unable to play the two stopped notes G and A *fortissimo*, and that the effect of the sudden change of tone was as if they had a 'bad cold in the head'.[1] It is interesting to discover that Mahler, when he rescored all four symphonies, restored this passage to its original pitch a major

[1] Letter to Mendelssohn, 22nd October 1845.

third lower in view of the greater capabilities of modern valve horns and trumpets.

Far more questionable than isolated examples of this kind is the thickness which characterizes Schumann's scoring as a whole – a thickness not part and parcel of the substance of the material as with Brahms, but one which is apt to obscure the structural outlines of the music and destroy the character of certain sections requiring clear colouring. Brass instruments are used far too frequently for no better purpose than padding, filling out and over-emphasizing unimportant middle parts, as in much of the scherzo of the C major Symphony. The bass line itself is frequently too prominent as the result of string basses being reinforced by bassoons and trombones. This bottom-heaviness is made worse by Schumann's tendency to weaken his top by using woodwind instruments in their less effective lower registers, or by doubling which tends to blur rather than sharpen the outline of a tune. Perhaps the perfect example of miscalculation is the staccato semiquaver section forming the trio in the scherzo of the 'Rhenish' Symphony. The delicacy of the passage is lessened by woodwind and strings playing together, with horns and trumpets adding redundant notes in the middle of the score. Mahler removes both woodwind and brass in his revised version, and the resulting lightness and clarity are typical of many other similar improvements in the four scores.

In fairness it must be admitted that there are several instances where the substance of Schumann's music is actually enhanced by the scoring, such as the ravishing high trills for the violins at the climax of the first section of the *Adagio* in the C major Symphony or the entry of the solo violin in the *Romanze* of the D minor Symphony. There is also a great deal of expressive writing for bassoons and trombones, from the 'doleful bassoon' in the slow movement of the C major Symphony to the impressive opening of the 'cathedral' movement in the 'Rhenish' and the solemn quartet towards the end of the slow movement of the 'Spring' Symphony. In this last work there is the delightful contrast of strings and wind in the first trio from the scherzo, and not least the triangle in the first movement – a comparative stranger in the dignified ranks of a symphony orchestra, but one which brings with it here much of the sparkle of the dew in an early morning in spring.

Of the seven works for solo instruments and orchestra, that in

A minor (Op. 54) for piano stands head and shoulders above the rest and ranks amongst Schumann's most happy works. The opening movement, *allegro affettuoso*, originally an independent *Phantasie*, dates from the year of the 'Spring' and D minor Symphonies, so that it is not surprising to discover in it the same economy with new material which characterized those two works. It would be an exaggeration to claim that the whole movement is monothematic because of the significance of several links in the argument, yet the first subject:[1]

Ex. 60

is in supreme command of the situation throughout. Transposed into C major it takes the place of a second subject, and apart from a few references to the peremptory figure with which the piano opens the movement, the development could be described as a set of variations on the same idea. Even in the coda Schumann is content to use it in 2–4 *allegro molto* rhythm, instead of indulging in his liking for a new tune at this spot. The uprising staccato quavers of its second bar generate the dialogue between piano and orchestra at the start of the gracious slow movement, at the end of which it returns to form a link with the finale. Even the finale's lively main theme:

Ex. 61

[1] Its continuation brings reminders of the five-note falling 'Clara' theme.

145

is indebted to the motto for its fall of a third (x) and rise of a fifth (y). The second subject in the dominant key of E major:

Ex. 62

is sufficiently syncopated to create an illusion of converting the 3–4 time into 3–2, so that unfortunately the subtlety of the device can only be fully appreciated on paper, or by watching the conductor's down beat coming off the beat in alternate bars. The ear by itself is all too ready to accept the passage as simple 3–2 time. Agile fingers are required for the brilliant quavers in the finale – but nowhere in the work is virtuosity as important a factor as in most concertos. Even the one and only cadenza (in the first movement) was written by the composer himself to ensure that the poetry of the music should not be disturbed by mere prestidigitation – it is the test of a musician rather than a technician. The scoring is outstanding for its delicacy and restraint, and in no other work does Schumann show such understanding of the personality of each instrument as an individual.

The other two works for piano and orchestra, the *Introduction und Allegro appassionato* (*Concertstück*) (Op. 92) of 1849 and the *Concert-Allegro mit Introduction* (Op. 134) of 1853, are less frequently played. Though in need of pruning, the former is as delicately scored and graciously romantic as the piano concerto, with virtuosity always subservient to poetic feeling. Cast in traditional first movement form, both works are preceded by a slow introduction to which the ensuing *allegro* makes frequent reference, in accordance with Schumann's ideals of unity. Even the later and at times more laboured D minor work (dedicated to Schumann's new young friend, Brahms) deserves occasional revival for the plangent beauty of the main theme of the brooding introduction. This work includes a *quasi* cadenza.

The year 1849 saw also the completion of a novelty, the *Concertstück* for four horns and orchestra (Op. 86). It was an extraordinarily fruitful year when Schumann seemed intent on adventure off the beaten track in his experiments with a great variety of wind instruments[1] – particularly the valve-horn. It is highly probable that Wagner was responsible for his interest in this comparatively new development of the horn, since in his Dresden scores Schumann makes more frequent use of it than he did at Leipzig. Were it not for some falling off of invention in the finale, it would be easy to understand why Schumann himself considered it one of his 'best things'.[2] The writing for the four solo valve-horns is highly original, and in the two faster flanking movements sometimes even recklessly brilliant; the central *Romanze* (characteristically linked to the finale) grows from a winsome start into a remarkable pre-echo of the 'cathedral' movement in the 'Rhenish' Symphony.

The cello Concerto in A minor (Op. 129) of 1850 is also let down by its finale (with a typically Schumannesque overworked rhythmic figure), and throughout the work Schumann's concern that the low-voiced solo instrument shall not be submerged results in rather too meagre orchestral support. Yet the subject matter of the first two movements is of rich nostalgic beauty, with the cello's ruminative cantabile often coming near to speech in its eloquence. The work is also interesting as a further experiment in formal compression, for all three movements (which share a few turns of phrase even if not complete themes) are most skilfully merged into one. As in the piano Concerto, the first movement's main theme is recalled as the link between the last two movements. The cadenza near the end has the additional interest of an orchestral accompaniment.

The two works for violin and orchestra, the *Phantasie* in C major (Op. 131) and the Concerto, were both inspired by

[1] See Chapter 6, p. 132, and Chapter 8, p. 152.
[2] Letter to Hiller, April 1849.

Joachim, whose performance of Beethoven's violin Concerto at the Düsseldorf Festival in the spring of 1853 made a deep impression on Schumann. The tribute was a gracious gesture, but both works fall short of the idea behind them. After a noble introduction, the *Phantasie* degenerates into short-breathed, laboured trivialities. As for the Concerto, Joachim, Brahms and even Clara eventually agreed that it should be withheld from publication, and the manuscript remained in the Prussian State Library in Berlin until Joachim's great-niece, Jelly d'Aranyi, in defiance of Eugenie Schumann's wishes, secured its publication and performance in 1938. Apart from the link between the second and third movements, the form of the work is unadventurous, and the finale only keeps going by repeating its three themes five times over. But throughout Schumann's last, laboured compositions there are moments of extraordinarily poignant beauty reminiscent of 'old, unhappy far-off things', and it would be wrong to dismiss this Concerto without mention of such a one towards the end of the nostalgic slow movement when the melody originally stated in the major recurs a third lower in the minor:

Ex. 63

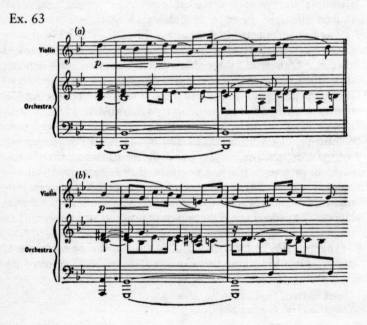

Of Schumann's seven orchestral overtures only two seem to have survived in the modern orchestral repertory: those to the opera *Genoveva* (Op. 81) and to *Manfred* (Op. 115). It is not hard to understand why these two overtures have long outlived the rest of the works for which they were intended, because each was written in the first flush of enthusiasm for the subject, when the poetic idea itself was most vivid in the composer's mind. The *Genoveva* overture, in fact, was sketched in April 1847, before Schumann had even sorted out the final details of his libretto. Each overture falls quite happily into regular first movement form, with a slow introduction. The actual structural skeleton is less obtrusive in *Manfred* than in *Genoveva* – the music flows more spontaneously and passionately, and the chromaticism provides a higher degree of tension. Added to this, the sombre orchestration enhances the character of the music more than is usual with Schumann, so that many people agree with the verdict of those (including Moscheles) who claimed that it was the 'most magnificent thing' he ever did.

Nevertheless 1851 was the year Schumann made the overture, as an art-form, his special preoccupation; and it is interesting to discover him once again turning to literature for inspiration after a period in which pure music had in the main been his ideal. Schiller and Goethe furnished him with subject-matter for his *Braut von Messina* (Op. 100) and *Hermann und Dorothea* (Op. 136) overtures, and from Shakespeare, newly translated into German, he selected *Julius Caesar* for his Op. 128. Richard Pohl, who had arranged the concert version of *Manfred* for Schumann, likewise made some adaptation of *Die Braut von Messina* and tried to persuade Schumann to write incidental music for it. Schumann rejected the idea,[1] but before doing so he read through the tragedy several times, and this eventually bore fruit in an independent overture. It is hard to understand nowadays why it was not immediately understood by the general musical public of Schumann's time,[2] for it is a straightforward work in classical first movement form and scarcely less emotionally appealing than *Genoveva*. Moritz Horn, the young poet whose *Pilgrimage of the Rose* Schumann had set as a cantata, discussed with Schumann in several letters the possibility of presenting Goethe's *Hermann und*

[1] Letter to Pohl, January 1851.
[2] Letter to Pohl, December 1851.

Dorothea as a *Singspiel* (as had been his intention in 1846), or alternatively as a concert oratorio. But again nothing came of the idea except the overture, written 'with great pleasure in a few hours'. Its chief musical interest is the introduction of the *Marseillaise* as part of the first subject. It was a tune which he had used three times before – not without his tongue in his cheek – but here he attributes its presence to the French revolutionary soldiers in the first scene of the projected play. *Julius Caesar* does not fulfil the promise of its majestic opening, and though there are some fine moments in the development section, the music has little inward driving-power to give it real continuity.

In 1853 Schumann made two final contributions to this genre: the first, the *Rheinweinlied* (Op. 123), being specially written for the Lower Rhine Festival held at Düsseldorf during the spring. The popular drinking song on which the work is based: 'Bekränzt mit Laub':

Ex. 64

is hinted at in the introduction, and the rhythm of its opening phrase becomes even more pronounced in the second subject. After the music has been worked out as a movement in sonata form, a tenor solo (singing Wolfgang Müller's connecting words, 'Was lockt so süss!' in the manner of a recitative suggested, perhaps, by Beethoven's approach to the big tune in the last movement of the choral Symphony) leads straight into a full statement of the rousing drinking-song, sung in three verses by the chorus. Even though the work is an occasional piece and frankly popular, it would well repay more frequent performances.

Schumann's last overture was that to his *Scenes from Faust*, completing a project that had intermittently preoccupied him for just on a decade. This is more academically conceived than his earlier overtures to *Genoveva* and *Manfred*, the two others closest

to his heart, at times betraying a certain mental tiredness in its
recourse to repetition. Even so, the music has a spiritual dignity
and gravity revealing his acute awareness of the magnitude of the
issues involved.

8

Chamber Music

Though occasionally flirting with chamber music in his younger days, and notably in the C minor piano Quartet (1828–9) of which sketches survive, Schumann waited until 1842 before turning to this medium with concentrated intensity. June and July saw the completion of three string Quartets in A minor, F major and A major, Op. 41. October brought the piano Quintet in E flat major, Op. 44, November the piano Quartet in E flat major, Op. 47, and January 1843 the first versions of two works subsequently revised, the *Phantasiestücke* for piano, violin and cello, Op. 88, and the *Andante and Variations* for two pianos, two cellos and horn, Op. 46. There was then a gap till 1847, when two piano Trios, in D minor, Op. 63, and F major, Op. 80, were written. In 1851 came a third piano Trio in G minor, Op. 110, also two violin and piano Sonatas, in A minor, Op. 105, and D minor, Op. 121. The third 'composite' violin Sonata in A minor followed in 1853, also the *Märchenerzählungen* for clarinet, viola and piano, Op. 132. All the other small pieces for single instrument and piano date from 1849.

Just as a study of Beethoven's orchestral scores had preceded Schumann's outburst of orchestral composition in 1841, so he began 1842 with a systematic study of quartets by Haydn, Mozart and Beethoven, nor was a copy of the '48' ever very far away. No longer was he the impetuous young man who claimed Jean Paul as his counterpoint teacher. Mendelssohn's polished craftsmanship had opened his eyes to many of his own technical shortcomings, and the goal now before him was mastery of form. In his 'Spring' Symphony of the previous year he had managed to clip the wings of the solitary butterfly so that it flew well within the bounds of classical form. But in his quartets he eschews all kinds of programme and concerns himself only with pure music.

This is best seen in the first two quartets – fine examples of disciplined thought, even if less characteristic of the composer than the last of the set, in A major. The first work opens with a slow contrapuntal introduction which would do credit to any student of Bach. Then with a complete change of key, mode, tempo, time and general character, the movement develops into an orthodox example of classical sonata form. Both this movement and the finale are extraordinarily close-knit – in both cases there is an intimate relationship between first and second subjects. In the first movement only the key and the quaver accompaniment betray where the continuation of the first subject:

Ex. 65

has given way to the second:

Ex. 66

and the two are linked by a short *fugato* clearly derived from bars three and four of the first subject. In the exhilarating finale the first subject:

Ex. 67

is inverted to form the second:

Ex. 68

The second Quartet reveals even greater economy of material in its first movement. Again, the first subject:

Ex. 69

dominates the movement, but this time Schumann overcomes his customary dislike of detaching limbs from his themes for separate development. Even in the exposition, the continuation of the first subject at bar nine:

Ex. 70

is inverted to become:

Ex. 71

Later the figure *c* from Ex. 70 is detached and developed:

Ex. 72

The fragment *a* from the first eight bars is then very cleverly merged into *b*, forming a counterpoint to imitative entries of the opening idea:

154

Ex. 73

Just before the development section the cello makes use of *a* to emphasize the dominant key:

Ex. 74

Both Quartets reveal an unusual mastery of the organic growth and development incumbent on sonata form, or first-movement form, and if the listener sometimes misses the essential Schumann in this intense preoccupation with craftsmanship, there is compensation in the truly beautiful slow movement in each. The scoring in the opening bars of the first of the two reveals that Schumann had not yet entirely freed himself from the habit of thinking through his ten fingers – the first two fiddles have the 'right-hand' melody in octaves over a Schumannesque type of arpeggio accompaniment. But no such criticism can be thrown at the *andante* and variations in the second Quartet. Sinuous, chromatic counterpoints enrich the significance of the theme, and some of the harmonious progressions, such as this from the second variation:

Ex. 75

are as novel as Schumann's youthful experiments, yet they have a
new, mature logic of their own. The finale of this happy F major
work is interesting for its recall of Beethoven's 'An die ferne
Geliebte' theme, quoted in the C major Phantasie for piano, Op.
17, and again in the finale of the C major Symphony, here as if in
joyous salute to his beloved Clara after their first painful period of
separation since their marriage.

The third Quartet stands on its own. The harmonization of the
expressive falling fifth in the first bar with a chord of the added
sixth:

Ex. 76

Andante espressivo

is so strongly reminiscent of the opening of Beethoven's E flat
major piano Sonata, Op. 31, No. 3, as to suggest that Schumann
had some special affection for this work – he had already quoted
from its third movement in *Faschingsschwank aus Wien*. This
falling fifth not only generates the main theme of the *allegro*, but is
also embodied in the second subject, and in its inversion it is again
prominent in both middle movements. In choosing such an
expressive opening Schumann betrays that heart as well as head
was involved in this first movement, and in consequence he does
not submit his material to quite such intellectual investigation as
in the first two Quartets. The short middle section merely

reiterates the main theme without any true development, and to avoid the risk of overstating it he only permits it one short appearance in the recapitulation. Emotion invariably breeds chromaticism, and there are passages in this movement, such as the approach to the development section:

Ex. 77

which reveal how the composer's questing mind could take him into new, unexplored harmonic regions. The scherzo has the unusual form of a set of variations on the interval of a rising fourth (the fifth inverted), and in the slow movement the abrupt change of tonality, where this same fourth interrupts the main theme, is very lovely. The melody of the *adagio*, in itself undistinguished, is completely transformed by its rich harmonic clothing, and the slow tempo permits the full beauty of the chromatic inner parts to be heard – particularly the viola. The fourth movement is a rondo – the only occasion in all the chamber music on which this form is used for a finale. The dotted rhythm of its main theme relates it to a figure of accompaniment in the slow movement, and the reappearance of the ascending fourth in the second episode gives even greater unity to the work as a whole. As Schumann had introduced a *musette* at the last minute in his first Quartet, it is interesting to observe that an episode in the style of a *gavotte* makes its way into this rather over-repetitive A major rondo.

In all the remaining chamber works Schumann incorporated

his own instrument, the piano. He was the first great composer to combine piano and string quartet, and his E flat major Quintet is his supreme achievement in the realm of chamber music. In fact it is hard to find a more satisfactory work among all his music, for there is in it a most happy reconciliation of content and form. The ideas glow with the youthful spontaneity of some of his early piano music, and he expresses them with the assurance and ease of a mature craftsman. Just occasionally the piano takes a little too much on its own shoulders – as in the development section of the first movement, but this is inoffensive owing to the extreme clarity of the texture: the five instruments do not all try to say the same thing at the same time. Especially graceful is the piano's lyrical continuation of the first subject in the exposition of the first movement – not least when the opening leap of a seventh is transformed into an octave:

Ex. 78

And the approach to the second subject betrays an equally felicitous romantic touch:

Ex. 79

The slow movement employs sonata-rondo form, and its episodes – both in material and scoring – provide admirable contrast from the funeral-march character of the main section. Ascending and descending scales constitute the main substance of the scherzo, which is lengthened by a second trio. But the main substance of the work is to be found in the finale, a movement curiously unorthodox in its key-scheme. The movement opens with a challenging first subject in G minor – not till a second section of the subject appears is the tonic key of E flat major established:

Ex. 80

The appearance of the second subject in G major for the viola prepares the listener for a bold excursion into sharps in the development section, possibly to correct the tonal balance after the extreme flatward veerings in the earlier movements. When the viola tune, differently phrased, appears in the development section it is accompanied by an entirely new melody in E major played by the first violin:

Ex. 81

and the recapitulation begins in a key as far removed from home as G sharp minor. The *pièce de résistance* is the coda itself, which towards the end reintroduces the theme of the first movement, augmented, as the subject of a *fugato*, with the first theme of the finale as a countersubject. It has been suggested that the idea came from Mendelssohn's string Quartet in E flat, but it is equally typical of Schumann's own experiments with interquotation of themes at this time, and reveals still more of his newly acquired contrapuntal skill.

In the following piano Quartet, Schumann was rather less successful in suppressing the pianist in himself. Indeed, the piano takes over full responsibility for the first twenty-two bars of the *allegro* (making the strings quite redundant), and throughout the work gets no respite whatsoever. The composer experiences particular difficulty in separating the bass line of the piano and the cello, and often the texture is inclined to be thick as a result of unnecessary doubling of all the string parts. How very much more effective the coda of the slow movement would have been had the two violins been permitted to climb above the sustained cello B flat without the assistance of the piano!

Ex. 82

Incidentally, at this moment the cello has to lower its bottom string to reach its B flat. However, the work has many fine points, among them a powerful and effective lead back to the recapitulation in the first movement; a scherzo with a delightfully graceful linking phrase between each section:

Ex. 83

and a slow movement with a melody full of sevenths as nostalgic as those in Elgar's 'Enigma' theme. The only structural weakness occurs in the finale, where Schumann reverts to a tiresome habit (noticed in the piano sonatas) of recapitulating the development section after the normal return of the exposition before adding the rightful coda.

The next two works, the *Phantasiestücke* for piano, violin and cello and the *Andante and Variations* for two pianos, two cellos and horn, both suffer from bad scoring. In eventually removing cellos and horn from the latter work Schumann himself realized that they were redundant in all but the last few variations – a fact which is proved by the very small alterations in the piano parts when the work was published in 1844 in its more familiar form for two pianos only.[1] Equally well could the piano part of much of the *Phantasiestücke* be played without violin and cello. As might be expected from the composer's choice of title when he revised the work in 1850, all four movements are of a slight and fanciful character.

Perhaps dissatisfaction with this work caused Schumann to experiment again with piano, violin and cello when he returned to the medium of chamber music in 1847. Of his three Trios, that in D minor has in it the most characteristic and distinguished material, ranging in emotion from the restless, introspective melancholy of the opening to the warm Schubertian geniality of the finale. Both first and second subjects in the first movement are extended melodies so heavily charged with emotional significance as to make their development a difficult problem. And here Schumann's solution is particularly interesting: he devotes the larger part of the development section to a seemingly new,[2] chorale-like tune which not only provides emotional respite but also variety of tone-colour with the piano playing *una corda* and the strings *sul ponticello*. The texture is inclined to be thick: how unneccesary, for example, for both piano and violin to provide background semiquavers to the second subject melody:

[1] See p. 118.

[2] Gerald Abraham has suggested that the entire first movement is 'controlled' by a secret idea found in Schumann's sketches, but never overtly stated in the finished work, a theory he supports with several other examples in Schumann's later works.

Ex. 84

But the chromaticism is particularly expressive. The finale, also in sonata form, is in complete contrast: D minor changes to D major, chromaticism to diatonicism, and the actual themes to purely musical organisms. In consequence, development is a comparatively straightforward matter and it is interesting to notice how Schumann detaches the two fragments *x* and *y* from the first subject:

Ex. 85

without any qualms when it suits his purpose. The two middle movements are equally outstanding: the scherzo for its unflagging

162

vitality and the slow movement for the searching beauty of its unusually (for Schumann) unmetrical opening melody – made to yield an even greater wealth of expression by the chromatic harmonization.

The second Trio, in F major, is less personal music, yet the rigours of first-movement form are unable to prevent the essential Schumann from breaking into the second subject with unexpected harmonies, or from introducing a third-subject melody with the initials R.S. invisibly embroidered in every bar, or from extending the recapitulation to permit experiments with rhythm – this time not syncopation, but the transformation of 6–8 into 2–4. The slow movement has an air of dignified nobility which is in no way disturbed by the enharmonic plunges from flats to sharps and back again, and the third movement invariably charms all listeners with its elfin melancholy. The whole work flows easily and is well written for all three instruments.

The turbulent opening of the G minor Trio gives promise of a work as characteristic and powerful as the earlier one in D minor, but the promise is not fulfilled. In the first movement, even the introduction of a new tune in steady quavers in the development does not provide the neccesary relief from the overworked rhythm ♩. ♫♫♩. ♫♫ and the scaffolding of sonata form is all too obvious. The slow movement has very little personality, and the scherzo says nothing that had not already been said far better in the scherzo of the second string Quartet. The episodic finale suffers from weakness of structure and rhythmic vagaries. But the work's main poverty lies in its lack of counterpoint. Schumann had never found it easy to think horizontally, and his study of Bach and subsequent exercises in fugue and canon, published as piano solos, reveal the determination with which he set out to overcome this weakness in middle life. His success can be measured by the good, independent contrapuntal movement of the string parts in all the other chamber works, in which harmony is largely (though not entirely) a by-product of combined melodies. But in the G minor Trio, violin and cello parts are merely a by-product of the harmony.

It is tempting to attribute the work's lack of inspiration to the decline in Schumann's health in 1851, but this is belied by the two violin Sonatas which followed shortly afterwards – both of them particularly virile and persuasive compositions. Nor is it possible to suggest that Joachim quickened his creative power, for it was not till the Düsseldorf Festival in the spring of 1853 that the two men became closely acquainted. The first Sonata, in A minor, shows a real understanding of each instrument's peculiar capabilities (even though there is a little too much doubling), and the material is presented logically without any startling departures from traditional procedure. If the agitated character of first and last movements is indicative of the fears and forebodings which clouded the composer's last years, the slow movement is equal testimony to other moments of pure happiness during that same time. It is full of 'delight in simple things', but in its simplicity it comes as near to human speech as music ever can. The second work, in D minor, runs through a wider gamut of emotion and is also more ambitious in structure. The main point of interest is the close interconnection of the middle movements. In his 'Spring' Symphony Schumann had anticipated the third movement, the scherzo, by introducing its main theme in less energetic form at the end of the slow movement. In the D minor Sonata not only does the second movement, the scherzo, introduce the theme of the slow movement *ff* just before its close, but the slow movement also twice refers back to the scherzo with considerable vehemence. The theme of the slow movement is that of the chorale 'Gelobet seist du, Jesu Christi' (used by Bach) turned into triple time, and the lovely variations of it which follow are notable for their sensitive scoring – including *sul ponticello* and *una corda* effects of tone-colour.

It was after the Düsseldorf Festival that Schumann paid his homage to Joachim, primarily in the violin *Phantasie* and Concerto for violin and orchestra, but also by contributing a Romance and Finale to a Sonata for violin and piano (based on Joachim's 'Frei aber einsam' motto) which came as joint tribute from Schumann, Brahms and Dietrich; soon afterwards he composed a new opening movement and scherzo to replace those of Dietrich and Brahms.[1] Like the *Märchenerzählungen* for piano, clarinet and viola (Op. 132), also of 1853, this music is that of a tired mind – though a mind still capable of creating moments of a strangely poignant kind of beauty, such as in the third of the *Märchenerzählungen*, marked 'Ruhiges Tempo, mit zartem

[1] In this form the work had its first London performance at the Wigmore Hall on 20th March 1956, as his Sonata No. 3 in A minor.

Ausdruck'. The *Adagio and Allegro* for horn and piano (Op. 70), the *Phantasiestücke* for clarinet and piano (Op. 73), the *Drei Romanzen* for oboe and piano (Op. 94) and the *Fünf Stücke im Volkston* for cello and piano (Op. 102), all of 1849. are pleasing miniatures, written with understanding of each instrument's personality – though in the *Volkston* pieces cello and piano are apt to stay too much in the same register. The last of the four *Märchenbilder* for viola and piano (Op. 113), marked 'Langsam, mit melancholischem Ausdruck', is very lovely, though the rest of the set tend to overwork certain rhythmic features in the same way as the first movement of the G minor Trio, also of 1851.

9

Choral and dramatic music

Schumann's choral and dramatic music forms a fair proportion of his larger works. *Das Paradies und die Peri* (Op. 50), *Der Rose Pilgerfahrt* (Op. 112) and the *Scenes from Goethe's 'Faust'* loom large among ten other choral cantatas and ballads on a smaller scale; there are also the opera *Genoveva* (Op. 81) and the incidental music to Byron's *Manfred* (Op. 115), as well as a *Mass* (Op. 147) and a *Requiem* (Op. 148) for chorus and orchestra. Yet all these works are almost unknown to present-day audiences. To what extent does the composer who showed such fine feeling for words in his songs deserve this neglect of his more ambitious choral works?

Paradise and the Peri, with its full paraphernalia of soloists, chorus and orchestra, was his first essay in this direction, dating from 1843. The poem itself comes from Thomas Moore's oriental romance, *Lalla Rookh*, where it stands as one of the several perfumed effusions with which the fictitious, mysterious Feramorz (in reality the noble bridegroom in disguise) regaled the beautiful princess Lalla Rookh on the long journey from her father's home in Delhi to her nuptials in Cashmere. Appearing in 1817, *Lalla Rookh* had so instantaneous a success that it was translated into innumerable languages, both European and Oriental, and it was the German version which was sent to Schumann in 1841 by his old school friend, Emil Flechsig. Schumann's delight was twofold. In the first place the exoticism of the East had an irresistible lure for all writers, musicians and artists of the German romantic movement, always anxious to blend an element of strangeness with the beautiful. In the second place, *Paradise and the Peri* is a story with an underlying moral of repentance as the road to heaven. Moore's Peri (like all her sisters in Persian mythology) is an outcast spirit, a fallen angel, anxious to gain readmission to Paradise; this she can only do by returning from her earthly wanderings with 'the gift that is most dear to heaven'. From India she brings back the last drop of a hero's blood shed in the cause of liberty, from Egypt she returns with the last sigh of a maiden who has chosen to die beside her plague-stricken lover. But it is not till the Peri returns from Syria with the tear of a repentant sinner that the gates of Paradise open to let her in. At no time in his life could Schumann be described as an orthodox believer, and not till coming into contact with Roman Catholicism in Düsseldorf in later years did he turn to the setting of liturgical words. Yet his characteristically German, middle-class sense of moral piety grew increasingly strong after he settled down to middle life and marriage, and rarely did any subject attract him for extended musical setting unless it was ennobled by awareness of guilt, remorse, repentance or self-sacrifice. Besides *Paradise and the Peri*, his *Faust*, *Genoveva*, *Manfred*, *The Pilgrimage of the Rose* and the *Requiem für Mignon* all contain some moral message beyond their purely narrative interest.

In attempting to place *Paradise and the Peri* Schumann described it as 'an oratorio – not for the conventicle, but for bright, happy people'. His model may well have been Löwe's *John Huss*, which in his review of 1842 he described as half way between oratorio and opera, more suitable for performance in the concert hall than the church. Besides a certain amount of cutting as well as re-translation of the text, Schumann and his poet friend and collaborator, Adolph Böttger, also amplified it in places so as to allow all protagonists to speak for themselves instead of merely being described. But within the three sections conditioned by the Peri's three separate journeys, the music is more or less through-composed, with choruses and arias flowing into each other without sharp break, and with a lyrical kind of arioso taking the place of conventional recitative. Such innovations earned harsh criticism from 'Philistine' critics like Rellstab. Schumann himself nevertheless far-sightedly recognized this continuity of style as 'an advantage showing genuine and palpable improvement'. 'It is my biggest work, and I hope my best' were his words to his Dutch friend, Verhulst. In his personal diary he went on to say: 'Except for certain oratorios of Löwe's, which, however, have for the most part a didactic flavour, I know nothing in music that is like it . . . my wish is that it may do some good in the world and assure me of a loving place in the memory of my children'.

To what extent can posterity substantiate the composer's

estimate of this his first important essay in an extended choral form? There is no doubt whatsoever that the memorable moments are those in which Schumann became a youthful romanticist again, with his imagination taking light from poetic imagery —notably in the evocation of the subtle mystery and splendour of the East. Early in the work a drastic enharmonic modulation from the three sharps of A major into the four deep-hued flats of A flat major at the Peri's words

'I know the wealth hidden in every urn
Wherein the red rubies of Chilminar burn'

gives forewarning of Schumann's feeling for the exotic, but it is with the seductive ripple of the waters of the Nile (sung by a chorus of the Genii of the Nile to words added to Moore's text by Böttger and the composer himself) early in the second part, and still more with the chorus of Houris at the start of part three (to words again added by Schumann and Böttger) with its reiterated rhythmic bare fifths in the bass, and triangle, big drum and cymbals in the orchestral accompaniment, that the composer is at his most original and daring.

Ex. 86

There are other bold, descriptive strokes in the battle music in the first part, and in the bleakly orchestrated chromatic chords depicting the plague-stricken region in the second. And for purely emotional expression, the chorus of lament after the hero's death in the first part should not be overlooked. In the writing for solo voices there is much that is delicately and often plangently beautiful, though here the overall similarity of both arioso and aria results in a certain monotony; without resorting to anything as archaic as recitative for contrast, the composer could profitably have pitched his characters' personal reflective observations in a

higher emotional key than that of the arioso used for imperson?'
commentary.

The only serious disappointments in the work are those massiv
homophonic choruses in which Schumann was aiming and
striving to get highest, i.e. by directing thoughts from earth to
heaven through the employment of a more conventionally
academic, oratorio-like style. There is a gallant attempt at fugal
texture at 'For blood must holy be' in the conclusion to part one,
but Schumann's belated effort to acquire contrapuntal mastery in
middle life only too often (as here) weakened the originality and
individuality of his harmonic idiom. In sum, then, the listener can
greatly enjoy Schumann's earthly travels with the Peri, but he will
not quite get to Paradise.

Just as the Faust legend preoccupied Goethe for the greater part
of his life, so Schumann, too, dwelt on it longer than anything else.
As early as 1832 he had written Gretchen's words 'Meine Ruh' ist
hin' over the middle section of his E minor *Intermezzo* for piano,
Op. 4. For a while he thought of it as the ideal subject for the opera
he always longed to write. And when in 1844 he eventually
embarked on a choral setting, in the manner of *Paradise and the
Peri*, it was not till 1853 and the completion of the overture that
he eventually bid it all farewell.

What fired his imagination in 1844 was not any of the more
familiar and easily understood incidents in the drama but
Goethe's mystical closing scene, which no musician had
approached before. This, according to Clara's diary, was
sketched by August 1844, 'by the sacrifice of his last strength'. At
the end of that year he moved to Dresden, assuming conductorship of a men's choral society and also a mixed choir of his own
founding: together with the impending national celebrations in
honour of the centenary of Goethe's birth, this prompted him to
revise the concluding 'Chorus mysticus' in 1847 and to amplify
sketches of Nos. 4–6 in 1848, so that the whole of what is now
known as Part III was ready for trying out at a private party in
June 1849. The official première was reserved for the centenary
itself in August, with simultaneous performances in Dresden,
Leipzig (under Rietz) and Weimar (under Liszt). 'How I wish I
could have had Faust's mantle for that day in order to be
everywhere and hear everything' was Schumann's subsequent
comment. Only in Leipzig was there some disappointment,

largely, in his own opinion, because it was placed at the beginning of the programme when its entire character was one of conclusion, and because, owing to parts not being copied, Rietz had to use the original version of the 'Chorus mysticus', and mistook its proper tempo at that. In Dresden Schumann was particularly thrilled because people told him his music had made the meaning of Goethe's final scene clear to them for the first time. In a letter to his friend Brendel he confessed that he had secretly feared the reproach 'why music to such perfect poetry?'

Not surprisingly, all this excitement inflamed his imagination anew. Already by the end of July 1849 he had dipped into Goethe's first part for three numbers providing a composite study of Gretchen in love, remorse and despairing fear of retribution. Between 1849 and 1850 he returned to Goethe's second part for a similar tripartite study of the regenerated Faust. These two sections now stand as Parts I and II of Schumann's complete trilogy. The overture followed in 1853. But no complete performance of *Scenes from Faust* in its entirety was given until Hiller conducted it in Cologne in 1862, six years after Schumann's death. He himself is known not to have favoured such an undertaking, conceding 'at the most it might be done only as a curiosity'. Perhaps he was secretly aware of the discrepancy of style between Part III and the later Parts I and II. For what strikes home most strongly nowadays in any complete performance is just how much Schumann's direction changed after leaving Leipzig, where Mendelssohn was uncrowned king, for Dresden. Though reluctant to admit any good in Wagner's operatic innovations, Schumann was still totally unable to resist the lure of the Dresden Court Theatre's Kapellmeister. While Part III belongs wholly to the concert platform, Parts I and II are often more genuinely dramatic than anything to be found in his one and only opera, *Genoveva*, which preoccupied him in between.

If separately entitled, Part I could only have been called *Gretchen*. No. 1 brings first avowals of love in Martha's garden and ends with a few snatches from Goethe's subsequent summer-house scene: lyrical without four-squareness, the music comes to a climax in Gretchen's 'He loves me, loves me not, loves me' followed by the glowing cantilena of Faust's invitation to sensual surrender (marked *Innigkeit*). For No. 2 Schumann jumps to the scene where joy has already dissolved into remorse as Gretchen puts fresh flowers before a picture of the Mater Dolorosa in a niche in the city wall. Again Schumann allows every passing shade of feeling to determine the course of the free-flowing continuous melody, with impassioned octave leaps at the climactic 'Save me from shame and death in one!' In Goethe this is followed by the duel scene (in which Valentine, avenging his sister's honour, is killed by Faust). Hence the turning of the screw when Schumann jumps for his own No. 3 to the Cathedral Scene: here Gretchen, going to pray, is taunted by an evil spirit as the choir chants the *Dies Irae* with ominously threatening persistence. The orchestral contribution is also strongly tell-tale, with one or two details of figuration almost assuming the importance of *leitmotif*.

Part II is designed as a character study of Faust as encountered in the allegorical second part of Goethe's drama, which is to say a Faust after Schumann's own heart, well on the way to salvation, as self-seeking yields to service. No. 1, 'A Pleasant Landscape', is in fact the opening scene of Goethe's own second part, in which Ariel and attendant spirits seek to rekindle the weary Faust's creative impulse by hymning the wonders of nature. Here Schumann responds to Goethe's indications 'song, accompanied with Aeolian harps' (for Ariel) and 'singly, by twos and many together, alternately and collectively' (for the spirits) with some of his most translucent scoring (including harps) and texture in the whole work. Ariel's final invocation and Faust's response are couched in ecstatic speech-melody wholly Wagnerian in inspiration. For No. 2 Schumann makes a big leap forward in the text to Faust's midnight scene with the four grey hags, Want, Debt, Care and Need, who awaken his earlier disquiet. Care eventually blinds him, but with physical darkness comes the first great dawning of spiritual light and a vision of the ideal society he hopes to create. From the opening quartet for the four grey hags, with its sinisterly chromatic tremolando motif for accompanying strings, the whole scene is strongly atmospheric, not least the eerie moment of blinding and Faust's deeply poignant reaction ('Die Nacht scheint tiefer'). The subsequent switch from minor to major as hope dawns anew is even more stirring than in the previous number. No. 3, following consecutively in Goethe, is the scene of Faust's death, wisely curtailed by Schumann so as to end at its dramatic climax. The blinded Faust believes the clink of spades to be workmen carrying out his grandiose schemes for the reclaiming of land from the sea for life's betterment: in reality it comes from the lemures brought by Mephistopheles to dig his grave. For the lemures (skeleton-like ghosts of the wicked dead with minds as sub-normal as their bodies) Schumann writes a mocking, four-square ditty. Mephistopheles and Faust in their turn soar direct into realms of embrionic Wagnerian *unendliche Melodie*. Nothing in Schumann's entire output is more dramatic than the actual moment of Faust's death and the eerie hollowness that follows, with orchestration, textural lay-out, harmony and dynamics all playing their part.

Speaking of his own Part III, Schumann once confessed that he was initially drawn to it because of the sublime nature poetry of Goethe's last scene, in which Faust's redeemed soul is wafted to regions of the blessed and the waiting Gretchen. But since the closing words are 'Das Ewig-Weibliche zieht uns hinan' (the eternal womanly leads us upwards and on) he no doubt glimpsed a vision of his own beloved Clara behind Gretchen. Though divided into seven sections the music is continuous, with chorus and solos flowing into each other as in *Paradise and the Peri*. In a complete performance of *Scenes from Faust*, the more regular rhythm, blander lyricism, smoother harmony and discreeter orchestration of this section all initially help to transport the listener from earthly trauma into a purer, tensionless realm of holy anchorites, angels and blessed boys. But despite exceptional suavity of craftsmanship and moments of genuine spiritual insight and beauty, gradually the influence of Mendelssohn and the 'establishment' in this section reveals itself as no match for that of the exploratory Wagner in Parts I and II. Within a continuously reflective mood, the music's progress is too symmetrical and predictable.

Goethe's opening scene (thought to have been suggested by a description of the Mount of Montserrat in Barcelona) is headed 'Forest, Rock, Wilderness: Holy anchorites, disposed here and there, at different heights among the chasms'. But though the ensuing text evokes the elemental wildness of the scene, Schumann emphasizes only its all-pervading holiness as a 'refuge of love and grace'. No. 2, a tenor solo for Pater Ecstaticus, is interesting for an undulating figure of accompaniment (perhaps suggested by Goethe's stage direction 'floating up and down') that reappears like a *leitmotif* in Part I and the overture. In No. 3

Schumann takes his cue from Goethe as to voice types, with Pater Profundus ('from the depth') a bass and Pater Seraphicus ('at middle height') a baritone besides the treble and alto blessed boys. But here, as in so much else in this section, four-square phraseology takes its toll. No. 4, an extended chorus in praise of Faust's redemption, was the most important of the several 1848 additions. For Mater Glorioso's final 'Come then! To higher spheres conduct him!' in No. 6, Schumann finds a startling harmonic progression marvellously evocative of divine regeneration.

Ex. 87

Both original and revised versions of the concluding 'Chorus mysticus' (No. 7) share the slow, searching introduction wholly at one with the metaphysical nature of Goethe's own thought. Whereas the first version brought a pronounced change midway to a sturdily contrapuntal, animated conclusion, Schumann himself preferred his longer, more continuous and less classically argued revised ending. Clara was inclined to agree with him, but added 'all the same I am sorry to give up the first, and if it lay with me both choruses would be printed', as indeed they eventually were, for every conductor to make his choice.

As for the overture, added last, Schumann confessed that he found it the hardest part of all since 'the elements that have to be mastered are too many and too gigantic'. At one time he thought of fugue ('the most deeply thoughtful form of music') as a solution, but eventually chose abbreviated sonata form with D minor conflict resolved in a spiritually triumphant D major coda. The undulating second subject, derived in the first place from the accompaniment to Pater Ecstaticus's solo (III, 2), can also be briefly observed in the original version of the 'Chorus mysticus' (III, 7) besides introducing Mephistopheles in the garden scene (I, 1) and the evil spirit in the Cathedral scene (I, 3). Several conductors have felt impelled to thin the scoring slightly, notably the excessive tremolando in middle strings and some of the woodwind too. But Schumann's overture has a nobility of thought worthy of its subject. Like so many of his later works, the complete *Scenes from Faust* can be made or marred in performance. But given dedicated advocacy, there is no doubting its status as a masterpiece, albeit not without flaws.

Inevitably Dresden and Wagner rekindled Schumann's long cherished dreams of a genuine German school of opera and desire to contribute to it himself. Finding a worthy subject nevertheless troubled him as much as Beethoven. Besides *Doge and Dogaressa* (from Hoffmann's *Serapions-Brüder*) obsessing him in the early months of 1840 and Byron's *Corsair*, which even progressed as far as an aria and chorus, the subjects listed in his notebook for consideration included Faust, Till Eulenspiegel, El Golan, Hanko, Nibelunglied, The Wartburg War, The Bridge of Mantible, Abélard and Héloïse, The False Prophet (from Lalla Rookh), The Last Stuart, Kunz von der Rosen, Atala, The Noble Bride, The Pariah, Maria Stuart, Sacontala, War of the German Peasants, Sardanapalus, The Robbers of the Bell, The Stone Guidepost, The Smith of Gretna Green, The Dead Guest, King Arthur, and even Tristan and Isolde.

The search ended in 1847 with his discovery of Hebbel's forceful play on the medieval legend of *Geneviève*, on which Tieck had also written a more tender kind of dramatic poem. In the original tale Genoveva, wife of Count Siegfried of Brabant, was falsely accused of adultery by Golo, the major-domo, in her husband's absence, and sentenced to death. But her executioner abandoned her in a forest in the Ardennes, where for six years she lived in a cave with her son, who in infancy was nourished by a roe, until her husband on a hunting expedition pursued this roe into the cave and was happily reunited with wife and child. It was from Hebbel, Tieck and the legend itself that Schumann asked the poet, Robert Reinick, to compile a libretto, leading to sufficient disagreements about plan (Schumann wanted both exile and reconciliation relegated to the last act so as to accommodate more of Hebbel's interest in the passion-wracked Golo and his sinister witch-mother) and also general style for Schumann to appeal to Hebbel for assistance. As he put it 'Though the adapter has the best possible intentions, still I cannot say I like much of what he has done; above all there is a want of *strength*, and the conventional libretto style is not at all to my taste. I can find no music for such tirades, and won't put up with them.' But Hebbel would not oblige and Schumann was driven to making the final version himself, a hotch-potch including direct quotations from both Hebbel and Tieck, some folk-song words, some of Reinick's text and some of his own – and over it all the shadow of Weber's *Euryanthe*, for which at this time his enthusiasm was unbounded. On seeing the result, Reinick withdrew his name entirely. More interesting still was Wagner's opinion. As he subsequently wrote in *Mein Leben*: 'When, however, out of a genuine desire for the success of the work, about which I had grave misgivings, I called his attention to some grave defects in it, and suggested the necessary alterations, I realized how matters stood with this extraordinary person: he simply wanted me to be swayed by himself, and deeply resented any interference with the product of his own ideals, so that henceforth I let matters alone.'

The first of Schumann's four acts shows Siegfried departing with his knights to help drive Saracen invaders out of France: Genoveva is left in the care of Golo, whose secret passion for her is encouraged by his evil, black-magic dabbling un-wed mother, Margaretha. In the second act Genoveva is gradually driven to repel Golo's late-night advances with the phrase 'Zurück, zurück, ehrloser Bastard', stinging him into a revengeful plot whereby Drago, the faithful old steward, is discovered in Genoveva's bedroom and killed by angry retainers, and she herself led off to imprisonment. In the third act Siegfried, wounded in a victorious battle, is nursed in Strasburg by the evil Margaretha in disguise, who, when Golo arrives with news of the supposed infidelity, conjures up false visions of Genoveva and Drago in her magic mirror, which Siegfried finally smashes in despair crying that his wife must die. In the fourth act Genoveva, having again rejected Golo and his proposals of escape, is miraculously saved from the sword of Siegfried's appointed huntsmen-executioners by a dumb youth as off-stage horns (no doubt suggested by Beethoven's off-stage trumpet in *Fidelio*) announce the return of Siegfried just in time for a happy ending.

As for musical style, Schumann divides the opera into numbers succeeding each other without discernible break, as in *Paradise and the Peri*, with an orchestrally accompanied kind of arioso serving as recitative. It is unnecessary to look for Italian influences: his contempt for that country's emphasis on vocal display at the expense of everything else is summed up in a remark to Weber's son-in-law who was enthusing over Cimarosa's *Matrimonio segreto*: 'Let me alone with your canary-bird music and your tunes out of the waste-paper basket.' Nor had he any sympathy with the ostentatious French style of Meyerbeer, condemned once and for all in his celebrated article on *Les Huguenots* (it was ironical that the production of *Genoveva* should have been postponed for several months in favour of Meyerbeer's *Le Prophète*). *Genoveva* is, in fact, wholly German, as Schumann wished it to be, and can be placed between Weber and Wagner. It was surely from Weber that he took the idea of introducing *quasi* folk-songs – the duets of Genoveva and Golo 'Wenn ich ein Vöglein wär' (Act II) and of the huntsmen Caspar and Balthasar, 'Sie hatten Beid' sich herzlich lieb' (Act IV). The choruses of knights, nobles and retainers in the first act, on the other hand, are strongly reminiscent of *Tannhäuser*. Of the arias, Genoveva's two prayers, 'O du, der über Alle wacht' (Act II) and 'Die letzte Hoffnung schwindet' (Act IV) and Golo's 'Frieden zieh' in meine Brust' (Act I) are the most ambitious in scope and rewarding to operatic voices, but they owe more to middle period Wagner, such as exemplified in Elsa's prayer, than to the grand 'show-piece' style of Weber's dramatic arias. Like both Weber and Wagner, Schumann was also keenly aware of the possibilities of thematic reminiscence, or *leitmotif*, though his use of it is somewhat looser and less dramatic than Wagner's at this same time. Golo has not just one but several themes, of which this potent motif perhaps contributes most theatrically, not least when he vows vengeance after Genoveva's cry of 'bastard':

Ex. 88

(Overture, bar 4)

Her main motif, introduced at the climax of her first act duet with
Siegfried, is reminiscent of the opening phrase of 'Süsser Freund'
in *Frauenliebe und -leben*. It generates the whole of her second act
prayer, which incidentally ends romantically to the distant chimes
of midnight.

Ex. 89

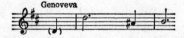

At its Leipzig première in 1850, the opera's first two acts were
warmly acclaimed, the last two rather less so. That judgement still
holds good. For despite Schumann's dramatic inexperience, most
notably revealed in inability to contrast characters sharply
enough in musical terms and reluctance to resort to theatrical
tricks to heighten points of climax, tension is nevertheless
cumulatively sustained until the second act denouement. Nothing
in the work is finer than Golo's late night visit to the lonely
Genoveva, alarmed by her roistering servants, in the second act.
Her relief at the arrival of a supposed friend, their mutual pleasure
in singing a folk-song to the accompaniment of Golo's zither,
Golo's sudden, passionate outburst, Genoveva's mounting distress at his advances culminating in her 'Away, you faithless
bastard', and finally Golo's stunned brooding over that verbal
whip-lash and his vow of vengeance, are all conveyed with a
psychological insight and musical skill worthy of Wagner. Golo's
'stolen kiss' scene in the first act, with its arresting orchestration,
also shows the influence of Wagner: it is important to remember
that Schumann heard several performances of *Tannhäuser* after

its first production in October 1845. And though Margaretha, Golo's evil genius, emerges as little more than a pantomime witch, at least in her *molto vivace* arrival in the first act finale, with its scintillating scoring, Schumann manages to establish that she inhabits a different world.

As often in Schumann's larger, later projects, so again here invention is less consistently sustained in the last two acts, particularly the fourth. The basic stumbling block, as Wagner so well knew, was the scenario itself, descending through a charade of magic to a last minute triumph of right over wrong, the heroine by this time too pale to invite sympathy, the villain and villainess sentimentally weakened by remorse. But despite its contrived situations, the third act briefly brings Siegfried to life, first in his hunting-horn-inspired 'Bald blick' ich dich wieder mein Heimatschloss', and then as tormented victim of falsely sown suspicion. The finale of this act, set in Margaretha's room 'fantastically decorated with appliances of magic', opens as spookily as any horror scene in contemporary German romantic opera – the orchestration throughout Margaretha's dream is particularly striking. There is also a touch of the supernatural in Schumann's subtly seductive use of two off-stage sopranos, later joined by two tenors, for the pictures conjured in her magic mirror. But atmospheric evocation is not intensified enough in preparation for the final climax. Certainly Drago's ghost and the flames spurting from the mirror smashed by the frenzied Siegfried demand pictorial imagery of a much more vivid kind from the orchestra.

In the last act Schumann again shows insufficient sense of theatre. Not even the stage direction 'during the following scene the stage becomes darker and darker. A storm arises' brings any kind of descriptive response in the music. Equally disappointing is the progressive failing of lyrical inspiration. True, Genoveva's long aria near the start, 'Die letzte Hoffnung', soars to impassioned climaxes. But her last life-and-death encounter with Golo is sub-normal in emotional temperature (incidentally Schumann just lets Golo slip away 'to roam the world at large' rather than acknowledge his guilt, as in Hebbel, in a dramatic death). And all that can be said of her muted reunion with her husband is that it allows Schumann to revive memories of their first act duet, with its simple avowals of conjugal trust and affection, in the same key of D. The only truly dramatic stroke is Margaretha's high-pitched, off-stage cry of atonement, as stirring in its mere five notes as Leonora's 'Töt' erst sein Weib!' in *Fidelio*. The all-too-syllabic choral writing is unmemorable except for Schumann's masterly merging of the first chorus of rejoicing country-folk into the second chorus of knights and retainers singing the chorale with which the opera began. In view of what seems like frequent quotation from the opera itself, it is surprising to discover that the fine overture was in fact written first. It is no mere curtain-raiser, but a résumé of the whole drama.

In 1848, hard on the heels of *Genoveva*, came the incidental music to Byron's *Manfred*. It is not hard to see why Schumann was attracted to this poem. In the first place there is the obvious affinity between it and *Faust* (which Goethe himself noticed) both in the characters of Manfred and Faust and in the breath-taking beauty of the nature poetry in each. Also, possibly Schumann's own secret fears in times of illness were those of the 'restless, wandering, distracted man, tormented by fearful thoughts' which Byron portrays. Wasielewski quotes Schumann as having remarked: 'I never devoted myself to any composition with such lavish love and power as to *Manfred*,' and tells of how when reading the poem to two Düsseldorf friends 'his voice suddenly faltered, he burst into tears and was so overcome that he could read no farther'.

Though Byron's poem is written in dramatic form, he never intended it to be placed on a stage – there are far too many incorporeal beings which appear from and disappear into mid-air to make a stage representation practicable. Yet Schumann's adaptation of the text shows that he had a stage performance in mind, and the work has been performed several times in Germany in this way with his incidental music. There is also a concert version of the work, with the connecting text between the musical numbers arranged by Richard Pohl.

In selecting where to introduce music Schumann was sometimes guided by Byron's imaginatively musical indications in the poem. This was so with the songs of the spirits near the beginning at Byron's 'A star is seen at the darker end of the gallery: it is stationary; and a voice is heard singing', and again Schumann introduces the *ranz des vaches* at Byron's indication 'The shepherd's pipe in the distance is heard.' For the rest, he used his own discretion and on the whole showed good judgment, selecting other spirit passages or else those parts of the text where music could help to intensify the emotion or contribute generally to the atmosphere. The sum total of his incidental music amounts to four numbers for Act One, seven for Act Two and four for Act Three as well as the overture.

In the overture Schumann shows absolute understanding of the profound psychological issues of the poem, but the remaining music does not go quite so deep as Byron. Yet it has all that delightful spontaneous freshness which characterized the composer's earlier piano music and songs, and it is not difficult to explain the reason why. Most of the numbers are mere fragments, each a poetic idea dissolved into music and then dismissed without further development – in *Papillons* style. And it was in this direction that so much of Schumann's genius lay. Moreover, the orchestration has a wonderful delicacy in keeping with the quality of the ideas.

He is at his best in the melodramas, where he provides only an instrumental background against which the words are declaimed. The appearance of a spirit in the form of a beautiful female figure: 'Oh heaven! if it be thus' (No. 2), the calling up of Astarte and Manfred's address to Astarte (Nos. 10 and 11) and Manfred's soliloquy: 'There is a calm upon me' (No. 12), are all particularly moving examples of this somewhat problematical art-form. But for Schumann melodrama solved rather than created problems. It enabled him to preserve the rhythmic freedom of the words without sacrificing the metrical flow of the music, and is more satisfactory in effect than many of his later experiments with arioso.

Apart from the songs of the spirits (No. 1), there are no solo songs. But the Incantation 'When the moon is on the wane' (No. 3), sung by four bass voices, is worthy of mention for the solemn atmosphere evoked by the accompaniment, at first strongly reminiscent of the opening of the theme of the *Études symphoniques* for piano. Of the choruses the most outstanding is the final cloister hymn, 'Requiem aeternam' (No. 15), of which both words and music were added to Byron's poem by Schumann for the purpose of making the ending more effective and conclusive.

It must be regretted that Schumann did not live in the age of radio, since the most satisfactory way of presenting *Manfred* with his incidental music is as a radio play. Could he have conceived it in this way, he would not have found it necessary to make his several cuts in the poem, such as leaving out three of the seven spirits in the first act or omitting the whole of Byron's third scene from the second act, where again the poet calls for 'a voice without singing', or cutting four verses from the Incantation as well as smaller passages from Manfred's speeches towards the end. These are explainable only on the grounds of his desire to prevent the music from unduly holding up the action in a stage performance.

Schumann wrote no other dramatic works. Possibly he realized his talent did not really lie in this direction; moreover, as conductor of choral and orchestral societies at Dresden and Düsseldorf he was probably not blind to the many opportunities which surrounded him for performances of choral works written for the concert platform. So between 1847 and the time of his death he returned again to the path he had trodden with such success (at the time) in *Paradise and the Peri*.

The most ambitious of these remaining choral works is *The Pilgrimage of the Rose* (Op. 112) of 1851, the poem of which was sent to Schumann for consideration by the young poet Moritz Horn. The story is of a rose who, unsatisfied with her lot, asks to be changed into human form that she may taste the delights of love. The Fairy Queen warns her of the sorrows of human love, but eventually grants her request, giving her a magic rose which will ensure happiness for her so long as she keeps it, but death should she part with it. After being driven away by an old woman she eventually finds shelter for her first night on earth with an old grave-digger, who soon suggests to a miller and his wife that they should adopt the girl in place of their own daughter who has died of a broken heart. Her happiness in her new home is complete when she eventually meets a young forester and marries him and bears his child. But she chooses to pass on the magic rose to her baby and dies through her self-sacrifice. Both in subject-matter and style the poem is an example of that weak and sickly sentimentality which characterizes the less distinguished of the German romantic poets. Schumann's sneaking sympathy with this type of thought dates from his choice of Chamisso's *Frauenliebe und -leben* for his Op. 42 song-cycle, and by 1851 it was sufficiently developed for Horn's poem to give him immediate pleasure. He asked for certain cuts and a more dramatic treatment of the ending, but could write to the poet: 'The poem is so fresh in my mind that the sooner you could undertake these alterations the better I should be pleased.'[1]

In general style of setting *The Pilgrimage of the Rose* is akin to *Paradise and the Peri*, though considerably shorter, and, in Schumann's estimation, 'more rustic and German'. It is divided into numbers which succeed each other without perceptible break, and again Schumann uses his soloists both as actors in the story and as outside commentators. The regular rhythm of the verse made it unsuitable for any other than a metrical setting; the music is thus consistently lyrical with even less differentiation between dramatic and reflective passages than in the *Peri*. Moreover, the characters in the poem are insipid and their emotions anaemic, with the result that the composer had little chance for vivid or varied emotional colour in the music. Within a pale pink limitation some of the numbers have a certain virginal charm, such as the delightfully fresh A major trio for two trebles and alto which opens the work. And the more robust wedding-feast chorus, No. 22, in *Volkslieder* style, is worthy of mention, for it is as 'rustic and German' in spirit as ever Schumann succeeded in being. The work was first performed with only its original piano accompaniment. Later in 1851 Schumann orchestrated it, and in this complete form it was first heard in February 1852 at a Düsseldorf subscription concert.

Schumann's correspondence during 1851 shows that his mind at this time was overflowing with ideas for choral works of all kinds. In letter to Richard Pohl he discussed the possibility of a Reformation trilogy on Luther's life, a project which was eventually abandoned. And it was to Pohl that he first confessed his feeling that 'many a ballad might, with a little trouble, be treated with good effect as a concert piece for solo voices, chorus and orchestra',[2] ending the letter with a request that Pohl would help him to arrange Uhland's *Des Sängers Fluch*. The outcome of this idea was four choral ballads: Uhland's *Der Königssohn* (Op. 116) in 1851, the same poet's *Des Sängers Fluch* (Op. 139) in

[1] 21st April 1851.
[2] Letter of 25th June 1851.

1852, Geibel's *Vom Pagen und der Königstochter* (Op. 140) in 1852 and Uhland's *Das Glück von Edenhall* (Op. 143) in 1853. Hasenclever assisted Schumann in adapting the text of *Das Glück von Edenhall* as Pohl had done in *Des Sängers Fluch*, but Schumann himself, as far as is known, arranged the other two.

By far the most successful of the four, musically, is *The Minstrel's Curse*. In changing the poem into dramatic form Pohl gave Schumann opportunities for clear characterization – the parts of the king, the queen, the harper and the youth are maintained by solo voices. Moreover, the story is held together by means of a narrator, an alto soloist, while the chorus provides the impersonal comments on the situation. There are some delightful bass and treble solos and duets in strophic form from the old harper and the boy, such as the boy's 'In the fair Provençal valleys' (No. 4), in answer to the queen's requests for songs, though whether or not Pohl was justified in introducing other of Uhland's poems to provide texts for these songs is another matter. Schumann himself thought it an excellent idea. The frequent use of solo harp in the orchestral accompaniment adds further freshness and variety to the music, and mention must also be made of the descriptive chromatic harmonies in the accompaniment to the harper's final curse solo, 'Woe, woe, thou haughty palace' (No. 13). In fact the whole work is an extraordinarily vivid musical conception of the text to have come from Schumann in 1852.

The King's Son, completed before *The Minstrel's Curse*, is on the other hand a very poor composition. Not only does all the music show signs of forced invention, as opposed to spontaneous inspiration, but it is full of inferior craftsmanship. Several of the solos have no feeling whatsoever for the metre of the poem, such as this from the end of No. 2:

Ex. 90

183

There is some attractive descriptive music in the last two of the four numbers comprising *Of the Page and the King's Daughter*, but neither this work nor *The Luck of Edenhall* (the shortest of the four ballads, and through-composed) has any distinguishing qualities calling for comment, though each is a correct enough setting of the text.

His other choral works are all of a predominantly reflective rather than a narrative or descriptive kind. Feuchtersleben's short poem *Beim Abschied zu singen* (Op. 84), of 1847, has only two flutes, oboes, clarinets, bassoons and horns for accompaniment instead of full orchestra, but it is hardly suitable for performance in this form, since the wind instruments do little but double the voice-parts all the way through. Hebbel's *Nachtlied* (Op. 108) and the *Requiem für Mignon* (Op. 98B), from Goethe's *Wilhelm Meister*, both of 1849, are very much more satisfactory, particularly the latter, which is an enchanting cantata-like presentation of Mignon's funeral (from the eighth chapter of the eighth book of the novel) for soloists, chorus and orchestra. Mignon's selfless devotion to Wilhelm, which eventually overtaxed the mysterious child's frail constitution, awakened an immediate response in the tender-hearted Schumann, and he went so far as to evoke the scene in a quotation from the book prefixed to the score. 'The obsequies of Mignon took place in the evening. The company proceeded to the Hall of the Past, and found it magnificently illuminated and ornamented. The walls were hung with azure tapestry almost from ceiling to floor, so that only socle and frieze were visible. In the four candelabra in the corners large wax lights were burning, and smaller wax lights in the four smaller candelabra which surrounded the sarcophagus. Near the sarcophagus stood four boys, dressed in blue and silver, and over a figure which was resting upon the sarcophagus they were waving broad fans of ostrich feathers. The company sat down, and two choruses began to sing with sweet voices.'

Goethe's ensuing text was a ready-made gift, since it takes the form of a dialogue between the four young boys who bring their playmate to her resting place and an invisible choir which, without using liturgical words, offers a message of solace and hope. The children (represented in the cantata by a solo quartet of two sopranos and two altos) bewail their lost companion in the minor key, the choir brings comfort in the major (at one time even approaching the style of a chorale), till eventually the children are persuaded to 'turn back to life' in a radiant F major concluding chorus – in striking contrast to the funereal C minor of the opening number. The six sections of the work flow into each other without any break in the continuity, and the scoring is full of telling, expressive details – even to the inclusion of harp, since Mignon was a harper's daughter.

Though this work is a 'secular' Requiem, with not even a passing reference to liturgical works such as is found in the final *Manfred* chorus, it is significant that the word *religioso* appears twice among the expression marks. Schumann had always accepted the ethical code of Christianity. But there is reason to believe that from about 1847 onwards he began to focus his thoughts rather more closely on the Christ behind the Christian ethic. Rather than go direct to the Bible he chose at first to make his approach through the medium of poetry, selecting three of Rückert's sacred poems for his *Adventlied* (Op. 71) of 1848, for chorus and orchestra, also the *Motet* (Op. 93) of 1849 for double male-voice choir, organ *ad lib.* and orchestra[1] and the *Neujahrslied* (Op. 144) of 1849–50, for chorus and orchestra. All three works adopt the same kind of musical procedure as of old: the numbers succeed each other without discernible break and the text is shared among choruses, duets and solos. The only musical clue to the sacred significance of the words is the interpolation of a chorale-like chorus as the fourth number of the *Adventlied*, and also the introduction of the chorale tune 'Nun danket alle Gott' – at first in the bass part only, while the remaining voices add free counterpoint above, and finally taken up triumphantly by the whole choir – in the final number of the *Neujahrslied*. Of the three the *Neujahrslied* is the most deserving of performance because of its interesting orchestral accompaniment and the variety of the vocal material, which even includes some formal recitative.

Finally, in 1852, he turned to the words of the liturgy for his Mass (Op. 147) and Requiem (Op. 148). Though he was not a Catholic, his duties at Düsseldorf included the direction of performances of sacred music in connection with festivals of the Roman Catholic Church, and it was undoubtedly with these

---

[1] The work was not orchestrated until 1852.

occasions in mind that he embarked on the composition of Catholic rather than Protestant music.

As well as the Kyrie, Gloria, Credo, Sanctus and Agnus Dei of the Ordinary, Schumann also includes an Offertory between the Sanctus and Agnus Dei in his Mass. The Requiem is made up of nine shorter movements, not arranged in the traditional order. Each work is thus plainly a concert work, not suitable for use in the regular services of the Roman Catholic Church. On the concert platform both demand much help from their interpreters. The important vowel sounds of the Latin language need to be sustained over long flights of vocal polyphony, and Schumann was insufficiently skilled as a contrapuntist to be able to keep his music afloat for these extended periods. In consequence some of the numbers suffer from the inevitable short-windedness of small-term construction applied to large-scale movements. This can be seen at its worst in the Gloria of the Mass, a movement in which the flow is completely disrupted by the over-frequent strong harmonic cadences. In the Credo the syllabic setting, i.e. one syllable, one note, resulting in a prominence of consonants which the Latin language does not require, again helps to destroy the continuity of the vocal line. As exercises in the polyphonic style the opening and ending of the Sanctus and the final Agnus Dei are the most successful movements, but the short Offertory, set in simple lyrical style for soprano solo and strings, is far more typical of Schumann and of what he was best able to do.

Schumann considered the Requiem a more personal work and therefore did not try to imbue it with the same classical restraint that he had attempted in all but the Offertory of the Mass. Rushing minor scale-passages make their way into the accompaniment of the 'Dies irae' for atmospheric effect, and the flames of hell are also represented pictorially in the middle of the fifth number at the words 'Confutatis maledictis, flammis acribus addictis'. But again Schumann shows little understanding of the special demands of the Latin language. Apart from some of the solo writing, notably the alto's 'Que Marium absolvi' in the fifth number, the only other really memorable music is the gravely sustained opening 'Requiem aeternam', and still more, the final 'Benedictus', with a feeling of wonderful calm at its beginning and end. Reissmann[1] has drawn attention to the sketchy nature of the orchestration in this work, and there is every reason to believe that Schumann left it uncompleted.

[1] In his book *Schumann's Life and Works*.

10

Schumann as Critic

Though Schuman's début as music critic dates from a fanciful article on Chopin, printed in the *Allgemeine musikalische Zeitung* in 1831 when he was only twenty-one years old, it was the founding of the *Neue Zeitschrift für Musik* in April 1834 which gave him his real chance to make his voice heard. By this time there were no doubts in his mind as to his life-work. Law had been abandoned in 1830 – music had been selected in its place. And when the accident to his hand in 1832 made a pianist's career out of the question, he knew he was destined to be a composer. But his early environment had not been without its influence. The many hours spent in his father's bookshop during his schooldays had given him a much wider knowledge of both classical and contemporary literature than the comparatively small town of Zwickau could offer him musically and, furthermore, he had inherited from his father an ability to express himself in words which far exceeded his ability to express himself in terms of music at that time. In these circumstances it was not surprising that Schumann should wish to write about music as well as compose it, nor was it surprising that with true youthful intolerance he should deem the general musical condition of Germany, including its musical press, to be unhealthy and in dire need of reform. His own introduction to *Music and Musicians*, a collection of his essays and articles he assembled in 1852 and eventually published in four volumes in the spring of 1854, best describes how he felt:

> Towards the end of the year 1833 [he writes] a number of
> musicians – most of them young – met together, as though by
> accident, every evening at Leipzig; these meetings were partly the
> result of a desire for social intercourse, as well as for the exchange
> of ideas in regard to that art which was the meat and drink of life to
> them – Music. The musical situation was not then very encourag-
> ing in Germany. On the stage Rossini reigned, at the pianoforte
> nothing was heard but Herz and Hünten, and yet but a few years

had passed since Beethoven, Weber and Schubert had lived among us. It is true that Mendelssohn's star was ascending, and wonderful things were related of Chopin, but the deeper influence of these only declared itself afterwards. Then one day the thought awakened in a wild young heart, 'Let us not look on idly, let us also lend our aid to progress, let us bring the poetry of art to honour among men!'

Such is the story behind the *Neue Zeitschrift* which Schumann edited for its first ten years, and it is through the pages of this enterprising music journal that we are able to know the composer in the rôle of critic and observer of musical life around him.

In writing of the paper's aims and aspirations, which were so vigorously debated during those winter evenings of 1833–4, Schumann first stresses the importance of the past: 'Our plan was . . . to recall the old times and its works with great emphasis, thus to draw attention to the fact that fresh artistic beauties can be strengthened only at such pure sources.' And this was no empty statement. The spirit of Bach in particular, in a bright halo, hovers over many pages – Leipzig is described as 'this little corner of the earth once consecrated by the spirit of Bach'. Handel is pictured 'firm as the heavenly vault above us, and Gluck not less so'. Secondly, the paper resolved 'to attack as inartistic the works of the present generation, since they proceed from the praises of superficial virtuosos'. The most cursory glance through Schumann's writings shows him to be over-generous, if anything, in his criticisms; as a composer he was too well aware of what an artist has to give of himself in his work to tread wantonly on other people's toes. But he was equally unable to apply a blind eye to the telescope: where he knew there was superficiality he did his utmost to expose it. He begins the now famous article on Meyerbeer's *Huguenots* with the words: 'I feel today like a brave young warrior who draws his sword for the first time in a great cause,' and in another article the sentence 'We are tired of world-weary, pallid virtuoso faces' comes as a profound *cri du coeur*. It was an age of ostentatious display in composing and performing, and today, in the light of over a hundred years, we are bound to admire Schumann's remarkably clear sight in distinguishing between the showman and the true artist. Finally the paper resolved 'to assist in hastening the dawn of a new poetic age'. This clause comes last as if, in spite of the encouragement he wished to offer younger artists, Schumann realized the necessity of caring for the roots and clearing away weeds before the new shoots could flourish. And even his conception of a new poetic age steered a temperate, midway course – being founded not so much on that 'roughly scrawled materialism which the French new romantics favour', but asking for a 'new kingdom, suspended like Mohammed's earth, on wondrously interlaced diamond fillets, and concealing within it strange things yet unseen, though faintly foretold by Beethoven's prophetic spirit and whispered by the gifted Franz Schubert in his own wise, yet childlike, fairylike manner'.

Plainly the policy of the *Neue Zeitschrift* was not one of ruthless iconoclasm, even though Schumann was determined to put an end to the 'critical honey-daubing' in which most of the other music papers excelled. But the conservative reader must have been curiously puzzled and at times exasperated by the streak of fancy running through its pages – a streak of fancy which radiated from the mysterious society of Davidites whose purpose it was to tease and provoke the false Philistines of art whenever opportunity arose. Schumann explained that the society existed 'only in the heart of its founder, but that it seemed a fit idea in order to express different views of art – to invent opposite artistic characters', furthermore, that it 'wound itself like a red thread through the musical paper, binding together truth and poetry in a humorous manner'. The fantasy of literary romanticism, in particular of Jean Paul, had not been wasted on Schumann – no flights of fancy were too extravagant for his impressionable young mind. Since this chapter is concerned with his own criticism there can be no discussion of the contributions of his many friends under their various Davidsbündler pseudonyms. The spotlight must be concentrated on the articles signed with his own *noms de guerre*: Florestan, signifying his impulsive, active self; Eusebius, his contemplative, introspective self, Master Raro, the mediator between the two (at times this name also hid the identity of Wieck); Figure 2 or 12 his disinterested self; Jeanquisit and Jonathan, borrowed occasionally from Hiller and Schunke respectively; and also on his unsigned contributions written in editorial capacity.

In whatever guise he writes, it is immediately apparent that his interest lies in the aesthetic rather than the technical aspects of music, in each composer's contribution to the *sum* rather than to the development of art. There are isolated instances of close, analytical criticism, notably the article on Berlioz's *Fantastic Symphony*. But even here his comment is: 'I believe that Berlioz, when a young student of medicine, never dissected the head of a handsome murderer with greater unwillingness than I feel in analysing his first movement.' Intuition was Schumann's greatest attribute as a critic, and in consequence he prefers to discuss not the means but the end, and in describing the end he relies on the evocative qualities of words, the poetry of words, rather than the usual labels of musicology. In an article on Hiller Schumann writes:

> The editors of this paper have been reproached with laying too much stress on the poetical side of music, to its disadvantage as a science. . . . This blame touches precisely those points that distinguish this paper from others. We will not venture to decide in what manner art is best and most quickly served, but we must declare that we regard that criticism as the highest which leaves behind it an impression resembling that awakened by its subject. In this sense Jean Paul, by means of a poetic companion-picture, may contribute more to the understanding of a Beethoven symphony or fantasia (even without mentioning either symphony or fantasia) than a dozen so-called art critics, who place their ladders against the Colossus and measure him carefully by the yard. But to awaken such impressions a great poet, somewhat similar in gifts, is required.

Articles on Schubert's C major Symphony and on Chopin, Henselt and Sterndale Bennett as well as shorter fragments such as 'Letters of an Enthusiast' or 'Dorn's "Tone-Flowers" ' best reveal how Schumann combines 'truth and poetry' on an extended scale, and how his points are subtly woven into a rich, ornamental tapestry. Yet as a nutshell example, how vividly he epitomizes the difference between Beethoven's third and fourth Symphonies through the adjectives 'Roman' and 'Grecian'. His beloved Schubert inspired particularly fanciful imagery, such as 'the imaginative painter, whose pencil was steeped now in moonbeams and then in the full glow of the sun'; on another occasion Schubert's first waltzes are called 'little, lovely genii, floating above the earth at about the height of a flower'. Even adverse criticism could be administered with grace and fantasy, the pill hidden within the poetry. Of Rossini and Beethoven, Eusebius s~ys: 'The butterfly flew in the way of the eagle; he moved aside lest he should crush the insect with the beating of his wings.' And again:

> See the lovely, floating butterfly! yet brush away his coloured dust, and he becomes a miserable, unregarded creature; but after the flight of centuries the skeletons of gigantic creations exist, to the astonishment and admiration of posterity.

Humour is never far distant. Of a prima donna's embellishments in Rossini's *Barbiere di Siviglia* we read:

> Viardot transformed the entire opera into a great variation; she scarcely left one melody untouched. What a false view of the liberty of a virtuoso! Yet this is her best character.

And again on inaccuracy in manuscripts:

> It is quite natural that among the hundred thousand dots that a composer writes in an incredibly short space of time, a dozen or so should be scribbled down a little too high or too low; indeed they sometimes write the wildest harmonies.

Referring to Liszt's difficult arrangements of Schubert's songs:

> a witty fellow wonders whether an easier arrangement could not be published, and also whether the result of such a one would be the original Schubert song again.

When faced with the laborious task of reviewing a whole collection of mediocre dance music, Schumann is found weaving his criticism into an attractive account of an imaginary ball, in which the tunes of the dances are discussed by the characters as they drift in and out of the ballroom. Chopin is the hero of the evening with his bolero and a waltz and two polonaises; Liszt suffers another good-humoured dig when

> Ambrosia hammered more out of the Liszt waltz than she was aware of, perspiring visibly meanwhile. 'Such a monster can only be vanquished by the courageous,' I whispered in her ear, 'and you do well not to spare yourself.'

And when reviewing a collection of studies by Cramer, Schumann pretends to have lost the title-page, and thus in mock ignorance of the composer wonders if the duller bits were written by 'old fogies'.

But perhaps of greater interest now than his method of

expressing himself is what he actually had to say of paramount musical challenges of his time. Each age has its own particular conditions and its problems; and an eye-witness's account of the situation and his surmises about their resolution are the more intriguing to posterity, which has the privilege of knowing what hitherto lay beyond the eye's horizon. Just as music and its relation to political ideology is a subject of considerable interest in eastern Europe today, so music and nationalism occupied many thoughtful minds a hundred years earlier. It was a time which saw the beginning of the end of the hegemony of Germany and Italy, and Schumann was fully aware of both the good and the bad side of the impending change. 'Until now', he writes, 'we have had three principal schools of music – Italian, French, German. How will it be when other nations step in, even from Patagonia?' And later:

> We see quite a novel artistic character before us. It really begins to look as if the nations bordering on Germany desired to emancipate themselves from the influence of German music; this might annoy a German nativist, but it could only appear natural and cheering to the more profound thinker, if he understood human nature. So we see the Franco-Pole Chopin, Bennett the Englishman, Verhulst the Dutchman, besides the representatives of Hungarian music, giving promise and performance that must lead them to be regarded as most worthy embodiments of the artistic tendency of their native lands. And though they all seem to regard Germany as their first and favourite teacher of music, we cannot wonder that they try to speak their own musical language to their own nation, without becoming untrue to their former instructor. For no land can yet boast masters that equal our greatest ones: who will declare the contrary?

Though Bennett and Verhulst did not fulfil Schumann's expectations, this was a prescient observation for 1843. But he is fully aware of the dangers of the over-local flavour and in an article on Chopin stressed the need for art to remain universal:

> Many of Chopin's earlier creations bear this impress of the sharpest nationality. But art requires more. The cosmopolitan must sacrifice the small interests of the soil on which he was born. . . . The further he removes from it, the greater will his consequence in the general world of art become.

This last sentence caps his views on the subject, and is an instance of his penetrating insight into fundamental issues.

Nationalism still lay on the horizon, but romanticism had already arrived. Schumann was one of its foremost exponents both in notes and words, and his neat summarization of the position must be quoted:

> It is well known that in the years 1830–4 a reaction took place in opposition to the reigning taste. On the whole the struggle was not a difficult one; it was principally waged with that empty flourish of manner that displayed itself in nearly every department of art.

But the revolution, to use a stronger word than Schumann's, stirred up considerable strife not only in the minds of the superficial virtuosos and their easy-going public, but also of the academicians. In an amusing little article entitled 'The Devil's Romanticists' Schumann says: 'Some people twaddle about the "torment and martyrdom of this epoch of transition" . . . if you are not satisfied, old gentlemen, why not give us works yourselves – works, works, not only words?'

All his writings give evidence of a profound conviction that music was a language – not a language of material things, but a medium whereby more subtle and elusive emotions than those of words might be conveyed. As a keen follower of Goethe's philosophies he undoubtedly agreed with that poet's remark: 'Music begins where words end.' Or to quote Florestan: 'That would be but a small art indeed which merely possessed sounds, but no speech, no symbol fitted to express the varying movements of the soul.' But here too he is against the excessive emphasis laid on meaning in music by the *avant-garde* of the romanticists. He writes:

> Beethoven understood the danger he ran with his Pastoral Symphony. In the few words with which he headed it, 'Rather expressive of the feeling than tone-painting', lies an entire aesthetic system for composers. But how absurd it is of painters to make portraits of him sitting beside a brook, his head in his hands, listening to the bubbling water!

In that now historic article on Berlioz's *Fantastic Symphony* he explains at length just to what extent the eye can safely influence the ear and what part a programme can legitimately play in music:

> The more elements are congenially related to music which the thought or picture created in tones contains within it, the more poetic and plastic will be the expression of the composition; and in

proportion to the imaginativeness and keenness of the musician in receiving these impressions will be the elevating and touching power of his work.

Note this employment of the word 'plastic'. Schumann was deeply interested in the extent to which romanticism would affect the actual shape of music – and he makes several references to the future of symphonic form in particular. He even entertains grave doubts whether such an extended form would survive. 'Great spaces require great minds to fill them,' he writes in the early part of his article on the *Fantastic Symphony*. The great 'Ninth' appeared for the time to have exhausted all symphonic possibilities, and Beethoven's immediate followers – Ries, Schubert, Spohr, Kalliwoda, Maurer, Schneider, Moscheles, Müller, Hesse, Lachner – though each contributing something mildly personal [Schubert more than mild] in the way of content, had not been able to make any developments in actual symphonic form. He describes how Mendelssohn, perceiving that nothing was to be gained on this road, had turned to the concert overture, in which 'he compressed the idea of the symphony within a smaller circle', and with which 'he won crown and sceptre above all the other instrumental composers of the day'. He then describes how in France and Italy composers preferred to write operas, and ends with the remark: 'It began to look possible that the name of the symphony would soon become a merely historical one.' And finally, with great generosity, as he was not even then entirely in sympathy with Berlioz's eccentricity, he finds sufficient originality in the 'Fantastic' – with regard to both structure and programme – to hope that German composers would follow a similar trail to preserve the symphony as an art-form from mere pedantry, if not from actual extinction. This was written in 1835 when Schumann was only twenty-five. As he grew older, we know that his views on romanticism were considerably modified; or rather that, while remaining aware that Beethoven had changed the direction of the symphony, he foresaw a cul-de-sac in music too closely tied to 'programme'. Schumann's own D minor Symphony, an essay in concentrated purely musical logic, was his most effective personal contribution to the solution. From Elysian fields he undoubtedly watched Sibelius's progress in the same direction with a knowing smile on his face.

Every age has its particular musical evils – its charlatans – and from the second point in the paper's original policy, 'to attack as inartistic the works of the present generation', we get a fore-glimpse of Schumann's bitter dislike of the commercial artists of his day. These he divides into two kinds. First, the composers of 'superficial' operas, like Rossini[1] and Meyerbeer, who, to cater for popular taste, merely debase their subjects 'in order to raise money and noise'. But equally stringent abuse is showered upon the travelling virtuoso – the 'pedlars in art', who composed brilliant cascades of notes and trills merely because all existing music was too limited to display their dazzling capabilities as technical acrobats. Schumann attacks this degraded art whenever opportunity arises; at times he will even branch off from an unrelated subject in his effort to convince the public of their misdirected applause. On one occasion he mentions a 'recently awakened fancy among virtuosos to emigrate to America', and adds humorously, 'and many of their friends secretly hope they will remain over there'. But Schumann cannot be accused of harbouring a mere prejudice: it was a deep-rooted conviction, as he himself puts it, that 'the distractions and unsettled nature of the virtuoso life are opposed to and injure lofty research and productiveness, which requires happiness and complete isolation from the world'.

He hated superficiality in every sphere of life, even in the loose critical gossip of the public at a concert. In 'Letters of an Enthusiast' he writes:

> So, so my Public, I have you again! once more we can harass each other; how long have I not desired to found concerts for the deaf and dumb, to set you an example of good behaviour, of which you display so little – even in the finest concerts! And if you dared to gossip about the wondrous things you heard in the enchanted land of music, I would have you petrified, like Tsing-Sing, into a stone pagoda.

The 1835 article 'Shrovetide Speech by Florestan' was written entirely for the purpose of condemning those members of the public who dared to decry, or even praise, Beethoven after a performance of the D minor Symphony, and it reveals all the ardour of the youthful Schumann prepared to live or die for his convictions. But in calmer mood he is able to discuss applause

[1] Schumann failed to perceive the good in Rossini.

objectively. Of one of Liszt's concerts he writes: 'The Viennese is less sparing of his hands than any other German, and, like an idolater, prides himself on the torn gloves that he has sacrificed to Liszt.' And again, referring to German lethargy: 'Certainly a dozen of applauding Frenchmen accomplish more than a room full of German Beethovenians falling asleep with rapture.'

So much for his review of general conditions in the earlier part of the nineteenth century. Now we must examine what he has to say of individual composers, since nowadays we admire him most as a critic for his ability to differentiate between genius and mediocrity, and to bestow just praise and blame. His respect for the past has already been mentioned, and his esteem for Bach in particular amounted to reverence. Though it is Mendelssohn who is usually associated with the nineteenth-century Bach revival, Schumann was his loyal lieutenant and frequently pleaded that the numerous Bach manuscripts stored away in the library of the Berlin Singakademie should be brought out, and an authentic edition published of his complete works. (This was realized in 1852.) Handel, Scarlatti, Couperin and Gluck are all favourably mentioned in the *Neue Zeitschrift*. In his account of concerts given by the society known as *Euterpe* at Leipzig from 1837 to 1838 he mentions that Mozart was played more often than Haydn, and suggests that he is in sympathy with the choice. But in the case of these composers he had the perspective of time to influence his estimates. More praise is due to him for his appreciation of representatives of the immediate past: Beethoven, Schubert and Weber, who were not then receiving universal recognition. In 'A Monument to Beethoven' his four selves discuss the project of erecting some permanent memorial to Beethoven (which was eventually carried out in 1845). Florestan is of the opinion that his greatness could never be matched in mere stone; Jonathan says parabolically that his spirit could never be tied down to one place only; Eusebius is full of stupendous schemes of carving his likeness in colossal proportions, 'that he could gaze above the mountains as he did when living'; while Raro insists that all reverence needs some kind of practical, outward manifestation. Behind this fanciful exterior it is obvious that Schumann regarded Beethoven's genius as transcendental. Schubert we know was his youthful god, yet in his mature 1840 article on Schubert's C major Symphony he gives a just account of the composer's measure beside Beethoven. In associating Weber with these two names he was perhaps over-generous; yet when writing of *Euryanthe*: 'The opera cost him a piece of his life. True, but through it he is immortal,' he willy-nilly betrays that composer's more slender claim to immortality.

Prophecy is a dangerous pastime in artistic matters: as with material things, only time can really prove what will wear well. When writing of his fellow composers Schumann did not play for safety. He gave fearless opinions and was prepared to run the risk of their being wrong. Usually he was astonishingly right: only with Mendelssohn did a warm personal regard cause him to overrate his relative importance as a composer. In this he was not alone. Wherever he went, Mendelssohn was acclaimed as a divine genius – few composers have met with such spontaneous success in their lifetime. The frequent bouquets Schumann throws to him for his work as conductor of the Gewandhaus concerts, and not least for his insistence on adequate orchestral rehearsal, were fully deserved. But such extravagant praises of his music coming from a man of infinitely subtler cast of mind are regrettable, and the description of 'I waited for the Lord' from the *Hymn of Praise* as 'a glance into a heaven filled with the Madonna eyes of Raphael' is perhaps the most unfortunate sentence Schumann ever caused his pen to place on permanent record.

His enthusiasm for Chopin dates from his very first article of 1831, containing the now famous sentence: 'Off with your hats, gentlemen – a genius,' and in all his subsequent writings he acknowledges Chopin as a true representative of the 'new poetic age' which the paper set out to hasten. Of Berlioz he wishes he could 'restrain his inclination towards eccentricity'; but he realizes that there is strength in his music and says: 'It is vain to seek to refine it by art, or to confine it forcibly within bounds, until it has learned to be prudent with its means and to find the right direction and the goal in its own way.' One of the most forceful prophecies he ever made was that 'it will be as impossible to cause Berlioz to be forgotten, by ignoring him, as to sink an historical fact in oblivion by passing it over'.

Liszt he praises unreservedly as a pianist: 'The instrument glows under his hands.' He admires his noble head and general appearance and even goes so far as to say: 'He must be heard – and also seen; for if he played behind the scenes a great deal of the poetry of his playing would be lost.' He is fascinated by Liszt's elaborate transcriptions of other people's music, but of Liszt's original compositions he aptly writes: 'If, with his eminently musical nature, Liszt had devoted the same time to composition and to himself that he has given to his instrument and to the works of others, he would have become a very remarkable composer.'[1]

It was not till Schumann had given up the *Neue Zeitschrift* that he came to know Wagner and his music; consequently it is only in his private letters that he reveals his disapproval of the many consecutive fifths and octaves scattered throughout the score of *Tannhäuser*. If the two composers could have met when younger, it is probable that they would have had much more in common. The older, more conservative Schumann was bound to admit that the operas on the stage had a certain 'mysterious magic that overpowers our senses', and yet in his heart he not only deplored their apparent lack of form, but also felt that in achieving his ends Wagner at times overstepped the limits of good taste. For Brahms, on the other hand, he had nothing but admiration, even though at the time of their first meeting Brahms was but a youth of twenty with little to show for himself. Yet Schumann's confidence in his ability was so great that after nearly ten years of silence he returned to music criticism to proclaim Brahms as the chosen member of the younger generation who alone was worthy to carry on the more seemly traditions of romanticism. This article, entitled 'New Paths', was a veritable *Nunc dimittis*, for Schumann died three years later.

Provided that they shared his own belief in the 'dawn of a new poetic age', lesser composers too came in for generous praise, though today we can see that his delight in the romantic inclinations of people like Bennett, Moscheles, Henselt, Vieux-temps, Gade and Berger occasionally caused his pen to transform their miniatures into masterpieces. Of course he had his blind spots, and prejudices too. He was once honest enough to admit that criticism stems basically from the simple phrase 'I do not like', and as a composer it was inevitably the kind of music most removed from his own style that he hated most – notably the operatic music then coming out of France (excepting Berlioz) and Italy. Meyerbeer suffered nastier knocks than anyone, and

---

[1] Written long before Liszt's withdrawal from the concert platform and subsequent development into 'a very remarkable composer'.

Schumann's outspoken article on *Les Huguenots* (which placed its composer among 'Franconi's circus people') gave rise to equally outspoken criticism against himself. His operatic note-book for 1850 mentions that Meyerbeer's *Le Prophète* was performed at Dresden in February, but in place of the customary review Schumann drew just a small black cross – more eloquent than pages of abuse. Czerny, Hertz and Hünten, the virtuoso pianist-composers, were also once dismissed as 'amongst music's weeds'.

In his dual role of composer-critic, Schumann was also occasionally reproached for running with the hare and hunting with the hounds. Lobe went as far as to say that his fame as a composer was achieved 'through the pens and journal of a famous coterie'. This was wholly unjust, for while the paper's policy was naturally in support of the new poetic music which Schumann himself wrote, references to his own compositions are infrequent. His nature was above self-advertisement and professional rivalry of any kind; all his journalism was inspired by dedication to a cause.

Schumann gave up the editorship of the *Neue Zeitschrift* in 1844, when he realized that his limited time and energy would have to be conserved for composition and practical music-making. But it is interesting to observe how his style changed during those ten years of criticism. As the influence of Jean Paul begins to wane, so his articles become more direct and penetrating; they contain less fancy, if not more truth. And he had the courage to admit modifications of opinion, sometimes even changes of mind. He confesses that in his younger days his enthusiasm for Schubert was so unbounded that 'his name, I thought, should only be whispered at night to the trees and stars'. Later he realizes that Schubert's music is of the kind which appeals first and foremost to youth, and wonders what he might have written had he reached maturity. He begs Moscheles's pardon for previously judging his *Maid of Orleans* overture merely from the piano score. He expresses a fear that Chopin, in his love for smaller piano forms, 'will not rise any higher than he has risen'. Of Bennett he says much the same: 'Though we love fairy sports, we prefer manly deeds.' And he even criticizes his revered Mendelssohn's setting of *When Israel went out of Egypt* with the words 'it falls somewhat behind *As pants the hart*, and even remind us of some things by Mendelssohn we have already heard'.

Oscar Wilde once defined the true critic as 'he who can translate into another manner or a new material his impression of beautiful things', and this in the final resort is where Schumann's talent for criticism lay. He could not, as a young man, accept the view that music was an abstract art with only tone and rhythm for its subject-matter – for him it was essentially an expression of 'the great goings-on of nature and of human affairs'. Just as in much of his own music he sought to translate extra-musical impressions and experiences into sound, so in his criticism he attempted to reveal the significance of other people's music in comprehensible human terms. And that, surely, is one of the critic's most valuable functions.

APPENDICES

APPENDIX A

(Figures in brackets denote the age reached by the person mentioned during the year in question.)

Year	Age	Life	Contemporary Musicians
1810		Robert Alexander Schumann born, June 8, at Zwickau, Saxony, son of Friedrich August Schumann (37), bookseller and publisher.	Chopin born, Feb. 22; Nicolai born, June 9; Wesley (S. S.) born, Aug. 14. Adam aged 7; Auber 28; Balfe 2; Beethoven 40; Bellini 9; Benedict 6; Berlioz 7; Bishop 24; Boieldieu 35; Catel 37; Cherubini 50; Clementi 58; Donizetti 13; Dussek 49; Field 28; Glinka 7; Gossec 76; Grétry 69; Halévy 11; Hérold 19; Hummel 32; Lesueur 50; Loewe 14; Lortzing 7; Marschner 15; Méhul 47; Mendelssohn 1; Mercadante 15; Meyerbeer 19; Onslow 26; Paer 39; Paisiello 69; Rossini 18; Schubert 13; Spohr 26; Spontini 36; Vogler 61; Weber 24; Zelter 52.
1811	1		Hiller born, Oct 24; Liszt born, Oct 22; Thomas (Ambroise) born, Aug. 5.
1812	2		Dussek (51) dies, March 20; Flotow born, April 27.
1813	3		Dargomizhsky born, Feb. 14; Grétry (72) dies, Sept. 24; Verdi born, Oct. 10; Wagner born, May 22.
1814	4		Henselt born, May 12; Vogler (65) dies, May 6.
1815	5		Franz born, June 28; Heller born, May 15.
1816	6		Bennett (Sterndale) born April 13; Paisiello (75) dies, June 5.

Year	Age	Life	Contemporary Musicians
1817	7	Is sent to the private school of Archdeacon Döhner.	Gade born, Feb. 22; Méhul (54) dies, Oct. 18.
1818	8	Begins to receive some desultory instruction in music from Johann Gottfried Kuntzsch (43), a school master and organist.	Gounod born, June 17.
1819	9	Begins to make some attempts at composition. Visit to Carlsbad with his father (46), where he hears Moscheles (25), summer.	Offenbach born, June 21.
1820	10	Passes from Döhner's school into the Lyceum, Easter.	Serov born, Jan. 23; Vieux-temps born, Feb. 20.
1821	11	Plays the piano well by this time and tries over much music found in his father's (48) shop. He plays the piano in a patched-up performance of Schneider's (35) *Last Judgment*.	
1822	12	Plays the piano and recites at concerts given at the Lyceum.	Franck born, Dec. 19; Raff born, May 27.
1823	13	Becomes acquainted with the best classical chamber music at the house of Carl Erdmann Carus (49), a wealthy manufacturer.	Kirchner born, Dec. 10; Lalo born, Jan. 27.
1824	14	Is now an accomplished pianist and plays at Carus's (50) house as well as at school concerts. With the aid of books at his disposal at his father's (51) shop, he develops a literary taste.	Bruckner, born, Sept. 4; Cornelius born, Dec. 24; Reinecke born, June 23; Smetana born, March 2.
1825	15	Progresses in improvisation and composition. Weber (39) is approached with a view to teaching him, but gives an evasive answer. Literary society formed with the pupils of the Lyceum, Dec. 12.	Strauss (Johann ii) born, Oct. 25.

Year	Age	Life	Contemporary Musicians
1826	16	Suicide of his sister Emilie (19), who has been bodily and mentally afflicted. His father's (53) ill-health is accelerated by the shock and he dies, Aug. 10.	Weber (40) dies, June 4/5.
1827	17	Acquaintance with Dr Ernst August Carus and his wife Agnes, with whom he plays and studies much music, especially that of Schubert (30). Holiday at their house at Colditz, summer, and visit to Prague, Aug. He conceives a literary passion for Jean Paul, whose style he imitates in his letters, falls readily in and out of love and cultivates a liking for champagne.	Beethoven (56) dies, March 26.
1828	18	Leaves the Lyceum and goes to Leipzig, where he enters the university as a law student, March. Friendship with Gisbert Rosen, with whom he tours Bavaria, meeting Heine (31) in Munich, April–May. Back in Leipzig, he meets Wieck (43) and his daughter Clara (9), who is already a remarkable pianist. He sends songs to Gottlob Wiedebein (49) at Brunswick for criticism.	Schubert (31) dies, Nov. 19.
1829	19	Takes piano lessons with Wieck (44) and neglects his university studies. He moves to Heidelberg, to continue them there and to rejoin Rosen, May. Frequents the very musical home of Thibaut (55), who is a professor there. Holiday in Switzerland and Italy, Aug.–Oct.	Gossec (95) dies, Feb. 16.

Year	Age	Life	Contemporary Musicians
		First part of *Papillons* for piano (Op. 2) composed.	
1830	20	University studies again neglected. He hears Paganini (46) at Frankfort, Easter. Returns to Leipzig, Oct. He has obtained his mother's permission to make a six months' trial for a professional musician's career, and he again studies under Wieck (45), at whose house he lodges. He develops into a virtuoso and composes the Variations on the name of 'Abegg' (Op. 1) and the Toccata (Op. 7, first version) for piano. He runs badly into debt.	Catel (57) dies, Nov. 29; Goldmark born, May 18; Rubinstein born, Nov. 28.
1831	21	Wieck (46) advises him to study composition under Weinlig (51), the St Thomas cantor, but he prefers to go to Dorn (27). He contributes to G. W. Fink's (48) *Allgemeine musikalische Zeitung*. Second part of *Papillons* (Op. 2) and Allegro (Op. 8) for piano composed.	
1832	22	Dorn (28) leaves Leipzig and S. continues to study without a master, spring. He injures his hand with an unscientific contrivance invented by himself for mechanical finger development, June, and is unable to continue his piano studies. Visit to Zwickau, where part of a Symphony in G minor is performed at a concert given by Wieck and his daughter Clara (13), Nov. 18. Studies on Caprices by Paganini (48) for	Clementi (80) dies, March 10; Zelter (74) dies, May. 5.

Year	Age	Life	Contemporary Musicians
		piano (Op. 3) and *Intermezzi* (Op. 4) composed.	
1833	23	The Symphony, which had failed at Zwickau, rewritten and performed in Leipzig, April. S. forms a circle of young intellectuals who found the *Neue Zeitschrift für Musik. Impromptus sur une Romance de Clara Wieck* (14) for piano (Op. 5) composed for Wieck's (48) birthday, Aug. Death of brother, Julius (28), Nov. Toccata (Op. 7) revised and dedicated to Ludwig Schunke (23), with whom S. has made friends. Concert Studies on Caprices by Paganini (49) for piano (Op. 10) composed and piano Sonatas (Opp. 11 and 22) begun.	Borodin born, Nov. 12; Brahms born, May 7; Hérold (42) dies, Jan. 19.
1834	24	First number of the *Neue Zeitschrift für Musik* published April 3. S. invents the imaginary league of the 'Davidsbündler' as contributors, among whom are Mendelssohn (25), Wagner (21) and Heller (19). He falls violently in love with Ernestine von Fricken, and begins the composition of the *Études en forme de Variations* (12 *Études Symphoniques*) for piano (Op. 13) on a theme by Baron von Fricken. *Carnaval* (Op. 9) is also begun. Death of Schunke (24) Dec. 7.	Boieldieu (59) dies, Oct. 8; Ponchielli born, Sept. 1.
1835	25	*Carnaval* (Op. 9) finished. Engagement to Ernestine broken off. Meeting with Chopin (25), who visits	Bellini (34) dies, Sept. 24; Cui born, Jan. 18; Saint-Saëns born, Oct. 9.

Year	Age	Life	Contemporary Musicians
		Leipzig, Sept. 12. First meeting with Mendelssohn (26), Oct. 3, and Moscheles (41). Piano Sonata, F sharp minor (Op. 11), finished and dedicated to Clara Wieck (16); Sonata, G minor (Op. 22) completed (not with the present finale); *Troisième grande Sonate* (*Concert sans Orchestre*), F minor (Op. 14), composed.	
1836	26	Death of S.'s mother at Zwickau, Feb. 4. Wieck (51), aware that S. is falling in love with Clara (17), has sent her to Dresden, but on discovering that S. went to meet her there, he recalls her to Leipzig and cuts off all communication with him. Second visit of Chopin (26), Sept. Friendship with Sterndale Bennett (20), Nov. *Phantasie* for piano (Op. 17) begun.	Delibes born, Feb. 21.
1837	27	Engagement to Clara Wieck (18) against her father's will, Aug. 14. They decide to wait some two years and then to be married with or without Wieck's (52) consent. *Études Symphoniques* (Op. 13) published with a dedication to Sterndale Bennett (21). The quotation from Marschner's (42) opera, *Der Templer und die Jüdin*, in the finale, is a reference to England, Bennett's country. *Davidsbündlertänze* (Op. 6) and *Phantasiestücke* (Op. 12) composed. The former work is dedicated to Walther von Goethe (19),	Balakirev born, Jan. 12; Field (55) dies, Jan. 11; Jensen born, Jan. 12.

Year	Age	Life	Contemporary Musicians

who studies music at Leipzig, the latter to Robena Laidlaw (18), an English pianist.

1838   28   *Kinderscenen* for piano (Op. 15) and *Kreisleriana* (Op. 16) composed. *Phantasie* (Op. 17) finished and a new finale to the G minor Sonata (Op. 22) written, March. Visit to Vienna, Sept. He discovers Schubert's C major Symphony, which he sends to Mendelssohn (29) for performance in Leipzig. Meeting with Thalberg (26). *Arabeske* (Op. 18) and *Novelletten* (Op. 21) composed.   Bizet born, Oct. 25; Bruch born, Jan. 6.

1839   29   Return to Leipzig, March, his intention to settle in Vienna not having materialized. Composition of *Blumenstück* (Op. 19), *Humoreske* (Op. 20), *Nachtstücke* (Op. 23), *Faschingsschwank aus Wien* (Op. 26) and 3 Romances (Op. 28), all for piano. Clara Wieck (20) and S. take legal proceedings to force Wieck (54) to consent to their marriage. Her father disowns her, winter.   Mussorgsky born, March 21; Paer (68) dies, May 3; Rheinberger born, March 17.

1840   30   Song cycle, *Myrthen* (Op. 25), composed, Feb. Visit to Dresden to meet Liszt (29), who returns to Leipzig with him, March. Liszt plays several number of the *Carnaval* (Op. 9) at his recital, March 30. Wieck (55), still violently opposing S.'s marriage to his daughter, now resorts to slander and   Götz born, Dec. 17; Svendsen born, Sept. 3; Tchaikovsky born, May 7.

Year	Age	*Life*	*Contemporary Musicians*

seeks to make their union illegal by proving that S. is a drunkard. By Aug. his schemes are frustrated and S., having received the honorary doctor's degree from the University of Jena, is married to Clara Wieck (21), Sept. 12. Song cycles (Opp. 24, 27, 29–31, 33, 35, 36, 39, 40, 42, 45, 48, 49 and 53) composed.

1841 31 Symphony No. 1, B flat major (Op. 38), finished, Feb., and performed at Clara Schumann's (22) concert under Mendelssohn's (32) direction, March 31. Overture, Scherzo and Finale for orchestra (Op. 52), May. *Phantasie* in A minor (later first movement of piano Concerto) composed and second Symphony, D minor (later No. 4) begun, spring. S. reads Thomas Moore's (62) *Lalla Rookh* and decides to compose parts of *Paradise and the Peri* as a choral work. Birth of daughter, Marie, Sept. 1.

Chabrier born, Jan. 18; Dvořák born, Sept. 8; Pedrell born, Feb. 19.

1842 32 S. and Clara (23) study Haydn's and Mozart's string quartets. 3 Quartets (Op. 41) completed, July. S. having overworked himself, they visit the Bohemian spas, Aug. Piano Quintet, E flat major (Op. 44), finished, Oct. Meeting with Wagner (29), Nov. Piano Quartet, E flat major (Op. 47), and *Phantasiestücke* for violin, cello and piano (Op. 88)

Boito born, Feb. 24; Cherubini (82) dies, March 15; Massenet born, May 12; Sullivan born, May. 13.

Year	Age	Life	Contemporary Musicians

composed, Nov. and Dec. *Lieder und Gesänge* (Op. 51).

1843 33 Crisis of mental exhaustion following on prolific last three years. S. is obliged to give up composition for a time. Meeting with Berlioz (40), who visits Leipzig, end of Jan. Unable to resist inspiration, S. composes the Andante and Variations for two pianos, two cellos and horn (Op. 46) and then sets to work on *Paradise and the Peri* (Op. 50), Feb. Opening of the new Leipzig Conservatory founded by Mendelssohn, April 3. S. is appointed professor of composition. Birth of second daughter, Elise, April 25. First performance of the Andante and Variations (Op. 46) in a version for two pianos only, by Clara Schumann (24) and Mendelssohn at a concert given by Pauline Viardot (22), Aug. 19. First performance of *Paradise and the Peri*, Dec. 4, with Livia Frege (25) in the soprano part.

Grieg born, June 15; Sgambati born, May 28.

1844 34 Departure for Russia, where Clara (25) has undertaken a concert tour, Jan. 25. Meeting with Henselt (30) at St Petersburg, where Clara appears at court and where S.'s first Symphony is given at a concert arranged by the Vielhorsky family. Visit to various Russian cities. Return to Leipzig, May 30. Editorship of the *Neue*

Rimsky-Korsakov born, March 18.

Year	Age	Life	Contemporary Musicians
		Zeitschrift für Musik given up, June. Serious breakdown, which brings him to the verge of insanity, Aug. But he composes the final chorus of the *Scenes from Goethe's 'Faust'*. Visit to the Harz Mountains, Sept., does not improve his condition. A visit to Dresden, Oct., proves more beneficial. S. and Clara decide to settle there. Removal to Dresden, Dec. 13.	
1845	35	Hiller (34) becomes a devoted friend. He introduces Félicien David (35) to S., who now comes more frequently into touch with Wagner (32), but finds no real contact with him. Intermezzo and finale added to the A minor *Phantasie* for piano and orchestra (see 1841), May and June. The work thus becomes the piano Concerto (Op. 54), first perf. by Clara under Hiller in Dresden on Dec. 4. *Studien* and *Skizzen* for pedal piano (Opp. 56 and 58) composed. Symphony No. 2, C major (Op. 61), begun, Dec.	Fauré born, May. 12.
1846	36	Repeat perf. by Clara of the pf. Concerto at a Leipzig Gewandhaus concert under Gade, Jan. 1. Symphony No. 2, C major (Op. 61), finished and dedicated to Oscar I of Norway and Sweden (47). 5 Songs on poems by Burns (Op. 55) and 4 Partsongs (Op. 59).	

Year	*Age*	*Life*	*Contemporary Musicians*
1847	37	Nervous complaint progresses and makes him more and more retired and taciturn. Visit to Zwickau, his native town, where a festival in his honour is held, July. On Hiller's (36) departure from Dresden, S. becomes conductor of the 'Liedertafel'. Opera, *Genoveva* (Op. 81), begun. The libretto, by S., is based on Tieck (74) and Hebbel (34). Piano Trios, D minor (Op. 63) and F major (Op. 80).	Mackenzie born, Aug. 22; Mendelssohn (38) dies, Nov. 4.
1848	38	Opera, *Genoveva* (Op. 81), finished, Aug. 4. Incidental music to Byron's *Manfred* (Op. 115) begun, Aug. S. gives up the conductorship of the 'Liedertafel', but continues to direct a choral society founded by himself. *Bilder aus Osten* for piano duet (Op. 66); *Album für die Jugend* for piano (Op. 68); Rückert's (60) *Adventlied* for solo voices, chorus and orchestra (Op. 71).	Donizetti (51) dies, April 8; Duparc born, Jan. 21; Parry born, Feb. 27.
1849	39	An enormous increase in S.'s creative activity indicates an improvement in his health and mental condition, but also threatens their further deterioration through overwork. Much work done at Kreischa, where the family has taken refuge during the revolution. Hiller (38) offers S. his conductorship at Düsseldorf, autumn. *Waldscenen* for piano (Op. 82) and incidental music to Byron's *Manfred* (Op. 115) completed. Work on *Scenes*	Chopin (39) dies, Oct. 17; Nicolai (39) dies, May 11.

Year	Age	*Life*	*Contemporary Musicians*
		from Goethe's 'Faust' progresses. More than 20 works between Opp. 67 and 146 composed.	
1850	40	Concert tour with Clara (31), including Leipzig, Bremen and Hamburg, Feb. and March. At Altona they meet Jenny Lind (30). S. has accepted the post at Düsseldorf and begins to draw his salary, April 1. *Genoveva* produced at Leipzig, June 25, and received with cold respect. Removal to Düsseldorf, Sept. 1. S. takes up his duties as conductor of the subscription concerts, the choir practices and occasional performances of church music. After a visit to Cologne, Sept. 29, the composition of the third ('Rhenish') Symphony, E flat major (Op. 97), is begun. *Scenes from Goethe's 'Faust'* completed with the exception of an overture. Songs (Opp. 77, 83, 87, 89, 90 and 96). Violoncello Concerto, A minor (Op. 129).	
1851	41	Albert Dietrich (22) becomes S.'s pupil. Differences begin to arise between S. and the orchestra as well as the committee, who become aware of his unsuitability for the conductor's post, due to his mental instability. Obstinately confirmed by Clara (32) in his opinion of himself, he can attribute their attitude only to a desire for persecution. The choir	d'Indy born, March 27; Lortzing (48) dies, Jan. 21; Spontini (77) dies, Jan. 14.

Year	*Age*	*Life*	*Contemporary Musicians*
		also begins to grow recalcitrant. Overture to Schiller's *Braut von Messina* (Op. 100) received with indifference. Symphony in D minor rescored and called No. 4 (Op. 120). Piano Trio No. 3, G minor (Op. 110); violin Sonatas, A minor (Op. 105) and D minor (Op. 121); Overtures to Shakespeare's *Julius Caesar* (Op. 128) and Goethe's *Hermann und Dorothea* (Op. 136); Songs (Opp. 104, 117, 119, 125 and 127); *Fantasiestücke* for piano (Op. 111); Cantatas, *Der Rose Pilgerfahrt* (Op. 112) and *Der Königssohn* (Op. 116).	
1852	42	Oratorio on the subject of Luther considered. Conducts the first performance of his Overture to Byron's *Manfred* at a Gewandhaus concert in Leipzig. The Düsseldorf committee, still unaware of his advancing mental deterioration, grows more and more dissatisfied with his apparent laxity and neglect of his duties. By the summer he is obliged to let Julius Tausch (25) deputize for him as conductor. He is asked to resign, winter, but the committee resigns instead and he is reinstated by the new one. Mass (Op. 147); Requiem (Op. 148); Songs (Opp. 107, 135 and 142); Cantatas, *Des Sängers Fluch* and *Vom Pagen und der Königstochter* (Opp. 139 and 140); *Bunte Blätter* for piano (Op. 99).	Stanford born, Sept. 30.

Year	Age	*Life*	*Contemporary Musicians*
1853	43	Symphony No. 4, D minor (Op. 120), performed with success at the Lower Rhenish Festival held at Düsseldorf, spring. But S.'s committee is now thoroughly alarmed by the spreading rumours of his incapacity as a conductor and the impending deterioration of Düsseldorf's musical reputation. He has auditory delusions, begins to find speech difficult and is often melancholy and vaguely terrified. Brahms (20) visits S. and Clara (34) with an introduction from Joachim (22) and becomes much attached to them, Sept. Violin Sonata for Joachim written jointly by S., Brahms and Dietrich (24), Oct. The committee now asks S. tactfully to give up conducting for a time, but he suspects intrigues and stays away from rehearsals at once, Nov. Concert tour with Clara in Holland, Nov. and Dec. Overture added to *Scenes from Goethe's 'Faust'*. Introduction and Allegro for piano and orchestra (Op. 134); Overture on the *Rheinweinlied* (Op. 123); Cantata, *Das Glück von Edenhall* (Op. 143).	
1854	44	Visit to Hanover, where Joachim (23) conducts the fourth Symphony (Op. 120) and plays the *Phantasie* for violin and orchestra (Op. 131). Back at Düsseldorf, alarming signs of mental de-	Humperdinck born, Sept. 1; Janáček born, July 4.

Year	*Age*	*Life*	*Contemporary Musicians*

rangement show themselves, Feb. He writes down a theme he believes to have been sent him by angels, Feb. 17, asks to be taken to an asylum, Feb. 26, and runs out in the rain only half dressed and throws himself into the Rhine, Feb. 27. He is rescued and brought home by strangers. At his own request he is taken to a private asylum at Endenich near Bonn, March 4. Brahms (21) hastens to Düsseldorf to assist Clara (35). S. has lucid days during which he works quietly at music, but produces nothing of any value. For a time hopes of his recovery are entertained.

1855 45 At first the doctors continue to hope for S.'s recovery, but later they abandon all hope.

Bishop (69) dies, April 30; Chausson born, Jan. 21; Liadov born, May 11.

1856 46 Clara (37), who has to support the family by accepting as many professional engagements as possible, is in England when she is informed that her husband has not much longer to live. She returns to Düsseldorf, July 14. She is summoned to Endenich by telegram, July 23, but the crisis passes and she returns home. Tortured by foreboding, she goes to see S. again, July 27. He shows signs of recognition, but cannot speak coherently. Schumann dies in his sleep at Endenich, July 29.

Martucci born, Jan. 1; Sinding born, Jan. 11; Taneiev born, Nov. 25. Adam aged 53; Auber 74; Balakirev 19; Balfe 48; Benedict 52; Bennett 40; Berlioz 53; Bizet 18; Boito 14; Borodin 23; Brahms 23; Bruch 18; Bruckner 32; Chabrier 15; Chausson 1; Cornelius 32; Cui 21; Dargomizhsky 43; Delibes 20; Duparc 8; Dvořák 15; Fauré 11; Flotow 44; Franck 34; Franz 41; Gade 39; Glinka 53; Goldmark 26; Götz 16; Gounod 38; Grieg 13; Halévy 57; Heller 41; Henselt 42; Hiller 45; Humperdinck 2; d'Indy 5;

Year	Age	Life	Contemporary Musicians
			Janáček 2; Jensen 19; Kirchner 33; Lalo 33; Liadov 1; Liszt 45; Loewe 60; Mackenzie 9; Marschner 61; Massenet 14; Mercadante 61; Meyerbeer 65; Mussorgsky 17; Offenbach 37; Parry 8; Pedrell 15; Ponchielli 22; Raff 34; Reinecke 32; Rheinberger 17; Rimsky Korsakov 12; Rossini 64; Rubinstein 26; Saint-Saëns 21; Serov 36; Sgambati 13; Smetana 32; Spohr 72; Stanford 4; Strauss (J. ii) 31; Sullivan 14; Svendsen 16; Tchaikovsky 16; Thomas (A.) 45; Verdi 43; Vieuxtemps 36; Wagner 43.

APPENDIX B

(Dates refer to composition)

Piano Solo

Opus
1. Theme on the Name of 'Abegg' with Variations, 1829–30.
2. *Papillons*, 1829–31.
3. Six Concert Studies on Caprices by Paganini, 1832.
4. *Intermezzi*, 1832.
    1. A major. 2. E minor. 3. A minor. 4. C major. 5. D minor. 6. B minor.
5. Impromptus on a Theme by Clara Wieck, 1833 (rev. 1850).
6. *Davidsbündlertänze*, 1837 (rev. 1851).
    1. G major. 2. B minor. 3. G major. 4. B minor. 5. D major. 6. D minor. 7. G minor. 8. C minor. 9. C major. 10. D minor. 11. D major. 12. E minor. 13. B minor-major. 14. E flat major. 15. B flat major. 16. G major-B minor. 17. B major-minor. 18. C major.
7. Toccata, C major, 1829–32.
8. Allegro, B minor, 1831.
9. *Carnaval. Scènes mignonnes sur quatre notes*, 1833–5.
    1. *Préambule*. 2. *Pierrot*. 3. *Arlequin*. 4. *Valse noble*. 5. *Eusebius*. 6. *Florestan*. 7. *Coquette*. 8. *Réplique. Sphinxes*. 9. *Papillons*. 10. *A. S. C. H.–S. C. H. A. (Lettres dansantes)*. 11. *Chiarina*. 12. *Chopin*. 13. *Estrella*. 14. *Reconnaissance*. 15. *Pantalon et Colombine*. 16. *Valse allemande*. 17. *Intermezzo: Paganini*. 18. *Aveu*. 19. *Promenade*. 20. *Pause*. 21. *Marche des 'Davidsbündler' contre les Philistins*.
10. Six Concert Studies on Caprices by Paganini (Set II), 1833.
11. Sonata No. 1, F sharp minor, 1832–5.
12. *Phantasiestücke*, 1837.
    1. *Des Abends*. 2. *Aufschwung*. 3. *Warum?* 4. *Grillen*. 5. *In der Nacht*. 6. *Fabel*. 7. *Traumes Wirren*. 8. *Ende vom Lied*. (A title-less ninth piece, rejected by Schumann, was published in 1935.)
13. *Études en forme de variations* (12 *Études symphoniques*), 1834–7 (rev. 1852).
14. Sonata No. 3, F minor (*Concert sans orchestre*), 1835–6 (rev. 1853).
15. *Kinderscenen*, 1838.
    1. *Von fremden Ländern und Menschen*. 2. *Curiose Geschichte*. 3. *Hasche-Mann*. 4. *Bittendes Kind*. 5. *Glückes genug*. 6. *Wich-*

Opus

      tige Begebenheit. 7. *Träumerei.* 8. *Am Camin.* 9. *Ritter vom*
      Steckenpferd. 10. *Fast zu ernst.* 11. *Fürchtenmachen.* 12. *Kind*
      im Einschlummern. 13. *Der Dichter spricht.*

16. *Kreisleriana. Fantasien,* 1838.
      1. D minor. 2. B flat major. 3. G minor. 4. B flat major. 5. G minor.
      6. B flat major. 7. C minor-E flat major. 8. G minor.

17. *Phantasie,* C major, 1836–8.

18. *Arabeske,* C major, 1838.

19. *Blumenstück,* D flat major, 1839.

20. *Humoreske,* B flat major, 1838–9.

21. *Novelletten,* 1838.
      1. F major. 2. D major. 3. D major. 4. D major. 5. D major. 6.
      A major. 7. E. major. 8. F sharp minor-D major.

22. Sonata No. 2, G minor, 1833–8.

23. *Nachtstücke,* 1839.
      1. C major. 2. F major. 3. D flat major. 4. F major.

26. *Faschingsschwank aus Wien. Phantasiebilder,* 1839–40.
      1. *Allegro.* 2. *Romanze.* 3. *Scherzino.* 4. *Intermezzo.* 5. *Finale.*

28. Three Romances, 1839.
      1. B flat minor. 2. F sharp major. 3. B major.

32. *Vier Clavierstücke,* 1838–9.
      1. *Scherzo.* 2. *Gigue.* 3. *Romanze.* 4. *Fughetta.*

68. *Album für die Jugend,* 1848.
      Erste Abteilung: Für Kleinere.
      1. *Melodie.* 2. *Soldatenmarsch.* 3. *Trällerliedchen.* 4. *Ein*
      Choral. 5. *Stückchen.* 6. *Armes Waisenkind.* 7. *Jägerliedchen.*
      8. *Wilder Reiter.* 9. *Volksliedchen.* 10. *Fröhlicher Landmann.*
      11. *Sizilianisch.* 12. *Knecht Ruprecht.* 13. *Mai, lieber Mai.* 14.
      Kleine Studie. 15. *Frühlingsgesang.* 16. *Erster Verlust.* 17.
      Kleiner Morgenwanderer. 18. *Schnitterliedchen.*
      Zweite Abteilung: Für Erwachsenere.
      19. *Kleine Romanze.* 20. *Ländliches Lied.* 21. * * * 22.
      Rundgesang. 23. *Reiterstück.* 24. *Ernteliedchen.* 25. *Nach-*
      klänge aus dem Theater. 26. * * * 27. *Canonisches Liedchen.*
      28. *Erinnerung.* 29. *Fremder Mann.* 30. * * * 31. *Kriegslied.*
      32. *Sheherazade.* 33. *'Weinlesezeit-Fröhliche Zeit!'* 34. *Thema.*
      35. *Mignon.* 36. *Lied italienischer Marinari.* 37. *Matrosenlied.*
      38. *Winterszeit I.* 39. *Winterszeit II.* 40. *Kleine Fuge.* 41.
      Nordisches Lied (Gruss an G.). 42. *Figurierter Choral.* 43.
      Sylvesterlied.
      Additional pieces published in 1924. *Kuckuck im Versteck.*
      Lagune in Venedig. Haschemann. Kleiner Walzer. These four
      pieces appeared again in 1958, together with: *Für ganz Kleine.*
      Puppenschlafliedchen. Linke Hand. Soll Sich Auch Zeigen. Auf
      der Gondel. * * *.

Opus

72. Four Fugues, 1845.
    1. D minor. 2. D minor. 3. F minor. 4. F major.

76. Four Marches, 1849.
    1. E. flat major. 2. G minor. 3. B flat major (*Lager-Scene*). 4. E flat major.

82. *Waldscenen*, 1848–9.
    1. *Eintritt*. 2. *Jäger auf der Lauer*. 3. *Einsame Blumen*. 4. *Verrufene Stelle*. 5. *Freundliche Landschaft*. 6. *Herberge*. 7. *Vogel als Prophet*. 8. *Jagdlied*. 9. *Abschied*.

99. *Bunte Blätter*, 1838–49.
    1–3. *Drei Stücklein*. 4–8. *Fünf Albumblätter*. 9. *Novellette*. 10. *Präludium*. 11. *Marsch*. 12. *Abendmusik*. 13. *Scherzo*. 14. *Geschwindmarsch*.

111. *Phantasiestücke*, 1851.
    1. C minor. 2. A flat major. 3. C minor.

118. *Drei Clavier-Sonaten für die Jugend*, 1853.
    1. G major. 2. D major. 3. C major.

124. *Albumblätter*, 1832–45.
    1. *Impromptu*. 2. *Leides Ahnung*. 3. *Scherzino*. 4. *Walzer*. 5. *Phantasietanz*. 6. *Wiegenliedchen*. 7. *Ländler*. 8. *Lied ohne Ende*. 9. *Impromptu*. 10. *Walzer*. 11. *Romanze*. 12. *Burla*. 13. *Larghetto*. 14. *Vision*. 15. *Walzer*. 16. *Schlummerlied*. 17. *Elfe*. 18. *Botschaft*. 19. *Phantasiestück*. 20. *Canon*.

126. *Sieben Clavierstücke in Fughettenform*, 1853.
    1. A minor. 2. D minor. 3. F major. 4. D minor. 5. A minor. 6. F major. 7. A minor.

133. *Gesänge der Frühe*, 1853.
    1. D major. 2. D major. 3. A major. 4. F sharp minor. 5. D major.
    Canon on *To Alexis*, A flat major (posthumously pub. 1859).
    Scherzo und Presto passionato.
        (A rejected scherzo for the Sonata, Op. 14, and the original finale for the Sonata, Op. 22, posthumously pub. 1866).
    Theme and Variations,[1] 1854 (Theme posthumously pub. 1873, Variations, 1939).
    5 Variations (rejected) for Op. 13, 1834 (posthumously pub. 1873).
    Etüden in Form freier Variationen über ein Beethovensches Thema, 1833. (One pub. as Op. 124, No. 2 in 1854. The complete work posthumously pub. 1976.)

---

[1] The theme, which Schumann imagined to have been dictated to him by angels on 17th February 1854, is that of the slow movement of his violin Concerto. Brahms wrote a set of variations for piano duet (Op. 23) on it.

PIANO DUET

— Eight Polonaises, 1828 (posthumously pub. 1933).
66. *Bilder aus Osten.* Six Impromptus, 1848.
    1. B flat minor. 2. D flat major. 3. D flat major. 4. B flat minor. 5. F minor. 6. B flat minor-major.
85. *Zwölf vierhändige Clavierstücke für kleine und grosse Kinder,* 1849.
    1. *Geburtstagsmarsch.* 2. *Bärentanz.* 3. *Gartenmelodie.* 4. *Beim Kränzewinden.* 5. *Kroatenmarsch.* 6. *Trauer.* 7. *Turniermarsch.* 8. *Reigen.* 9. *Am Springbrunnen.* 10. *Verstecken's.* 11. *Gespenstermärchen.* 12. *Abendlied.*
109. *Ballscenen,* 1851.
    1. *Préambule.* 2. *Polonaise.* 3. *Walzer.* 4. *Ungarisch.* 5. *Française.* 6. *Mazurka.* 7. *Ecossaise.* 8. *Walzer.* 9. *Promenade.*
130. *Kinderball. Sechs leichte Tanzstücke,* 1853.
    1. *Polonaise.* 2. *Walzer.* 3. *Menuett.* 4. *Ecossaise.* 5. *Française.* 6. *Ringelreihe.*

TWO PIANOS

46. Andante and Variations, B flat major, 1843.

PEDAL PIANO

56. *Studien für den Pedal-Flügel,* 1845.
    1. C major. 2. A minor. 3. E major. 4. A flat major. 5. B minor. 6. B major.
58. *Skizzen für den Pedal-Flügel,* 1845.
    1. C minor. 2. C major. 3. F minor. 4. D flat major.

ORGAN (OR PEDAL PIANO)

60. Six Fugues on the name of 'Bach', 1845.
    1. B flat major. 2. B flat major. 3. G minor. 4. B flat major. 5. F major. 6. B flat major.

ORCHESTRA

— Symphony in G minor 1832–3. (Incomplete. The first two movements edited by Marc Andreae for pub. in 1972.)
38. Symphony No. 1, B flat major ('Spring'), 1841.
52. Overture, Scherzo and Finale, E major, 1841.
61. Symphony No. 2, C major, 1845–6.
81. Overture to *Genoveva.* See Opera.
97. Symphony No. 3, E flat major ('Rhenish'), 1850.

Appendix B—Catalogue of Published Works

Opus

100. Overture to Schiller's *Braut von Messina*, C minor, 1850–1.
115. Overture to Byron's *Manfred*. See Incidental Music.
120. Symphony No. 4, D minor, 1841 (rev. 1851).
123. Overture on the *Rheinweinlied*. See Choral Works.
128. Overture to Shakespeare's *Julius Caesar*, F minor, 1851.
136. Overture on Goethe's *Hermann und Dorothea*, B minor, 1851.
      Overture to Goethe's *Faust*. See Choral Works.

CONCERTOS, ETC.

— *Concertstück*, piano and orchestra, D minor, 1839 (Incomplete. First movement reconstructed for performance, 1988).
54. Concerto, piano and orchestra, A minor-major, 1841–5.
86. *Concertstück*, 4 horns and orchestra, F major, 1849.
92. *Introduction und Allegro appassionato* (*Concertstück*), piano and orchestra, G major, 1849.
129. Concerto, violoncello and orchestra, A minor, 1850.
131. *Phantasie*, violin and orchestra, C major, 1853.
134. *Concert-Allegro mit Introduction*, piano and orchestra, D minor-major, 1853.
— Concerto, violin and orchestra, D minor-major, 1853 (posthumously pub. 1937).

CHAMBER MUSIC

— Piano Quartet in C minor, 1828–30 (posthumously pub. 1979).
41. Three String Quartets, 1842.
      No. 1. A minor. No. 2. F major. No. 3. A major.
44. Quintet, piano and string quartet, E flat major, 1842.
47. Quartet, piano, violin, viola and cello, E flat major, 1842.
63. Trio No. 1, piano, violin and cello, D minor, 1847.
80. Trio No. 2, piano, violin and cello, F major, 1847.
88. *Phantasiestücke*, piano, violin and cello, 1842 (rev. 1849).
      1. *Romanze*. 2. *Humoreske*. 3. *Duett*. 4. *Finale*.
110. Trio No. 3, piano, violin and cello, G minor, 1851.
132. *Märchenerzählungen*, piano, clarinet (or violin) and viola, 1853.
      Andante and Variations, two pianos, two cellos and horn (original version of Op. 46, for two pianos), 1843.

ONE INSTRUMENT AND PIANO

70, *Adagio und Allegro*, horn (or violin or cello) and piano, A flat major, 1849.
73. *Phantasiestücke*, clarinet (or violin or cello) and piano, 1849.
94. *Drei Romanzen*, oboe (or violin or clarinet) and piano, 1849.

Schumann

Opus

102. *Fünf Stücke im Volkston,* cello (or violin) and piano, 1849.
105. Sonata No. 1, violin and piano, A minor, 1851.
113. *Märchenbilder,* viola (or violin) and piano, 1851.
121. Sonata No. 2, violin and piano, D minor, 1851.
　　Sonata No. 3, violin and piano, A minor, 1853 (posthumously pub. 1956).
　　Piano accompaniments to six unaccompanied violin Sonatas by Bach, 1853.
　　Piano accompaniments to six unaccompanied cello Sonatas by Bach, 1853.
　　Piano accompaniments to Paganini's unaccompanied violin caprices, 1853–5.

Songs

— Eleven songs, 1827–8 (posthumously pub. 1933).
　　1. *Sehnsucht* (Ekert). 2. *Die Weinende* (Byron). 3. *Erinnerung* (Jacobi). 4. *Kurzes Erwachen* (Kerner). 5. *Gesanges Erwachen* (Kerner). 6. *An Anna* (Kerner). 7. *An Anna* (Kerner). 8. *Im Herbste* (Kerner). 9. *Hirtenknabe* (Ekert). 10. *Der Fischer* (Goethe). 11. *Klage* (Jacobi).
24. *Liederkreis* (Heine), 1840.
　　1. *Morgens steh' ich auf.* 2. *Es treibt mich hin.* 3. *Ich wandelte unter den Bäumen.* 4. *Lieb' Liebchen.* 5. *Schöne Wiege meiner Leiden.* 6. *Warte, warte, wilder Schiffmann.* 7. *Berg' und Burgen schau'n herunter.* 8. *Anfangs wollt' ich fast verzagen.* 9. *Mit Myrthen und Rosen.*
25. *Myrthen,* 1840.
　　1. *Widmung* (Rückert). 2. *Freisinn* (Goethe). 3. *Der Nussbaum* (Mosen). 4. *Jemand (My heart is sair)* (Burns). 5. *Sitz' ich allein* (Goethe). 6. *Setze mir nicht* (Goethe). 7. *Die Lotosblume* (Heine). 8. *Talismane* (Goethe). 9. *Lieder der Suleika* (Goethe). 10. *Die Hochländer-Witwe* (Burns). 11. *Mutter! Mutter!* (Rückert). 12. *Lass mich ihm am Busen hangen* (Rückert). 13. *Hochländers Abschied* (Burns). 14. *Hochländisches Wiegenlied* (Burns). 15. *Mein Herz ist schwer* (Byron). 16. *Rätsel* (Catherine Fanshawe). 17. *Leis' rudern hier* (Moore). 18. *Wenn durch die Piazzetta* (Moore). 19. *Hauptmanns Weib* (Burns). 20. *Weit, weit* (Burns). 21. *Was will die einsame Träne* (Heine). 22. *Niemand* (Burns). 23. *Im Westen* (Burns). 24. *Du bist wie eine Blume* (Heine). 25. *Aus den östlichen Rosen* (Rückert). 26. *Zum Schluss* (Rückert).
27. *Lieder und Gesänge,* vol. i, 1840.
　　1. *Sag' an, o lieber Vogel mein* (Hebbel). 2. *Dem roten Röslein gleicht mein Lieb* (Burns). 3. *Was soll ich sagen* (Chamisso).

Opus

4.*Jasminenstrauch* (Rückert). 5. *Nur ein lächelnder Blick* (Zimmermann).

30. *Drei Gedichte* (Geibel), 1840.

1. *Der Knabe mit dem Wunderhorn.* 2. *Der Page.* 3. *Der Hidalgo.*

31. *Drei Gesänge* (Chamisso), 1840.

1. *Die Löwenbraut.* 2. *Die Kartenlegerin* (after Béranger). 3. *Die rote Hanne* (after Béranger).

35. *Zwölf Gedichte* (Kerner), 1840.

1. *Lust der Sturmnacht.* 2. *Stirb, Lieb' und Freud'.* 3. *Wanderlied.* 4. *Erstes Grün.* 5. *Sehnsucht nach der Waldgegend.* 6. *Auf das Trinkglas eines verstorbenen Freundes.* 7. *Wanderung.* 8. *Stille Liebe.* 9. *Frage.* 10. *Stille Tränen.* 11. *Wer machte dich so krank?* 12. *Alte Laute.*

36. *Sechs Gedichte* (Reinick), 1840.

1. *Sonntags am Rhein.* 2. *Ständchen.* 3. *Nichts schönerers.* 4. *An den Sonnenschein.* 5. *Dichters Genesung.* 6. *Liebesbotschaft.*

37. *Gedichte aus 'Liebesfrühling'* (Rückert), 1840 (nos. 2, 4, 11 by Clara Schumann).

1. *Der Himmel hat eine Träne geweint.* 2. *Er ist gekommen* (C.S.). 3. *O ihr Herren.* 4. *Liebst du um Schönheit* (C.S.). 5. *Ich hab in mich gesogen.* 6. *Liebste, was kann denn uns scheiden.* 7. *Schön ist das Fest des Lenzes.* 8. *Flügel! Flügel! um zu fliegen.* 9. *Rose, Meer und Sonne.* 10. *O Sonn', o Meer, o Rose!* 11. *Warum willst du andre fragen* (C.S.). 12. *So wahr die Sonne scheinet.*

39. *Liederkreis* (Eichendorff), 1840.

1. *In der Fremde.* 2. *Intermezzo.* 3. *Waldesgespräch.* 4. *Die Stille.* 5. *Mondnacht.* 6. *Schöne Fremde.* 7. *Auf einer Burg.* 8. *In der Fremde.* 9. *Wehmut.* 10. *Zwielicht.* 11. *Im Walde.* 12. *Frühlingsnacht.*

40. *Fünf Lieder*, 1840.

1. *Märzveilchen* (Andersen). 2. *Muttertraum* (Andersen). 3. *Der Soldat* (Andersen). 4. *Der Spielmann* (Andersen). 5. *Verratene Liebe* (Chamisso).

42. *Frauenliebe und -leben.* (Chamisso), 1840.

1. *Seit ich ihn gesehen.* 2. *Er, der Herrlichste von allen.* 3. *Ich kann's nicht fassen.* 4. *Du Ring an meinem Finger.* 5. *Helft mir, ihr Schwestern.* 6. *Süsser Freund, du blickest.* 7. *An meinem Herzen.* 8. *Nun hast du mir den ersten Schmerz getan.*

45. *Romanzen und Balladen*, vol. i, 1840.

1. *Der Schatzgräber* (Eichendorff). 2. *Frühlingsfahrt* (Eichendorff). 3. *Abends am Strand* (Heine).

48. *Dichterliebe.* (Heine), 1840.

1. *Im wunderschönen Monat Mai.* 2. *Aus meinen Tränen spriessen.* 3. *Die Rose, die Lilie.* 4. *Wenn ich in deine Augen seh'.* 5. *Ich will meine Seele tauchen.* 6. *Im Rhein, im heiligen*

Opus

    Strome. 7. Ich grolle nicht. 8. Und wüssten's die Blumen. 9. Das ist ein Flöten und Geigen. 10. Hör' ich das Liedchen klingen. 11. Ein Jüngling liebt ein Mädchen. 12. Am leuchtenden Sommermorgen. 13. Ich hab' im Traum geweinet. 14. Allnächtlich im Traume. 15. Aus alten Märchen winkt es. 16. Die alten, bösen Lieder.

49. *Romanzen und Balladen*, vol. ii, 1840.

    1. *Die beiden Grenadiere* (Heine). 2. *Die feindlichen Brüder* (Heine). 3. *Die Nonne* (Fröhlich).

51. *Lieder und Gesänge*, vol. ii. Nos 1–3, 1840; no. 4, 1846; no. 5, 1849.

    1. *Sehnsucht* (Geibel). 2. *Volksliedchen* (Rückert). 3. *Ich wand're nicht* (Christern). 4. *Auf dem Rhein* (Immermann). 5. *Liebeslied* (Goethe).

53. *Romanzen und Balladen*, vol. iii, 1840.

    1. *Blondels Lied* (Seidl). 2. *Loreley* (Lorenz). 3. *Der arme Peter* (Heine):*(a) Der Hans und die Grete; (b) In meiner Brust; (c) Der arme Peter wankt vorbei.*

57. *Belsatzar.* Ballad (Heine), 1840.

64. *Romanzen und Balladen*, vol. iv. Nos 1 and 2, 1847; no. 3, 1841.

    1. *Die Soldatenbraut* (Mörike). 2. *Das verlassene Mägdelein* (Mörike). 3. *Tragödie* (Heine): *(a) Entflieh mit mir; (b) Es fiel ein Reif*; *(c) Auf ihrem Grab* (duet) (derived from a choral work projected in 1841).

74. Nos. 6 and 7. See Vocal Quartets.

77. *Lieder und Gesänge*, vol. iii. Nos 1 and 4, 1840; nos 2, 3, 5, 1850.

    1. *Der frohe Wandersmann* (Eichendorff). 2. *Mein Garten* (Hoffmann von Fallersleben). 3. *Geisternähe* (Halm). 4. *Stiller Vorwurf* (anon.). 5. *Aufträge* (L'Egru).

79. *Liederalbum für die Jugend*, 1849.

    1. *Der Abendstern* (anon.). 2. *Schmetterling* (anon.). 3. *Frühlingsbotschaft* (anon.). 4. *Frühlingsgruss* (anon.). 5. *Vom Schlaraffenland* (anon.). 6. *Sonntag* (anon.). 7. *Zigeunerliedchen* (Geibel). 8. *Des Knaben Berglied* (Uhland). 9. *Mailied* (duet *ad lib.*) (C. A. Overbeck.). 10. *Käuzlein* ('Des Knaben Wunderhorn' anthology). 11. *Hinaus in's Freie!* (Hoffmann von Fallersleben). 12. *Der Sandmann* (Kletke). 13. *Marienwürmchen* ('Des Knaben Wunderhorn'). 14. *Die Waise* (Hoffmann von Fallersleben). 15. *Das Glück* (Hebbel). 16. *Weihnachtslied* (Andersen). 17. *Die wandelnde Glocke* (Goethe). 18. *Frühlingslied* (duet) (Hoffmann von Fallersleben). 19. *Frühlingsankunft* (Fallersleben). 20. *Die Schwalben* (anon.). 21. *Kinderwacht* (anon.). 22. *Des Sennen Abschied* (Schiller). 23. *Er ist's* (Mörike). 24. *Spinnenlied* (trio *ad lib.*) (anon.). 25. *Des Buben Schützenlied* (Schiller). 26. *Schneeglöckchen* (Rückert). 27.

Opus

      Lied Lynceus des Türmers (Goethe). 28. *Mignon* (Goethe).

83. *Drei Gesänge*, 1850.

    1. *Resignation* (anon.). 2. *Die Blume der Ergebung* (Rückert). 3. *Der Einsiedler* (Eichendorff).

87. *Der Handschuh.* Ballad (Schiller), 1850.

89. *Sechs Gesänge* (W. von der Neun [F.W.T. Schöpff]), 1850.

    1. *Es stürmet am Abendhimmel.* 2. *Heimliches Verschwinden.* 3. *Herbstlied.* 4. *Abschied vom Walde.* 5. *In's Freie.* 6. *Röselein, Röselein.*

90. *Sechs Gedichte* (Lenau), 1850.

    1. *Lied eines Schmiedes.* 2. *Meine Rose.* 3. *Kommen und Scheiden.* 4. *Die Sennin.* 5. *Einsamkeit.* 6. *Der schwere Abend.*
    Appendix: *Requiem* (after Héloïse?).

95. *Drei Gesänge* (Byron), 1849.

    1. *Die Tochter Jephthas.* 2. *An den Mond.* 3. *Dem Helden.*

96. *Lieder und Gesänge*, vol. iv, 1850.

    1. *Nachtlied* (Goethe). 2. *Schneeglöckchen* (anon.). 3. *Ihre Stimme* (Platen). 4. *Gesungen* (Neun). 5. *Himmel und Erde* (Neun).

98A. *Lieder und Gesänge aus 'Wilhelm Meister'* (Goethe), 1849.

    1. *Kennst du das Land?* 2. *Ballade des Harfners.* 3. *Nur wer die Sehnsucht kennt.* 4. *Wer nie sein Brod mit Tränen ass.* 5. *Heiss mich nicht reden.* 6. *Wer sich der Einsamkeit ergibt.* 7. *Singet nicht in Trauertönen.* 8. *An die Türen will ich schleichen.* 9. *So lasst mich scheinen.*

101. Nos. 1, 2, 4 and 6. See Vocal Quartets.

104. *Sieben Lieder* (Elizabeth Kulmann), 1851.

    1. *Mond, meiner Seele Liebling.* 2. *Viel Glück zur Reise.* 3. *Du nennst mich armes Mädchen.* 4. *Der Zeisig.* 5. *Reich' mir die Hand.* 6. *Die letzten Blumen starben.* 7. *Gekämpft hat meine Barke.*

107. *Sechs Gesänge*, 1851. No. 4, 1852.

    1. *Herzeleid* (Ullrich). 2. *Die Fensterscheibe* (Ullrich). 3. *Der Gärtner* (Mörike). 4. *Die Spinnerin* (Heise). 5. *Im Wald* (Wolfgang Müller). 6. *Abendlied* (Kinkel).

117. *Vier Husarenlieder* (Lenau).

    1. *Der Husar, trara!* 2. *Der leidige Frieden.* 3. *Den grünen Zeigern.* 4. *Da liegt der Feinde gestreckte Schaar.*

119. *Drei Gedichte* (Pfarrius), 1851.

    1. *Die Hütte.* 2. *Warnung.* 3. *Der Bräutigam und die Birke.*

125. *Fünf heitere Gesänge*, 1850. No. 3, 1851.

    1. *Die Meerfee* (Buddeus). 2. *Husarenabzug* (Candidus). 3. *Jung Volkers Lied* (Mörike). 4. *Frühlingslied* (Braun). 5. *Frühlingslust* ('Jungbrunnen' anthology).

127. *Fünf Lieder und Gesänge*, 1840. No. 4, 1850.

Schumann

  1. *Sängers Trost* (Kerner). 2. *Dein Angesicht* (Heine). 3. *Es leuchtet meine Liebe* (Heine). 4. *Mein altes Ross* (Strachwitz). 5. *Schlusslied des Narren* (*When that I was*) (Shakespeare).
135. *Gedichte der Königin Maria Stuart* (translated by Vincke), 1852.
  1. *Abschied von Frankreich.* 2. *Nach der Geburt ihres Sohnes.* 3. *An die Königin Elisabeth.* 4. *Abschied von der Welt.* 5. *Gebet.*
138. Nos. 2, 3, 5, 7 and 8. See Vocal Quartets.
142. *Vier Gesänge*, 1840.
  1. *Trost im Gesang* (Kerner). 2. *Lehn' deine Wang'* (Heine). 3. *Mädchen-Schwermut* (anon.). 4. *Mein Wagen rollt langsam* (Heine).
— *Soldatenlied* (Hoffmann von Fallersleben), 1845 or earlier.
— *Frühlingsgrüsse* (Lenau), 1851.

DECLAMATION WITH PIANO ACCOMPANIMENT

106. *Schön' Hedwig* (Hebbel), 1849.
122. No. 1. *Ballade vom Haideknaben* (Hebbel), 1853.
  No. 2. *Die Flüchtlinge* (Shelley), 1852.

VOCAL DUETS WITH PIANO

 29. No. 1. See Vocal Quartets.
 34. Four Duets, 1840.
  1. *Liebesgarten* (Reinick). 2. *Liebhabers Ständchen* (Burns). 3. *Unter'm Fenster* (Burns). 4. *Familien-Gemälde* (Grün).
 43. *Drei zweistimmige Lieder*, 1840.
  1. *Wenn ich ein Vöglein war'* (anon.).[1] 2. *Herbstlied* (Mahlmann). 3. *Schön Blümelein* (Reinick).

 64. No. 3*c*. See Songs.
 74. Nos. 1, 2, 4, 5 and 8. See Vocal Quartets.
 78. Four Duets, 1849.
  1. *Tanzlied* (Rückert). 2. *Er und sie* (Kerner). 3. *Ich denke dein* (Goethe). 4. *Wiegenlied* (Hebbel).
 79. Nos. 9 and 18. See Songs.
101. Nos. 3 and 7. See Vocal Quartets.
103. *Mädchenlieder* (Elisabeth Kulmann), 1851.
  1. *Mailied.* 2. *Frühlingslied.* 3. *An die Nachtigall.* 4. *An den Abendstern.*
138. No. 4 and 9. See Vocal Quartets.
  Liedchen von Marie und Papa (unacc. duet) (Marie Schumann), 1852.

---

[1] Subsequently used in *Genoveva*.

Appendix B—Catalogue of Published Works

Vocal Trios with Piano

29. No. 2. See Vocal Quartets.
79. No. 24. See Songs.
114. *Drei Lieder für drei Frauenstimmen*, 1853.
     1. *Nänie* (Bechstein). 2. *Triolett* (L'Egru). 3. *Spruch* (Rückert).

Vocal Quartets with Piano

29. *Drei Gedichte* (Geibel), 1840.
     1. *Ländliches Lied* (duet). 2. *Lied* (trio). 3. *Zigeunerleben* (quartet).
74. *Spanisches Liederspiel* (Spanish poems translated), 1849.
     1. *Erste Begegnung* (S.A.). 2. *Intermezzo* (T.B.). 3. *Liebesgram* (S.A.) 4. *In der Nacht* (S.T.). 5. *Es ist verraten* (S.A.T.B.). 6. *Melancholie* (S.). 7. *Geständnis* (T.). 8. *Botschaft* (S.A.). 9. *Ich bin geliebt* (S.A.T.B.). Appendix: *Der Contrabandiste* (Bar).[1]
101. *Minnespiel* (Rückert), 1849.
     1. *Lied* (T.). 2. *Gesang* (S.). 3. *Duett* (A.B.). 4. *Lied* (T.). 5. *Quartett* (S.A.T.B.). 6. *Lied* (A.). 7. *Duett* (S.T.). 8. *Quartett* (S.A.T.B.).
138. *Spanische Liebeslieder* (Spanish poems translated), with piano duet, 1849.
     1. *Vorspiel* (piano). 2. *Lied* (S.). 3. *Lied* (T.). 4. *Duett* (S.A.). 5. *Romanze* (Bar.). 6. *Intermezzo* (piano). 7. *Lied* (T.). 8. *Lied* (A.). 9. *Duett* (T.B.). 10. *Quartett* (S.A.T.B.).
— *Die Orange und Myrtle* (composer) (S.A.T.B.), 1853 (posthumously pub. 1942).

Partsongs for Mixed Voices

55. *Fünf Lieder* (Burns), unaccompanied, 1846.
     1. *Das Hochlandmädchen*. 2. *Zahnweh*. 3. *Mich zieht es nach dem Dörfchen hin*. 4. *Die alte gute Zeit*. 5. *Hochlandbursch*.
59. *Vier Gesänge*, unaccompanied[2], 1846.
     1. *Nord oder Süd* (Lappe). 2. *Am Bodensee* (Platen). 3. *Jägerlied* (Mörike). 4. *Gute Nacht* (Rückert).
67. *Romanzen und Balladen*, unaccompanied, vol. i, 1849.
     1. *Der König von Thule* (Goethe). 2. *Schön Rohtraut* (Mörike). 3. *Heidenröslein* (Goethe). 4. *Ungewitter* (Chamisso). 5. *John Anderson* (Burns).

---

[1] S.=soprano; A.=alto; T.=tenor; Bar.=baritone; B.=Bass.
[2] A fifth song intended for this set was published about 1929–30.

Schumann

Opus

75. *Romanzen und Balladen*, unaccompanied, vol. ii,1849.
    1. *Schnitter Tod* (Old German). 2. *In Walde* (Eichendorff). 3. *Der traurige Jäger* (Eichendorff). 4. *Der Rekrut* (Burns). 5. *Vom verwundeten Knaben* (Old German).

141. *Vier doppelchörige Gesänge*, unaccompanied, 1849.
    1. *An die Sterne* (Rückert). 2. *Ungewisses Licht* (Zedlitz). 3. *Zuversicht* (Zedlitz). 4. *Talismane* (Goethe).

145. *Romanzen und Balladen*, unaccompanied, vol. iii, 1849–51.
    1. *Der Schmidt* (Uhland). 2. *Die Nonne* (anon.). 3. *Der Sänger* (Uhland). 4. *John Anderson* (Burns). 5. *Romanze vom Gänsebuben* (Malsburg).

146. *Romanzen und Balladen*, unaccompanied, vol. iv, 1849–51.
    1. *Brautgesang* (Uhland). 2. *Bänkelsänger Willie* (Burns). 3. *Der Traum* (Uhland). 4. *Sommerlied* (Rückert). 5. *Das Schifflein* (with flute and horn) (Uhland).

— *Der deutsche Rhein*, solo voice, chorus and piano, 1840.

PARTSONGS FOR FEMALE VOICES

69. *Romanzen*, with piano *ab lib.*, vol. i, 1849.
    1. *Tamburinschlägerin* (Eichendorff). 2. *Waldmädchen* (Eichendorff). 3. *Klosterfräulein* (Kerner). 4. *Soldatenbraut* (Mörike). 5. *Merrfey* (Eichendorff). 6. *Die Capelle* (Uhland).

91. *Romanzen*, with piano *ad lib.*, vol. ii, 1849.
    1. *Rosmarin* (Old German). 2. *Jäger Wohlgemut* ('Des Knaben Wunderhorn'). 3. *Der Wassermann* (Kerner). 4. *Das verlassene Mägdelein* (Mörike). *Der Bleicherin Nachtlied* (Reinick). 6. *In Meeres Mitten* (Rückert).

PARTSONGS FOR MALE VOICES

33. *Sechs Lieder*, unaccompanied, 1840.
    1. *Der träumende See* (Mosen). 2. *Die Minnesänger* (Heine). 3. *Die Lotosblume* (Heine). 4. *Der Zecher als Doctrinair* (Mosen). 5. *Rastlose Liebe* (Goethe). 6. *Frühlingsglocken* (Reinick).

62. *Drei Lieder*, unaccompanied, 1847.
    1. *Der Eidgenossen Nachtwache* (Eichendorff). 2. *Freiheitslied* (Rückert). 3. *Schlachtgesang* (Klopstock).

65. *Ritornelle in canonischen Weisen* (Rückert), unaccompanied[1], 1847.
    1. *Die Rose stand im Tau.* 2. *Lasst Lautenspiel und Becherklang.* 3. *Blüt' oder Schnee.* 4. *Gebt mir zu trinken!* 5. *Zürne nicht des Herbstes Wind.* 6. *In Sommertagen.* 7. *In Meeres Mitten.*

[1] An eighth song, *Hätte zu einem Traubenkerne*, was pub. 1906.

Appendix B—Catalogue of Published Works

Opus

— *Zum Anfang* (Rückert), 1847 (posthumously pub. 1928).

137. *Jagdlieder*. Five Hunting Songs (Laube) with four horns *ab lib.*, 1849.
> 1. *Zur hohen Jagd*. 2. *Habet acht*. 3. *Jagdmorgen*. 4. *Frühe*. 5. *Bei der Flasche*.

— Three 'Revolutionary' Partsongs, with wind-band *ad lib.* 1848 (posthumously pub. 1913).
> 1. *Zu den Waffen* (Ulrich). 2. *Schwarz-Rot-Gold* (Freiligrath). 3. *Freiheitssang* (Fürst).

Choral Works with Orchestra

50. *Das Paradies und die Peri*, solo voices, chorus and orchestra, 1843. (Text adapted from Thomas Moore's *Lalla Rookh* in 1841.)
71. *Adventlied*, soprano solo, chorus and orchestra (Rückert), 1848.
84. *Beim Abschied zu singen*, chorus and wind instruments (Feuchtersleben), 1847.
93. *Motet. Verzweifle nicht im Schmerzenstal* (Rückert), double chorus and orchestra (originally organ), 1852.
98B. *Requiem für Mignon*, solo voices, chorus and orchestra (from Goethe's *Wilhelm Meister*), 1849.
108. *Nachtlied*, chorus and orchestra (Hebbel), 1849.
112. *Der Rose Pilgerfahrt*, solo voices, chorus and orchestra (Moritz Horn), 1851.
116. *Der Königssohn*, solo voices, chorus and orchestra (Uhland), 1851.
123. Festival Overture on the *Rheinweinlied*, orchestra and chorus (connecting text by Wolfgang Müller), 1852–3.
139. *Des Sängers Fluch*, solo voices, chorus and orchestra (Pohl, after Uhland), 1852.
140. *Vom Pagen und der Königstochter*, solo voices, chorus and orchestra (Geibel), 1852.
143. *Das Glück von Edenhall*, solo voices, chorus and orchestra (Hasenclever after Uhland), 1853.
144. *Neujahrslied*, chorus and orchestra (Rückert), 1849–50.
147. Mass, chorus and orchestra, 1852–3.
148. Requiem, chorus and orchestra, 1852.
— *Scenes from Goethe's 'Faust'*, solo voices, chorus and orchestra, 1844–53.

Opera

81. *Genoveva* (Schumann, after Tieck and Hebbel), 1847–9.

Incidental Music

115. Music to Byron's *Manfred*, 1848–9.

APPENDIX C

PERSONALIA

Alexis, Willibald (1798–1871), the pseudonym of Georg Wilhelm Heinrich Häring, German historical novelist.

Bendemann, Eduard (1811–89), painter of historical and other pictures, and a professor of art at Dresden. Later became director of Düsseldorf academy of art.

Bennett, William Sterndale (1816–75), English composer and pianist. Pupil of Mendelssohn in Leipzig. Professor of music at Cambridge University, 1856–75.

Berger, Ludwig (1777–1839), pianist and professor of his instrument in Berlin.

Breitkopf & Härtel, publishing firm at Leipzig, founded in 1719 by Bernhardt Christoph Breitkopf (1695–1777).

Brendel, Karl Franz (1811–68), critic at Leipzig, editor of the *Neue Zeitschrift für Musik* from 1845, in succession to Schumann.

Chamisso, Adalbert von (1781–1838), German poet, novelist and naturalist of French descent.

David, Ferdinand (1810–73), German violinist and composer, leader of the Gewandhaus orchestra in Leipzig and professor at the Conservatorium there.

Dietrich, Albert Hermann (1829–1908), composer and conductor, court musical director at Oldenburg from 1861.

Dorn, Heinrich Ludwig Edmund (1804–92), composer, teacher and conductor, pupil of Zelter in Berlin, operatic conductor at Leipzig, Hamburg and Riga, where he succeeded Wagner in 1839. Finally conductor of the Royal Opera in Berlin, 1849–68.

Fink, Gottfried Wilhelm (1783–1846), theologian and music critic, editor of the *Allgemeine musikalische Zeitung*, 1827–41. Professor of music at Leipzig University from 1842.

Gade, Niels Vilhelm (1817–90), Danish composer.

Grillparzer, Franz (1791–1872), Austrian poet and dramatist, with special interest in music and musicians.

Hauptmann, Moritz (1792–1868), German theorist, writer on acoustics, harmony, fugue and music in general.

Hebbel, Friedrich (1813–63), German poet and dramatist. His tragedy, *Genoveva*, was written in 1840.

Henselt, Adolf von (1814–89), German pianist and composer for his instrument, long settled in St Petersburg.

Herz, Henri (Heinrich) (1803–88), Austrian pianist and composer for his instrument, settled in Paris.

Hiller, Ferdinand (1811–85), German pianist and composer, pupil of Hummel, settled in Paris 1828–35, later at Frankfort, Leipzig, Dresden and Düsseldorf.

Hiller, Johann Adam (1709–1843), flautist, singer, author and composer.

Hoffmann, Ernst Theodor Wilhelm (1776–1822), German romantic novelist and amateur composer, changed his third name to Amadeus in homage to Mozart.

Horn, Moritz (1814–74), studied law, aesthetics and history, but later became interested in the theatre and made arrangements of other people's works for it. He wrote several poems.

Hübner, Julius (1806–82), brother-in-law of Eduard Bendemann (q.v.). Painter and director of the Dresden art gallery.

Hummel, Johann Nepomuk (1778–1837), Hungarian-German pianist and composer. Studied piano with Mozart and Clementi, and composition with Albrechtsberger, Haydn and Salieri.

Hünten, Franz (1793–1878), German pianist and composer, studied and worked in Paris until 1837, when he retired to his birthplace, Coblenz.

Jean Paul. See *Richter*.

Knorr, Julius (1807–61), originally a theological student, later a pianist, music teacher and writer on musical subjects.

Kuntzsch, Johann Gottfried (1775–1854), music teacher at the Lyceum of Zwickau, and Schumann's first music master there.

Laidlaw, Robena Anna (1819–1901), English pianist, pupil of Herz (q.v.) and Ludwig Berger (q.v.), played with much success on the Continent.

Lind, Jenny (1820–87), Swedish soprano singer. First specialized in opera, later became a concert singer.

Lipinski, Karol Joseph (1790–1861), Polish violinist and composer. Became leader of Dresden court orchestra in 1839.

Marschner, Heinrich (1795–1861), operatic composer and conductor. For a while assistant to Weber at Dresden, and from 1827 to 1831 conductor of the Leipzig theatre.

Moscheles, Ignaz (1794–1870), German pianist and composer, long settled in London.

Nottebohm, Gustav (1817–82), German teacher and writer on music, friend of Mendelssohn and Schumann in Leipzig, settled in Vienna in 1846.

Pohl, Richard (1826–96), writer on music and critic, student at Göttingen and Leipzig, then professor at Graz and critic successively at Dresden and Weimar. One of the editors of the *Neue Zeitschrift für Musik*. He wrote a connecting text for Schumann's *Manfred* music.

Pohlenz, Christian August (1790–1843), organist, teacher and conductor. Organist of St Thomas's church in Leipzig, where he preceded Mendelssohn as conductor.

Reinick, Robert (1805–52), poet and painter, better known in his lifetime for his paintings, of which 'Rachel and Jacob at the Well' was one of the best. His literary works include *Liederbuch für deutsche Künstler* (Berlin, 1833) and *Lieder eines Malers mit Randseichnungen seiner Freunde* (Düsseldorf, 1838).

Rellstab, Heinrich Friedrich Ludwig (1799–1860), writer on music in Berlin, appointed critic to the *Vossische Zeitung* in 1826.

Richter, Johann Paul Friedrich (1763–1825), German romantic novelist known under the pen-name of 'Jean Paul'.

Richter, Ludwig (1803–84), German painter, etcher and illustrator, famous in his time for his treatment of domestic and fairy-tale subjects.

Rietschel, Ernst Friedrich August (1804–61), sculptor, and a friend of the Schumanns in Dresden.

Rietz, Julius (1812–77), composer and conductor, many years at Düsseldorf, from 1847 in Leipzig and from 1860 in Dresden.

Schneider, Friedrich Johann Christian (1786–1853), German composer and organist.

Schröder-Devrient, Wilhelmine (1804–60), distinguished operatic singer, whose performance of Leonore in *Fidelio* in 1822 gave Beethoven great satisfaction. She also appeared in some of Wagner's early operas.

Schunke, Ludwig (1810–34), German pianist, pupil of Kalkbrenner and Reicha in Paris. Lived in Leipzig at the end of his short life and was an intimate friend of Schumann's. He left some promising works for his instrument.

Spitta, August Philipp (1841–94), German musical historian and editor.

Stamaty, Camille (1811–70), French pianist and composer of German descent. Came to Leipzig to study with Mendelssohn from 1836 to 1837.

Stegmayer, Ferdinand (1803–63), conductor of the Leipzig Opera after Dorn, and a lovable but dissolute character. He was the son of the Viennese court actor and poet who wrote the farce *Rochus Pumpernickel*. One of the original Directors of the *Neue Zeitschrift für Musik*.

Täglichsbeck, Thomas (1799–1867), violinist and composer.

Tausch, Julius (1827–95), conductor and composer, pupil of Schneider (q.v.) at Dessau and of the Leipzig Conservatorium. Successor of Rietz (q.v.) at Düsseldorf in 1847 and of Schumann.

Thibaut, Anton Friedrich Justus (1774–1840), writer on music. Professor of law at Heidelberg University.

Tieck, Ludwig (1773–1853), poet, novelist and critic, one of the chief figures of the German romantic school.

Verhulst, Johannes Josephus Herman (1816–91), Dutch composer and conductor at The Hague.

Weinlig, Christian Theodor (1780–1842), theorist and composer, cantor at St Thomas's Church in Leipzig from 1823. Taught both Schumann and Wagner for a short time.

Wieck, Friedrich (1785–1873), pianist and teacher of his instrument in Leipzig, father of Clara Schumann.

Wiedebein, Gottlob (1779–1854), *Kapellmeister* at Brunswick at the time Schumann wrote to him. Published one book of songs which were widely admired by professional and amateur singers of his day.

Zuccalmaglio, Anton Wilhelm Florentin von (1803–69), German critic of Italian descent, with particular interest in folksong.

APPENDIX D

BIBLIOGRAPHY

Abert, Hermann, 'Robert Schumann'. (Berlin, 1920).
Abraham, Gerald, 'On a Dull Overture by Schumann'. ('Monthly Musical Record', Vol. LXXVI, 1946.)
——, 'Recent Research on Schumann'. ('Proceedings of the Royal Musical Association, 1948–9.')
——, 'Schumann's "Jugendsinfonie" in G minor'. ('Music Quarterly', Vol. XXXVII, 1951.)
——, 'Schumann's Opp. II and III'. ('Monthly Musical Record', Vol. LXXVI, 1946.)
——, 'The Three Scores of Schumann's D minor Symphony'. ('Musical Times', Vol. LXXXI, 1940.)
——, Article in Grove's Dictionary. (Fifth and sixth editions, 1954 and 1980.)
——, 'Schumann, a Symposium' (edited Abraham). (Oxford University Press, 1952.)
Ambros, A. W., 'Robert Schumanns Tage und Werke,' in 'Cultur-historische Bilder aus der Gegenwart'. (Leipzig, 1860.)

Basch, Victor, 'Schumann: a Life of Suffering'. (New York, 1932.)
Beaufils, M., 'Schumann'. (Paris, 1932.)
Bedford, Herbert, 'Schumann'. (London, 1933.)
Boetticher, Wolfgang, 'Robert Schumann: Einführung in Persönlichkeit und Werk'. (Berlin, 1941.)
——, 'Robert Schumann in seinen Schriften und Briefen'. (Berlin, 1942.)
Brion, M., 'Schumann and the Romantic Age'. Translated by G. Sainsbury. (London, 1956.)

Chissell, Joan, Schumann's Piano Music. B.B.C. Music Guides. (London, 1972.)
——, 'Clara Schumann, A Dedicated Spirit'. (London, 1983.)
Colling, A., 'La Vie de Robert Schumann'. (Paris, 1931.)

Dahms, Walter, 'Schumann'. (6th edition, Stuttgart, 1925.)

Eismann, Georg, 'Ein Quellenwerk über sein Leben und Schaffen'. (2 vols., Leipzig, 1956.)
Erler, Hermann, 'Robert Schumann: aus seinen Briefen', 2 vols. (Berlin, 1887.

Fiske, Roger, 'A Schumann Mystery'. ('Musical Times', August 1964.)
Fuller-Maitland, J. A., 'Robert Schumann'. (London, 1884.)

——, 'Schumann's Pianoforte Works'. (Oxford and London, 1927.)
——, 'Schumann's Concerted Chamber Music'. (Oxford and London, 1929.)

Gertler, W., 'Robert Schumann in seinen frühen Klavierwerken'. (Wolfenbüttel, 1931.)

Hadow, W. H., 'Robert Schumann and the Romantic Movement in Germany'. 'Studies in Modern Music', Vol. I. (London, 1926.)
Herbert, May, 'The Life of Robert Schumann told in his Letters'. (London, 1890.)
Hueffer, F., 'Die Poesie in der Musik'. (Leipzig, 1874.)

Jansen, F. G., 'Die Davidsbündler: aus Robert Schumanns Sturm und Drang Periode'. (Leipzig, 1883.)

Kalbeck, Max, 'R. Schumann in Wien', in 'Wiener allgemeine Zeitung'. (September–October, 1880.)
Korte, Werner, 'Robert Schumann'. (Potsdam, 1927.)
Kötz, Hans, 'Der Einfluss Jean Pauls auf Robert Schumann'. (Weimar, 1933.)

Litzmann, Berthold, 'Clara Schumann: ein Künstlerleben nach Tagebüchern und Briefen'. 3 vols. (Leipzig, 1902–8.) Abridged English translation by Grace E. Hadow. 2 vols. (London and Leipzig, 1913.)

Macleod, J., 'The Sisters d'Aranyi'. (London, 1969.)
MacMaster, Henry, 'La Folie de Robert Schumann'. (Paris, 1928.)
May, Florence, 'The Girlhood of Clara Schumann'. (London, 1912.)

Nauhaus, Gerd., 'Robert and Clara Schumann in Norderney'. (Badekurier Norderney, 1978.)
——, 'Die Interpretation: Sind Robert Schumanns Metronomangabungen richtig'. (Musik und Gesellschaft, 1980.)
Niecks, Frederick, 'Robert Schumann: a Supplementary and Corrective Biography'. (London, 1925.)

Oldmeadow, Ernest J., 'Schumann'. (London, 1910.)
Ostwald, Peter, 'Music and Madness'. (Boston, U.S.A. and London, 1985.)

Pitron, Robert, 'La Vie intérieure de R. Schumann'. (Paris, 1925.)
Pohl, Richard, 'Erinnerungen an R. Schumann', in 'Deutsche Revue'. (Berlin, 1878.)

Reich, Nancy, 'Clara Schumann: The Artist and the Woman'. (New York and London, 1985.)

239

Reissmann, August, 'Robert Schumann, sein Leben und seine Werke'. (Leipzig, 1879.) Translated as 'The Life of Schumann' by A. L. Alger. (London.)

Sams, Eric, 'Did Schumann use Ciphers?' ('Musical Times', August 1965.)
——, 'The Schumann Ciphers'. ('Musical Times, May 1966.)
——, 'The Schumann Ciphers: A Coda'. ('Musical Times', December 1966.)
——, 'The Songs of Robert Schumann'. (London, 1969.)
——, 'Schumann's Hand Injury'. ('Musical Times', December 1971.)
Schauffler, Robert Haven, 'Florestan: the Life and Work of Robert Schumann'. (New York, 1945.)
Schoppe, Martin, 'Zwickau'. Article in *The New Grove* (edited by Stanley Sadie, London, 1980.)
Schumann, Eugenie, 'Memoirs'. Translated by Marie Busch. (London, 1930.)
——, 'Ein Lebensbild meines Vaters'. (Leipzig, 1931.)
Schumann, Robert, 'Gesammelte Schriften'. (5th edition, Leipzig, 1914; 3rd edition translated into English by Fanny Raymond Ritter, London, 1883.)
——, 'The Musical World of Robert Schumann'. A selection from Schumann's own writings translated and edited by Henry Pleasants. (London, 1965.)
——, 'Jugendbriefe'. Edited by Clara Schumann. (Leipzig, 1885–6; English translation, London, 1888.)
——, 'Briefe: Neue Folge'. Edited by F. G. Jansen. (Leipzig, 1886; enlarged edition, 1904.)
——, 'The Letters of Robert Schumann'. Selected and edited by Karl Storck. Translated by Hannah Bryant. (London, 1907.)
——, 'Tagebücher'. Bd. I. Edited by George Eismann. (Leipzig, 1971.)
——, 'Haushaltbücher. Edited by Gerd Nauhaus. (Leipzig, 1982.)
——, 'Ehetagebücher und Reisenotizen'. Edited by Gerd Nauhaus. (Leipzig, 1987.)
Schwarz, W., 'Robert Schumann und die Variation'. (Kassel, 1932.)
Stricker, Rémy, Robert Schumann: Le musicien et la folie (Paris, 1984.)

Tessmer, H., 'Robert Schumann'. (Stuttgart, 1930.)

Wagner, K., 'Robert Schumann als Schüler und Abiturient'. (Zwickau, 1928.)
Walker, Alan (ed.), 'Robert Schumann, the Man and his Music'. (London, 1972.)
——, 'Schumann'. (London, 1976.)
Wasielewski, J. W. von, 'Robert Schumann: eine Biographie'. (4th edition, Leipzig, 1906.)

Wolff, V. E., 'Robert Schumanns Lieder in ersten und späteren Fassungen'. (Leipzig, 1914.)

Wörner, Karl H., 'Robert Schumann'. (Zürich, 1949.)

Young, P. M., 'Tragic Muse. The Life and Works of Robert Schumann'. (London, 1957.)

——, 'Schumann'. (London, 1976.)

Walsh, S., 'The Lieder of Schumann'. (London, 1971.)

Index

Index

Index